Studies in Torah Judaism

•

Modern Medicine and Jewish Law

MODERN MEDICINE
AND
JEWISH LAW

By

FRED ROSNER, M.D.

Published by
BLOCH PUBLISHING COMPANY
For
YESHIVA UNIVERSITY PRESS
NEW YORK

Copyright © 1972 by
FRED ROSNER, M.D.
SBN 0-8197-0389-3

Printed in the United States of America

Table of Contents

	Editor's Introduction	7
	Author's Preface	9
I	Who Heals the Sick — G'd or Man?	11
II	Cigarette Smoking and Jewish Law	25
III	Contraception in Jewish Law	32
IV	The Jewish Attitude Toward Abortion	53
V	The Morality of Abortion	79
VI	Artificial Insemination in Jewish Law	89
VII	Jewish Attitude Toward Euthanasia	107
VIII	The Definition of Death in Jewish Law	124
IX	Autopsy in Jewish Law and the Israeli Autopsy Controversy	132
X	Heart and Other Organ Transplantation and Jewish Law	155
XI	Suicide in Biblical, Talmudic and Rabbinic Writings	177
XII	Creation Versus Evolution	194

Editor's Introduction

In publishing this work on "Twentieth Century Medicine and Jewish Law," by our distinguished alumnus of Yeshiva University's Albert Einstein College of Medicine, Dr. Fred Rosner, we obviously do not intend to offer definitive halakhic views and decisions. To be sure, the subjects under consideration are so relevant that they require specific decisions by halakhic authorities. However, in this study we are presenting mere professional guidelines grounded in legal formulations and scientific research, that may set the stage for the halakhic process to become operative.

Accordingly, we are projecting two basic assumptions. First, that an authentic insight into a halakhic decision on modern problems requires some knowledge of scientific methodology and technological skill. No inductively conditioned halakhic judgment on contemporary problems can be made without reference to the relevant scientific disciplines.

A second assumption which is of utmost significance in any consideration of the halakhic process is that it serves a unique indispensable purpose for personal self-fulfillment and social concern. What man can do belongs to the scientific realm; what man ought to do is the property of the legal, ethical frame. In an age of massive technological development, as well as recent unprecedented advances by the life sciences, such as heart transplants, new drugs, manipulation of the genes and the creation of test tube babies, a traditional component of ethical concern for the individual, and social consciousness implicit in the legal process of Judaism, is of primary value. There is a growing consensus that the consequences of science are too important to be left to secularists. Religionists and social scientists are wondering whether scientific progress necessarily serves the good of man or society and whether it is the exclusive prerogative of the scientist to determine the direction it takes. Biological advances, for instance, may be used for a healthier world or for germ warfare. The increasing ability of neurologists to define precisely the areas of the brain that control certain aspects of behavior and the rapidly growing array of potent drugs that can change behavior, raise or lower intelligence and the learning process, involve ethical and legal problems which cannot be confined to a few isolated individuals in science.

Surely, the theologian, the halakhist, must be involved in the process of human behavior and conduct. There is a moral issue created by innovations in the sciences which must grapple with some of the fundamental assumptions underlying all sciences and technology. Among them are the beliefs that scientific progress is automatically good and that scientists are the best judges of the direction in which their research should go. The time has come to enlist the religionists and moralists to explore the moral, legal and social implications of developments in scientific pursuits.

Our author, an alumnus of Yeshiva University, is a product of both disciplines. As a *talmid muvhok* of our revered President, Dr. Belkin, Dr. Rosner has been exposed to the world of science at our Albert Einstein Medical School and the halakhic studies at Yeshiva University. Following in the footsteps of some of our great medieval luminaries who were medical men by profession and halakhists by avocation, our author has recently translated into English "The Medical Aphorisms of Moses Maimonides" jointly with Dr. Suessman Muntner of the Hebrew University, which we published. The publication has been hailed both here and abroad as a decisive contribution to Judaica. The second volume of "The Medical Aphorisms of Maimonides" has recently been published by Yeshiva University Press.

Dr. Fred Rosner is Director of Hematology of the Queens Hospital Center, Affiliation of The Long Island Jewish - Hillside Medical Center, Queens, New York; and Associate Professor of Medicine at the State University of New York College of Medicine at Stony Brook. He is the author of many articles that appeared in scientific and academic journals.

DR. LEON D. STITSKIN, Editor
Department of Special Publications
Yeshiva University Press

Author's Preface

Recent advances in medical knowledge and therapeutic procedures have created a veritable crisis in modern medicine. The moral and Jewish legal aspects of some of the most pressing of these issues are examined in detail in this book. Portions of the present work have previously been published in various scientific and religious journals.

The author is indebted to Rabbi Dr. Walter S. Wurzburger, editor of TRADITION, for permission to reprint articles on abortion (Winter 1968 issue), the definition of death (Fall 1969 issue), suicide (Summer 1970 issue), autopsy (Spring 1971 issue), the physician's license to heal and the patient's license to seek healing (Summer 1971 issue), and contraception (Fall 1971 isue); to Mr. Saul Bernstein, editor of JEWISH LIFE, for permission to reprint articles on heart transplantation (September-October 1969 issue), and the morality of abortion (January-February 1971 issue); to Dr. William Hammond, editor of the NEW YORK STATE JOURNAL OF MEDICINE for permission to reprint the article on euthanasia (September 15, 1967 issue); and to Mrs. Ruth B. Waxman, managing editor of JUDAISM, for permission to reprint the article on artificial insemination (Fall 1970 issue). The remaining portions of this book have not been published elsewhere.

I wish to extend my sincere thanks to Rabbi Dr. Leon D. Stitskin and to Rabbi Dr. Sidney B. Hoenig for their assistance.

To my dear loving wife, Saranne, I express my appreciation, love and devotion, for the continual and steadfast support and encouragement through the long hours of painstaking work.

Thanks are also due my secretary, Mrs. Sophie Falk, for the several typings of the manuscript.

This book is dedicated to the cherished memories of my

late father-in-law Rabbi Mitchel S. Eskolsky Z'TL, *Musmach* of Yeshiva University, and my sister-in-law Victoria Eskolsky Walter Z'L, whose untimely passings have been an inconsolable loss to their families and the Jewish community.

FRED ROSNER, M.D.

January, 1972
New York City

Chapter I

Who Heals the Sick — G'd or Man?

INTRODUCTION

Does man have a part in shaping his future? Is man's lifespan on this earth predetermined or can man alter the course of events during his stay in this world. The predetermination of a person's lifespan, or lack thereof, has been discussed at length by philosophers and theologians including Jewish savants such as Rav Hai Gaon,[1] Rav Saadia Gaon[2] and Moses Maimonides[3] with most scholars concluding that the duration of life is not predetermined. What can man do, then, to lengthen his life? One way is to behave in the manner prescribed by G-d and receive as a reward "added years." Another way is to improve one's health so as to live longer. These alternatives pose the following questions: Does a sick person have the right to secure healing of his body or should the illness run its course without interference? Should a person rely solely on Divine providence for his physical as well as spiritual healing? These questions pertain to the patient. From the physician's standpoint, a similar series of questions can be raised. Is a mortal allowed by Jewish law to become a physician and practice medicine or does such an act constitute "interference with the deliberate designs of Providence?"[4] Does a physician play G-d when he practices

---

1. Kaufmann, D., "Ein Responsum des Gaons R. Haya uber Gottes Vorherwissen und die Dauer des Menschlichen Lebens," Leipzig. *Zeitschr. Deutsche Morgenlandische Gesellschaft.* 49:73-84, 1895.
2. Weil, G., *Maimonides Uber die Lebensdauer.* Basel, S. Karger, 1953, 59 pp.
3. Rosner, F., "Moses Maimonides' Responsum on Longevity," *Geriatrics* 23:170-178, 1968.
4. Jakobovits, I. *Jewish Medical Ethics.* New York, Bloch Publishers, 1959, pp. 2-6.

medicine? Part I of this paper deals with the duties of the physician; Part II discusses the role of the patient.

In a Midrashic story[5] Rabbi Ishmael and Rabbi Akiba were walking through the streets of Jerusalem and met a sick man. The ill person asked: "Masters, tell me how I can be cured?" They answered: "Do thus and thus until you are cured." He said to them: "And who afflicted me?" "The Holy One, Blessed be He," they replied. He said: "And you interfered in a matter which is not your concern. G-d afflicted you and you wish to heal?" The Rabbis asked: "What is your vocation?" He responded: "I am a tiller of the soil. Here is the vine-cutter in my hand." They queried: "But who created the vineyard?" "The Holy One, Blessed be He," he answered. "You interfered in this vineyard which is not yours? He created it and you cut away its fruits?" they asked. "Do you not see the vine-cutter in my hands? Were I not to go out and plow and till and fertilize and weed, the vineyard would not produce any fruit," he explained. They said: "Fool, from your own work you have not learned what is written (Psalms 103:15): *'As for man his days are as grass.'* Just as the tree, if not weeded, fertilized and ploughed will not grow and bring forth its fruits ... so it is with the human body. The fertilizer is the medicine and the healing means, and the tiller of the earth is the physician."

Part I

For I am the Lord that healeth thee
(Exodus 16:26)

The extreme viewpoint, namely, total rejection of the permissibility of human healing, was espoused by the Karaites who vehemently objected to medicine and physicians. They relied entirely on prayer for their healing as (*Shabbat* 32a):

> Man must ever pray not to become ill for if he becomes so, it is demanded of him to show merit in order to be healed.

---

5. Eisenstein, J. D., *Otzar Midrashim*. New York, 1915, Vol. 2, pp. 580-581.

The Karaites must further have adhered to the literal interpretation of the following Biblical phrase (Exodus 16:26):

> And he said: if thou wilt diligently hearken to the voice of the Lord, thy G-d and wilt do that which is right in His eyes, and wilt give ear to His commandments and keep all His statutes, I will put none of the diseases upon thee, which I have put upon the Egyptians, for I am the Lord that healeth thee.

The last phrase "for I am the Lord that healeth thee" literally translated from the original Hebrew means *for I am the Lord thy physician.* In fact, Rabbi Abraham Ibn Ezra, in his commentary, states that just as G-d "healed" the undrinkable waters at Marah for the Israelites, so too G-d will remove or heal all plagues on the earth and there will be no need for physicians. This perhaps is the basis for the Karaitic objection to human healing and medicine.

Alternate interpretations of the above Scriptural verse are possible. The Talmud (*Sanhedrin* 101a) asks if we are told that G-d "will put none of the diseases upon thee," what need is there for a cure? Rabbi Yochanan answers that the verse means as follows: "If thou wilt harken (to the voice of the Lord), I will not bring disease upon thee, but if thou willt not, I will; yet even so, *I am the Lord that healeth thee.*" Rabbi Baruch Halevi Epstein in his *Torah Temimah* explains that the intent of this Biblical phrase is to show that the illness of the Egyptians was incurable as it is written (Deut. 28:27): "the boil of Egypt ... wherefrom one cannot be healed." However, afflictions of the Israelites can be healed by G-d.

The father of all Biblical commentators, Rashi, explains "for I am the Lord that healeth thee" to mean that G-d teaches the laws of the Torah in order to save man from these diseases. Rashi uses the analogy of a physician who says to his patient not to eat such and such a food lest it bring him into danger from disease. So too it is stated, continues Rashi, obedience to G-d "will be health to thy body and marrow to thy bones" (Prov. 3:8). In a similar vein, the extra Talmudic collection of Biblical interpretation known as the *Mechilta* asserts that the words of Torah are life as well as health as it is written (Prov. 4:22):

"For they are life unto those that find them and health to all their flesh." Other commentators (*Sifsei Chachamim,* and Rabbi Samson Raphael Hirsch among others) extend this thought by propounding that the Divine Law restores health, and certainly prevents illness from occurring, thus serving as preventive medicine against all physical and social evil.

Rabbi Jacob ben Asher, known as the *Ba'al Haturim,* states that heavenly cure comes easily whereas earthly or man-made cures come with difficulty. Finally, Rabbi Meir Leib ben Yechiel Michael, known as *Malbim,* in his commentary on the phrase "for I am the Lord that healeth thee" speaks of mental illness. He asserts that the Laws of the Torah were given by G-d to Israel not like a master ordering his slave but like a physician ordering his patient. In the former case, the master benefits, not the slave. In the latter case, the patient and not the physician is healed from illness. Similarly, G-d's statutes are for our benefit, not His.

The multitude of interpretations of the Scriptural phrase "for I am the Lord that healeth thee" indicates that this verse is not to be understood literally. There is no prohibition inherent in this verse against a mortal becoming a physician and healing the sick. In fact, specific permissibility and sanction for the physician to practice medicine is given in the Torah as described below. The physician, however, must always recognize that G-d is the true healer of the sick and that a doctor is only an instrument of G-d in the ministrations to the sick.

And heal he shall heal
(Exodus 21:19)

Compensation for personal injuries is described in the Bible in the following verses (Exodus 21:19-20):

> And if men quarrel and one smiteth the other with a stone or with his fist and he die not, but has to keep in bed . . . he must pay the loss entailed by absence from work and cause him to be thoroughly healed.

The last phrase translated literally reads "and heal he shall heal." The Talmud (*Baba Kamma* 85a) interprets this duplicate mention of healing as intended to teach us that authorization was granted by G-d to the physician to heal. Rashi extends the words of the Talmud when he asserts "lest it be said that G-d smites and man heals." Thus he implies that a need exists for specific Biblical sanctioning of human healing.

Many Biblical commentators including Rabbi Samson Raphael Hirsch and Rabbi Baruch Halevi Epstein (*Torah Temimah*) echo the above Talmudic teaching. That is, by the insistence or emphasis expressed in the double wording, the Torah uses the opportunity to oppose the erroneous idea that having recourse to medical aid shows lack of trust and confidence in Divine assistance. The Torah takes it for granted that medical therapy is used and actually demands it.

Other commentaries on the Scriptural phrase "and heal he shall heal," including those of the *Mechilta* and Rabbi Meir Leib ben Yechiel Michael (*Malbim*), explain that the repetition of the word "heal" means that the patient must be repeatedly healed if the illness or injury recurred or became aggravated. In discussing the above case concerning personal injury, the Talmud (*Baba Kamma* 85a) also requires that where ulcers have grown on account of the wound and the wound breaks open again, the offender would still be liable to heal it (*i.e.*, pay the medical expenses) even repeatedly.

The most popular interpretation of "and heal he shall heal" (*Rashi, Targum Onkelos*, Talmud *Baba Kamma* 85a and others) is that compensation for the injury must be paid by the offender. Such compensation consists of five items: the physician's fees and medical bills, payment for loss of time from work, the shame incurred by disfigurement, the pain suffered, and the physical damage produced. All agree, however, that human healing is sanctioned by this phrase of the Bible, if not explicitly, at least implicitly.

Rabbi Abraham Ibn Ezra seems to place a restriction on the permissibility for a physician to heal when he states that only external wounds can be healed by man. Internal wounds or ailments should be left to G-d. However, there is nearly universal acceptance that the sanctioning to the physician to heal is all inclusive, encompassing all internal and external physical and mental illness. In fact, a commentary on the Talmud by *Tosafot* specifically states (*Baba Kamma* 85a) that not only is it permitted to heal man-induced wounds but even heavenly-induced sicknesses and afflictions, *i.e.*, all illnesses.

> *And thou shalt restore it to him*
> (Deut. 22:2)

The above Scriptural phrase refers to the restoration of lost property. Moses Maimonides says that this law also includes the restoration of the health of one's fellow man, if he has lost it. Thus, Maimonides derives the Biblical sanction for human healing from a different phrase in the Scriptures than most other Jewish savants. Rabbi Baruch Halevi Epstein (*Torah Temimah*) in two separate places (Deut. 22:2 and Exodus 21:19) asks why Maimonides totally omits the phrase "and heal he shall heal" as a warrant for the physician to heal. Epstein offers an answer to his own question when he states that the verse in Exodus only grants permission for a physician to heal whereas "and thou shalt restore it to him" makes it obligatory.

Maimonides' reasoning is probably based upon a key passage in the Talmud (*Sanhedrin* 73a) where it states: "whence do we know that one must save his neighbor from the loss of himself? From the verse 'and thou shalt restore it to him.'" Thus, not only if one is sick is a physician required but also if someone is attempting suicide, one must provide psychiatric or other competent assistance to save the person's life and health. Maimonides' major pronouncement on this matter is found in his *Commentary on the Mishnah* (Nedarim 4:4). He states:

> It is obligatory from the Torah for the physician to heal the sick and this is included in the explanation of the Scriptural phrase "and thou shalt restore it to him," meaning to heal his body.

> *Neither shalt thou stand idly by the blood of thy neighbor*
> (Levit. 19:16)

Duties toward our fellowmen are described in Leviticus 19:11-16. According to Hertz,[6] these precepts restate the fundamental rules of life in human society that are contained in the Second Tablet of the Decalogue. These moral principles were expounded by the Sages and applied to every phase of civil and criminal law. One example, cited in the Talmud (*Sanhedrin* 73a) is:

> Whence do we know that if a man sees his neighbor drowning or mauled by beasts or attacked by robbers, that he is bound to save him? From the verse "thou shalt not stand idly by the blood of thy neighbor."

Maimonides codifies the above Talmudic passage in his *Mishneh Torah* (*Hilkhot Rotzeach* 1:14) where he states:

> Whoever is able to save another and does not save him transgresses the commandment "neither shalt thou stand idly by the blood of thy neighbor" (Levit. 19:16). Similarly, if one sees another drowning in the sea, or being attacked by bandits or being attacked by a wild animal and is able to rescue him . . . and does not rescue him . . . he transgresses the injunction "neither shalt thou stand idly by the blood of thy neighbor."

Such a case of drowning in the sea is considered as loss of one's body and therefore, if one is obligated to save a whole body, one must certainly cure disease which usually afflicts only one part of the body.

Code of Jewish Law and Medical Practice

From the discussion so far, it seems evident that permission for the physician to heal is granted in the Torah from the phrase "and heal he shall heal." Some scholars, notably Maimonides, claim that healing

---

6. Hertz, J. H., *The Pentateuch and Haftorahs*. London, Soncino Press, 2nd edit., 1962, pp. 499-501.

the sick is not only allowed but is actually obligatory. Rabbi Joseph Karo, in his Code of Jewish Law (*Shulchan Arukh, Yoreh Deah* No. 336) combines both thoughts.

> The Torah gave permission to the physician to heal; moreover this is a religious precept and it is included in the category of saving life; and if he withholds his services, it is considered as shedding blood.

Rabbi David ben Shmuel Halevi, known as *Taz,* asks: If it is a religious precept to heal, why did the Torah have to grant specific permission for the physician to do so? His answer is that true healing lies only with G-d, but G-d gives the physician the wherewithal to heal by earthly or natural means. Once permission has been granted, then it is a commandment on the physician to heal. A similar thought is expressed by Rabbi Abraham Maskil Le'aytan, known as *Yad Avraham,* who states that permission is only granted if the physician heals with his heart toward heaven.

Rabbi Shabtai ben Meir HaKohen, known as *Sifsei Kohen,* offers an alternate reason for the Torah granting permission to heal—that is in order to avoid the physician saying "who needs this anguish? If I err, I will be considered as having spilled blood unintentionally." In a similar vein, Karo, in his *Beth Yoseph* commentary on Jacob ben Asher's Code of Jewish Law called the *Tur* (*Yoreh Deah,* No. 336), quotes Nachmanides, himself a physician, who says that without the warrant to treat, physicians might hesitate to treat patients for fear of fatal consequences "in that there is an element of danger in every medical procedure; that which heals one may kill another."

The Jewish attitude toward the physician and his medical art, as well as the patient's responsibility to seek medical aid is beautifully depicted by Ben Sira (Eccles. 38) who perceived in the physician an instrument of Providence as he expresses it:[7]

---

7. Friedenwald, H., *The Jews and Medicine.* Baltimore, Johns Hopkins Press, 1944, Vol. 1, pp. 6-7.

Honor a physician before need of him
Him also hath G-d apportioned
From G-d a physician getteth wisdom
And from a king he shall receive gifts.
The skill of a physician shall lift up his head
And he shall stand before nobles
G-d bringeth out medicines from the earth
And let a prudent man not refuse them.
Was not water made sweet with wood
For to acquaint every man with His power?
And He gave man understanding
To glory in His might.
By them doth the physician assuage pain
And likewise the apothecary maketh a confection,
That His work may not fail
Nor health from among the sons of men.
My son, in sickness be not negligent
Pray unto G-d, for He will heal.
Flee from iniquity, and from respect of persons
And from all transgressions cleanse thy heart.
Offer a sweet savor as a memorial
And fatness estimated according to thy substance.
And to the physician also give a place
And he shall not remove, for there is need of him likewise,
For there is a time when in his hand is good success.
For he too will supplicate unto G-d
That He will prosper to him the treatment
And the healing, for the sake of his living.
He that sinneth against his Maker
Will behave himself proudly against a physician.

Part II

From the three Biblical citations cited and from Part I, it is perfectly clear that the Torah gave specific sanction to the physician to heal and, according to some authorities, made it obligatory upon him to provide his medical skills to cure disease. It is not evident from the above, however, that the patient is permitted by Jewish law to seek human healing. Is an individual who asks a physician to treat him denying Divine Providence? Is such an individual transgressing the Biblical teaching "For I am the Lord that healeth thee" (Exodus 15:26)? Is a person's illness an affliction by G-d that serves as punishment for wrongdoing? And does such a person remove his atonement for sin by not accepting the suffering imposed by Divine judgment? Should there be, or is there a distinction between heavenly afflictions and man-induced sickness in regard to the patient seeking medical aid? How does one define heavenly illness? What is cancer—G-d induced (*i.e.*, genetic) or man induced (*i.e.*, drugs, viruses, irradition), or both? The number of such questions is endless and lengthy prose could be written attempting to analyze them.

The two sides of the question are illustrated in the Talmud (*Berakhot* 60a) where it states that on going to be phlebotomized, a person should recite the following prayer:

> May it be Thy will, O Lord my G-d, that this operation may be a cure for me and mayest Thou heal me for Thou art a faithful healing G-d and Thy healing is sure since men have no power to heal but this is a habit with them.

From this passage it would appear that conflicting viewpoints could emerge. The fact that the Talmud describes a patient going to a physician for an operative procedure can be interpreted to mean that certainly this is permissible. The only requirement is for the patient to recognize that the physician is acting as an agent of the Divine healer. In fact, *Rashi* explains the Talmudic passage to mean that the afflicted person should have prayed for Heavenly intervention rather than human healing and perhaps the bloodletting might not have been necessary.

On the other hand, the Talmudic statement continues with an assertion by Abaye to the effect that a patient should not utter such a prayer because, in fact, the Torah gave specific consent for human healing in the phrase "and heal he shall heal." Therefore, says Abaye, a patient should seek the help of a physician. A similar but not identical prayer is found in the Codes of Jewish Law of Maimonides (*Hilkhot Berakhot* 10:21) and Rabbi Joseph Karo (*Shulchan Arukh Orach Chayim* No. 230:4).

A rather negative attitude to the question of the patient obtaining medical assistance is taken by Nachmanides who, in his commentary on the Scriptural phrase "and My soul shall not abhor you" (Levit. 26:11), states that G-d will remove sickness from among the Israelites as He promised "for I am the Lord that healeth thee" (Exodus 15:26). The righteous, continues Nachmanides, during the epochs of prophethood, even if they sinned and became ill, did not seek out physicians, only prophets. What therefore is the need for physicians if G-d promised to remove all sickness from man? To advise which foods and beverages to avoid in order not to get sick, answers Nachmanides, himself a physician. He explains the phrase "and heal he shall heal" to mean that the physician is allowed to practice medicine but the patient may not seek his healing but must turn to Divine Providence. Only people who do not believe in the healing powers of G-d turn to physicians for their cure, and for such individuals the Torah sanctions the physician to heal. The latter should not withhold his healing skills for fear lest the patient die under his care nor should he say that G-d alone heals.

Other than the Karaites who strongly objected to physicians and medicines, Nachmanides seems to stand alone in his apparent prohibition for patients to seek medical aid. It is possible that he refers only to the righteous who are free of illness because of their piety and who do not require human healing. Perhaps the general populace, however, even devout believers in G-d, are allowed to seek human healing. Such an interpretation of Nachmanides' discussion is found in the commentary of Rabbi David ben Shmuel Halevi (popularly known as the *Taz* or *Turei Zahav*) on Karo's Code of Jewish Law (*Yoreh Deah* No. 336:1). It may also be that Nachmanides refers only to heavenly illnesses, but for man-induced wounds and sicknesses healing may be sought.

Karo does not seem to make such a distinction when he states (*Orach Chayim* No. 571) that

> He who fasts and is able to tolerate the fast is called holy; but if not, such as if he is not healthy and strong, he is called a sinner.

It appears evident from this quote that it is an obligation upon man to take all possible action to insure a healthy body, and this includes the services of a physician. A less likely interpretation of Karo's statement is that if a person is able to tolerate sickness or pain, just as in the case of the fast, he should do so and not seek medical aid.

Another source that can be interpreted either in support or against the permissibility for a patient to obtain human healing is the following story related in the Talmud (*Berakhot* 5b). Rabbi Yochanan once fell ill and Rabbi Chanina went to visit him saying "Are your sufferings welcome to you?" Rabbi Yochanan replied "neither they nor their reward," implying that one who lovingly accepts sufferings in this world will be greatly compensated in the world to come. Rabbi Chanina then said "Give me your hand" which Rabbi Yochanan did, and he cured him. Why could not Rabbi Yochanan cure himself, asks the Talmud? The reply is "because the prisoner cannot free himself from jail," meaning the patient cannot cure himself. On the one hand, we see that Rabbi Yochanan required healing from Rabbi Chanina, and yet he did not use human healing as he cured Rabbi Yochanan by touching his hand.

The strongest evidence from Jewish sources that gives the patient permission to seek treatment from a physician is found in Maimonides' *Mishneh Torah*. He states (*Hilkhot Deot* 3:3) that a person should

> set his heart that his body be healthy and strong in order that his soul be upright to know the Lord. For it is impossible for man to understand and comprehend the wisdoms (of the world) if he is hungry and ailing or if one of his limbs is aching ...

He also recommends (*ibid.* 4:23), as does the Talmud (*Sanhedrin* 17b) that no wise person should reside in a city that does not possess a physician. Maimonides' position is further stated (*ibid.* 4:1) as follows:

Since when the body is healthy and sound (one treads in) the ways of the Lord, it being impossible to understand or know anything of the knowledge of the Creator when one is sick, it is obligatory upon man to avoid things which are detrimental to the body and acclimate himself to things which heal and fortify it.

An English translation of this entire chapter in Maimonides' Code that deals with hygienic principles is available for the interested reader (*Journal of the American Medical Association,* Vol. 194:1352-1354, Dec. 27, 1965).

There are numerous Talmudic citations which support the position that not only allows but requires the patient to seek medical aid when sick. We are told (*Baba Kamma* 46b) that he who is in pain should go to a physician. Further (*Yoma* 83b), if one is bitten by a snake, one may call a physician even if it means desecrating the Sabbath because all restrictions are set aside in the case of possible danger to human life. Similarly (*Avoda Zara* 28b), if one's eye becomes afflicted on the Sabbath, one may prepare and apply medication thereto, even on the Sabbath. When Rabbi Judah the Prince, compiler of the *Mishnah,* contracted an eye disease, his physician Samuel Yarchina'ah cured it by placing a vial of chemicals under the Rabbi's pillow so that the powerful vapors would penetrate the eye (*Baba Metzia* 85b). The Talmud also speaks (*Ketubot* 75a) of another physician curing a patient. Finally (*Baba Kamma* 85a), in a case of bodily injury where the offender says to the victim that he will bring a physician who will heal for no fee, the victim can object and say "a physician who heals for nothing is worth nothing." If the offender offers to bring a physician from far away, the victim may say "my eye will be blind before he arrives." If the injured person says to the offender "Give me the money and I will cure myself" the latter can retort "you might neglect yourself and remain a cripple." From these and other Talmudic passages, it seems evident that an individual is undoubtedly permitted and probably required to seek medical attention when he is ill.

Further support for this contention is mentioned by the present Chief Rabbi of Great Britain, Immanuel Jakobovits, who cites the

15th century philosopher Isaac Arama's work *Akedat Yitzchak*. Rabbi Arama proves from Biblical narratives such as the Patriarchs' efforts to save themselves when in danger, and legislation such as the duty to construct parapets around roofs (Deut. 22:8) for the prevention of accidents, that man must not rely on miracles or Providence alone, but must himself do whatever he can to maintain his life and health.

Rabbi Chayim Azulai, an 18th century commentator on Karo's *Code of Jewish Law*, writing under the pen name of *Birke Yoseph*, summarized Jewish thought and practice relating to our question. His views are cited in *Jewish Medical Ethics* as follows:

> Nowadays one must not rely on miracles, and the sick man is in duty bound to conduct himself in accordance with the natural order by calling on a physician to heal him. In fact, to depart from the general practice by claiming greater merit than the many saints (in previous) generations, who were cured by physicians, is almost sinful on account of both the implied arrogance and the reliance on miracles when there is danger to life. . . . Hence, one should adopt the ways of all men and be healed by physicians. . . .

One might arrive at the same conclusion if one were to literally interpret the Pentateuchal admonition "Take ye therefore good heed unto yourselves" (Deut. 4:15).

Chapter II

Cigarette Smoking and Jewish Law

Tobacco was first implicated as a cause of cancer in 1761.[1] There is no longer any doubt that cigarette smoking is a hazard to health. Overwhelming medical evidence has proved that cigarette smoking is associated with a shortened life expectancy. In January 1964, an Advisory Committee appointed by the Surgeon General of the United States Public Health Service issued its report[2] on the relationship between smoking and health. The conclusions of that report were summed up in the sentence: "Cigarette smoking is a health hazard of sufficient importance in the United States to warrant appropriate remedial action."

Nearly four years later, after reviewing more than 2,000 research studies published since the 1964 report, the U.S. Public Health Service published its follow-up report.[3] The report concludes that: "epidemiological evidence derived from a number of prospective and retrospective studies, coupled with experimental and pathological evidence, confirms the conclusion that cigarette smoking is the main cause of lung cancer in men." Other findings include the fact that cigarette smoking is the most important cause of chronic obstructive lung disease (emphysema) in the United States. It is also a significant risk factor contributing to the development of coronary heart disease, cancer of

---

1. Redmond, D. E. Jr. "Tobacco and Cancer: The First Clinical Report, 1761." *New Engl. J. Med.* 282:18-23, 1970.

2. *Smoking & Health.* Report of the Advisory Committee to the Surgeon General of the Public Health Service. 387 pages. U.S. Gov't. Printing Office, Washington, D.C. 1964.

3. *The Health Consequences of Smoking.* A Public Health Service Review: 1967. 199 pages. U.S. Gov't. Printing Office, Washington, D.C. 1968.

the larynx and probably cancer of the bladder. Pregnant women who smoke have smaller babies and greater fetal complications.

In the United Kingdom, the Royal College of Physicians of London followed its first report on smoking and health[4] with a new report[5] restating the medical hazards of smoking. The report claims that cigarette smoking has become as important a cause of death as the great epidemic diseases such as typhoid, cholera and tuberculosis.

The American Medical Association has prepared reading lists, pamphlets, booklets, films, posters and a variety of other educational materials to publicize the effects of smoking on health, and to help in the campaign to decrease or even eradicate cigarette smoking. Comparable materials are also available from the American Cancer Society, American Heart Association, National Tuberculosis Association and the National Clearinghouse for Smoking & Health. By act of Congress, the following warning appears on every pack of cigarettes manufactured for sale in the United States on or after November 1, 1970:

> *"The Surgeon General Has Determined That Cigarette Smoking is Dangerous to Your Health."*

Television advertising for cigarettes has been abolished by government decree as of January 1, 1971. Complete or partial bans on cigarette advertising are in effect in England, Holland, Norway, Sweden, Italy, Poland, Russia, Switzerland and probably others[6]—but people continue to smoke. To some people, cigarette smoking is the greatest single public health problem this nation has ever faced. The solution will not be simple nor easy but steps in the right direction are beginning to show results in a slight decrease in the number of smokers, particularly young smokers.

---

4. *Smoking & Health. Royal College of Physicians.* Pitman Medical Publishing Co., London. 1962.

5. *Smoking & Health Now*: A Report of the Royal College of Physicians. Pitman Medical Publishing Co., London. 1971.

6. Best, E. W. R. *A Canadian Study of Smoking & Health,* Dept. of National Health and Welfare. Ottawa. 1966.

The present essay is an attempt to show that in light of the overwhelming medical evidence proving the causal relationship of cigarette smoking to cancer of the lung, heart disease and chronic bronchitis, Jewish law absolutely prohibits this practice.

The Torah tells us not to intentionally place ourselves in danger when it states *take heed to thyself, and take care of thy life* (Deut. 4:9) and *take good care of your lives* (Deut. 4:15). The avoidance of danger is exemplified throughout the Bible, Talmud and Codes of Jewish Law in the positive commandment of making a parapet for one's roof (Deut. 22:8) so that no man fall therefrom. Moses Maimonides, in his classic *Mishneh Torah* enumerates a variety of prohibitions, all based upon the consideration of being harmful to life. They are quoted verbatim (*Hilchoth Rotze'ach,* chapter 11:4 ff) since they eloquently illustrate the point under discussion:

> "It makes no difference whether it be one's roof or anything else that is dangerous and might possibly be a stumbling block to someone and cause his death—for example, if one has a well or a pit, with or without water, in his yard—the owner is obliged to build an enclosing wall ten handbreadths high, or else to put a cover over it lest someone fall into it and be killed. Similarly, regarding any obstacle which is dangerous to life, there is a positive commadment to remove it and to beware of it, and to be particularly careful in this matter, for Scripture says, *Take heed unto thyself and take care of thy life* (Deut. 4:9). If one does not remove dangerous obstacles and allows them to remain, he disregards a positive commandment and transgresses the prohibition: *Thou bring not blood* (Deut. 22:8).
>
> "Many things are forbidden by the Sages because they are dangerous to life. If one disregards any of these and says, 'If I want to put myself in danger, what concern is it to others?' or 'I am not particular about such things,' disciplinary flogging is inflicted upon him.
>
> "The following are the acts prohibited: One may not put his mouth to a flowing pipe of water and drink from it, or drink at night from rivers or ponds, lest he swallow a leech while unable

to see. Nor may one drink water that has been left uncovered, lest he drink from it after a snake or other poisonous reptile has drunk from it, and die. . . .

"One should not put small change or *denar* into his mouth lest they carry the dried saliva of one who suffers from an infectious skin disease or leprosy, or lest they carry perspiration, since all human perspiration is poisonous except that coming from the face.

"Similarly, one should not put the palm of his hand under his arm, for his hand might possibly have touched a leper or some harmful substance, since the hands are constantly in motion. Nor should one put a dish of food under his seat even during a meal, lest something harmful fall into it without his noticing it.

"Similarly, one should not stick a knife into a citron or a radish lest someone fall on the point and be killed. Similarly, one should not walk near a leaning wall or over a shaking bridge or enter a ruin or pass through any other such dangerous place."

This quotation from Maimonides certainly emphasizes the point that placing one's health or life into possible danger is absolutely prohibited. Hence, the smoking of cigarettes, which constitutes a definite danger and hazard to life, should *a fortiori* be prohibited. The subterfuge of "it is no concern of others if I endanger myself" is specifically disallowed by Maimonides.

Similar prohibitions against endangering one's life are found in most later Codes of Jewish Law including Karo's *Shulchan Aruch*. The latter devotes an entire chapter (*Choshen Mishpat* #427) to "the positive commandment of removing any object or obstacle which constitutes a danger to life." Elsewhere, (*Yoreh Deah* #116), Karo reiterates the prohibitions against drinking water left uncovered, putting money in one's mouth, putting one's hand or a loaf of bread under the armpit, leaving a knife in a fruit, the consumption of unappetizing food or the use of dirty pots or dishes. He further states (*Orach Chayim* #170:16) that two people should not drink from the same cup, and (*ibidem* 173:2) that one should wait between eating fish and meat because of danger.

Rabbi Moses Isserles, known as the *Ramah*, in his glossary on Karo's *Shulchan Aruch* (*Yoreh Deah* 116:5) concludes:

> ". . . one should avoid all things that might lead to danger because a danger to life is stricter than a prohibition. One should be more concerned about a possible danger to life than a possible prohibition. Therefore, the Sages prohibited one to walk in a place of danger such as near a leaning wall (for fear of collapse), or alone at night (for fear of robbers). They also prohibited drinking water from rivers at night . . . because these things may lead to danger . . . and he who is concerned with his health (lit.: watches his soul) avoids them. And it is prohibited to rely on a miracle or to put one's life in danger by any of the aforementioned or the like . . ."

The *Ramah* thus rejects the contention of many that smoking is allowable because "the Lord guards the simple," since he prohibits reliance on miracles. The fact that so many Jewish people smoke is no justification for this dangerous and life-threatening practice. If many Jews commit a transgression, others should certainly not follow; rather they should try to teach the sinners to repent from their evil ways. The "pleasures" of adultery are not condoned by even the most liberal-minded Jew. Why then should the pleasures of smoking, which also involve Biblical prohibitions (*vide supra*), be relegated to an inferior status, to be treated more leniently?

Not only is the intentional endangerment of one's health or life, such as by smoking, prohibited in Jewish law, but also wounding oneself without fatal intent is also disallowed. The Talmud (*Baba Kamma* 91b) quotes Rabbi Elazar Hakapar Berabbi who maintains that a man may not injure himself. He learns this point from the Scriptural phrase *And make an atonement for him, for that he sinned regarding the soul* (Numbers 7:11) which refers to a Nazarite who is called a sinner because he deprived himself of wine. Certainly, says Rabbi Elazar Hakapar, a person who deprives himself of his health by injuring himself (through smoking) is considered a sinner.

Maimonides, in his *Mishneh Torah* (*Hilchoth Melachim* 6:10) states that he who smashes household goods, or destroys articles of food, with destructive intent, transgresses the commandment *Thou shall not destroy* (Deut. 20:19). Our Sages (*Shabbath* 140b) deduce from this phrase a prohibition against the wanton destruction of anything useful to man. The famous *Mishnah* commentator Rabbi Israel Lipshuetz, known as *Tifereth Yisroel*, extends this prohibition to the willful destruction of one's own body. An example of this is described in the Talmud (*Shabbath* 129a) where a footstool was broken up for Rabbah, whereupon Abaye said to Rabbah: "But are you not infringing on *Thou shalt not destroy?*" He retorted: "Thou shalt not destroy in respect of my own body is more important to me."

The prohibition against intentionally wounding onself or injuring one's health is codified by both Maimonides in his *Mishneh Torah* (*Hilchoth Chovel Umazik* 5:1), and Karo in his *Shulchan Aruch* (*Choshen Mishpot* #420:31 and *Orach Chayim* #571). Not only is smoking considered to constitute intentional injuring of one's health, but it may in fact constitute a slow form of suicide. Suicide, itself, whether slow or rapid, is absolutely prohibited in Jewish law,[7] based upon the Biblical phrase *And surely your blood, the blood of your lives, will I require* (Genesis 9:5).

Some argue that the following two Talmudic principles mitigate against the imposition of a Rabbinic ban against cigarette smoking:

(a) we must not impose a restrictive decree upon the community unless the majority of the community will be able to endure it (*Baba Kamma* 79b).

(b) it is better that they should transgress inadvertently rather than be deliberate sinners (*Shabbath* 148b).

Both arguments can be rejected,[8] since neither is applicable in the

---

7. Rosner, F. "Suicide in Biblical, Talmudic and Rabbinic Writings." *Tradition* 11(2):25-40 (Summer) 1970.

8. Aberbach, M. "Smoking and the Halakhah." *Tradition* 10(3):49-60 (Spring) 1969.

face of *Pikuach Nefesh* or danger to life. Furthermore, the smoking of cigarettes is not an inadvertent act, but an intentional practice of oral gratification which can lead to serious illness and even death.

What can be done about this problem? Physicians should urge their patients to stop smoking. Rabbis should deliver sermons urging their congregants to stop smoking, or for non-smokers not to begin this evil practice. Physicians and Rabbis must themselves give up smoking in order to practice what they preach and teach by example. Leading Rabbinic authorities should speak out on this subject without timidity. The Jewish community of this nation must marshal its forces in an attack on the promotional activities of the tobacco industry. Judaism must appeal to its people and educate them in the ways of our Torah which regards life and health to be sacred, and their preservation a Divine commandment.

Chapter III

Contraception in Jewish Law

INTRODUCTION

Controversy surrounding the problems associated with contraception is by no means on the decline. On the contrary, a veritable recent flood of books and articles in the medical and lay press, as well as innumerable programs on the mass communication media devoted to family planning, contraceptive practice and birth control, attest to the widespread and increasing interest in this subject. Introduction of "the pill" in the early 1960's revolutionized many people's thinking toward birth control, and had a major impact on the overall picture of world population limitation.

HISTORICAL ASPECTS

The classic work dealing with the history of contraception is that of Norman Himes,[1] first published in 1936 and reprinted in 1963. Himes' book, in which he gathers and describes relevant material on virtually every known culture and religion, is thought to be complete, accurate, scholarly and well written. It is an exhaustive survey of contraceptive usages and practices from antiquity until 1935. The dramatic changes that have occurred in medical contraception over the following quarter of a century are discussed from legal, religious, organizational, social and medical viewpoints by Alan Guttmacher in a lengthy preface to the 1963 edition of Himes' book.

---

1. Himes, N. E. *Medical History of Contraception.* New York, 1963. Gamut Press, L III and 521 pp.

There is no doubt that the medical history of conception control is much older than the social movement. Himes points out that the contraceptive knowledge of Greek, Roman, Islamic and Hebrew physicians was far more extensive than was suspected. Throughout history, particularly recent history, there has been a gradual drift toward the acceptance of various forms of birth control. The recent spectacular and revolutionary changes in the social and moral climate of the world we live in have provided complete democratization of the knowledge and practice of contraception.

Methods of Contraception Including "The Pill" and Intrauterine Devices

It is beyond the scope of this essay to provide the reader with a comprehensive discussion of the various contraceptive methods, their effectiveness or lack thereof, the physiological mechanisms involved and the possible side effects that may be encountered. For such information the reader is referred to the standard textbooks of obstetrics and gynecology. Suffice it simply to enumerate the major methods employed: the condom, coitus interruptus, the diaphragm and cervical caps, chemical contraceptives, the safe period or rhythm method, oral contraceptives and the intrauterine devices.[2] Sterilization and abortion should also be mentioned, as well as a variety of minor methods, such as douching, sponges and tampons, scrotal hyperthermia and coitus reservatus and saxonicus.

In 1960, oral contraceptives were first approved for prescription use in the United States. The "pill" is now probably the most widespread method of birth control. Approximately ten million, or one quarter of American women, in the childbearing years are thought to be taking some form of "pill." Feature articles in the lay press[3] propound the

---

2. Peel, J. and Potts, M. *Textbook of Contraceptive Practice.* Cambridge University Press, 1969, pp. XIII and 297.
3. *Time*, April 7, 1967; *McCalls*, March, 1967 and November, 1968; *Today's Health*, May, 1968.

virtues and side effects of the "pill." The facts and fallacies about today's oral contraceptives are considered in some detail by Kistner.[4] Editorials in four major medical journals[5] point out that no pharmacologic agents are free of toxicity and there is as yet no unanimity of medical opinion concerning the risks attending the use of oral drugs for contraception. However, there are many reports in the medical literature suggesting serious side effects caused by the pills. The National Library of Medicine, through its Medical Literature Analysis & Retrieval System (MEDLARS), provided this writer with 469 English language citations on adverse effects of oral contraceptives in humans, covering the literature from January 1967 to December 1969. More than fifty metabolic changes in biochemical processes in all body tissues have been recorded. These changes are not necessary for contraception, and their ultimate effect on the health of the user is unknown.

A statistically significant association has been demonstrated between the use of oral contraceptives and the incidence of potentially fatal blood clots, particularly to the lungs. [6,7] There are at least 159 papers in the medical literature from January 1964 to August 1968 dealing with blood coagulation during the use of oral contraceptives. Other adverse reactions known to occur in patients receiving the pill are gastrointestinal symtoms such as nausea, vomiting, abdominal cramps and bloating; breakthrough bleeding, spotting, change in menstrual flow, absent menses during and after treatment; edema, chloasma or melasma; breast changes such as tenderness, enlargement and secretion; weight gain or loss, changes in the uterine cervix, suppression of

4. Kistner, R. W. *The Pill.* Delacorte Press, New York, 1969, pp. XVIII and 329.

5. *New England J. Med.* 276:239-240, 1967; ibid. 281:1014-1015, 1969; *J.A.M.A.* 202:902-903, 1967; *Lancet* 2:783-784, 1969; *Annals Int. Med.* 65:863-864, 1966; ibid. 66:446-447, 1967.

6. Inman, W H. and Vessey, M. P. "Investigation of Deaths From Pulmonary Coronary and Cerebral Thrombosis and Embolism in Women of Childbearing Age." *Brit. Med. J.* 2:193-199, 1968.

7. Vessey, M. P. and Doll, R. "Investigation of Relation Between Use of Oral Contraceptives and Thromboembolic Disease." *Brit. Med. J.* 2:199-205, 1968.

lactation when given immediately after birth, jaundice, migraine, allergic rash, rise in blood pressure in susceptible individuals, and mental depression. Recently, the possible relation of oral contraceptives to breast cancer, has been raised.[5] A definitive answer to this question is not yet available.

The use of such powerful and effective drugs cannot be undertaken casually from the medical viewpoint. Alternative methods, though less convenient, should receive consideration. One such alternative is the intrauterine device. A concise but comprehensive review, including an excellent bibliography of several hundred references called "Report on Intrauterine Devices" was prepared in 1968 by the Advisory Committee on Obstetrics & Gynecology of the Food & Drug Administration. The intrauterine devices have proved far more reliable than the traditional methods (diaphragm and condom) and only slightly less reliable than the "pill."[8] Side effects include bleeding, pain, expulsion, infection and perforation. In a country such as India where the high cost of the "pill," and the unreliability of the patients make oral contraception impractical, the advantages of intrauterine devices are obvious. The Soviet Union has also selected intrauterine devices as the basis for its recent drive in launching a major birth control program.[9]

From the Jewish legal viewpoint, it is important to know the mechanism of action of oral contraceptives and intrauterine devices. The pill works by inhibiting ovulation through a complex hormonal feedback mechanism involving both the ovary and the pituitary gland. In addition, secretions in the cervix are affected in such a way to make it difficult for the sperm to penetrate the cervical os. The latest evidence suggests that intrauterine devices are in fact abortifacients, preventing proper implantation and growth of the fertilized egg. The Jewish perspective on the various methods of birth control is discussed below.

8. Allan, F. N. "Birth Control by Intrauterine Devices." *J.A.M.A.* 207:121-122, 1969.
9. "USSR Picks IUD over the Pill." *Medical World News,* Jan. 10, 1969, pp. 15-18.

Legal Aspects of Contraception

In the United States the Comstock Act of 1873 declares contraceptives obscene and prohibits their transmission through the mails or by public carriers. The ban also covers literature which describes birth control methods or advises where they may be obtained. Prior to 1936 the Comstock Act was rigidly enforced. However, on November 30 of that year, the U.S. Second Circuit Court of Appeals said that the act was not intended to prohibit "things which might intelligently be employed by conscientious and competent physicians." The Attorney General did not appeal the decision to the Supreme Court, and thus it constitutes the law of the land.

There are presently at least 30 states which have laws concerning contraception. In some states, contraceptive activities are prohibited but physicians are specifically exempted and birth control clinics operate freely. In other states the only ban is on advertising. No state interferes with *bona fide* medical practice.

In 1966, in his health and education message to Congress, President Johnson declared: "It is essential that all families have access to information and services that will allow freedom to choose the number and spacing of their children within the dictates of individual conscience." In 1968, Congress earmarked 24 million dollars for family planning services. Many State legislatures are now following this example and appropriating funds for such services.

The Food & Drug Administration controls the quality of all condoms and diaphragms as well as the sale of all contraceptive drugs. After reports of isolated cases of serious blood-clotting accidents, a committee of specialists appointed by the Food & Drug Administration in 1963 concluded that they could find no statistical evidence of a causal relation between the "pill" and blood-clotting problems, but urged continued study. Another advisory committee in 1966 concluded that "there is no adequate scientific data at this time proving these compounds unsafe for human use." The double negative seemed to imply doubt. On June 28, 1968 the Commissioner of the Food & Drug Administration mailed a letter to every American physician in which he stated, in part:

> "... the most recent data developed in studies conducted in Great Britain confirms what had been suspected: *there is a definite association between the use of oral contraceptives and the incidence of thromboembolic disorders...*"

The 1969 report of the above advisory committee entitled, "The Pill — A Second Look," arrived at a similar conclusion and, as a result, the Food & Drug Administration now requires a package insert warning for oral contraceptive users that advises them to consult with their physician about side effects. The insert is the first ever required to be placed in the patients' hands.

The American Medical Association and Contraception

The American Medical Association's policy on contraception was spelled out by the House of Delegates at the 1964 Clinical Convention in Miami Beach.

At that time, the House adopted a report prepared by the Committee on Human Reproduction. Among its policy statements were the following:

> "... the prescription of child-spacing measures should be made available to all patients who require them, consistent with their creeds and morals, whether they obtain their medical care through private physicians or tax or community-supported health services.
>
> An intelligent recognition of the problems that relate to human reproduction, including the need for population control, is more than a matter of responsible parenthood, it is a matter of responsible medical practice.
>
> The medical profession should accept a major responsibility in

matters related to human reproduction as they affect the total population and the individual family.

In discharging this responsibility, physicians must be prepared to provide counsel and guidance when the needs of the patients require it or refer the patients to appropriate persons.

The AMA shall take the responsibility for disseminating information to physicians on all phases of human reproduction, including sexual behavior, by whatever means are appropriate.

Emphasis (should) be given to teaching in medical schools the total subject of "reproduction" including sexual behavior. This teaching can be included in many of the present curricula and need not involve adding new courses."

The AMA makes available to physicians for distribution to their patients numerous booklets and pamphlets including *Contraceptive Drugs & Devices* (1967 and *What You Should Know About the "Pill"* (1970). In mid-January, 1970, in the wake of a nation-wide controversy over "the pill," the AMA Council on Drugs upheld the use of oral contraceptives stating they should continue to be prescribed by physicians for patients who require this type of contraception. It endorsed its own statement published in the February 27, 1967 issue of the Journal of the AMA indicating there was no reason to recommend any change in the present availability of oral contraceptives. It recommended that research into the possible side effects of these drugs continue.

The American College of Obstetricians and Gynecologists, in a policy statement in 1970, said that it considers "that the oral contraceptives are accepted therapeutic methods available to the patient under the supervision of her physicians."

The World Health Associaiton, in 1966, keenly aware of the world population problem, published two pamphlets (Technical Report Series #326 and 332) entitled *Clinical Aspects of Oral Gestogens* and *Basic and Clinical Aspects of Intra-Uterine Devices.*

Moral Aspects of Contraception

The morality (or immorality) of contraception is discussed at length by Fletcher[10] and McFadden.[11] All moral issues seem to boil down to a two-sided argument. On the one hand, many people claim that there is no moral difference between preventing the natural process of conception by contraception, and preventing the natural process of obesity by diet or pills.[10] On the other hand, traditional Judaic-Christian teaching maintains that by the mind and will of G-d there is an objective standard of right and wrong in the universe, and that men are possessed with the rational faculty to choose one or the other. Thus, if the Torah considers any interference with the act of procreation as morally wrong, then such interference is legally prohibited in Jewish law. The commandment of *be fruitful and multiply* (Genesis 1:28) interdicts the indiscriminate use of contraceptives.

The argument that contraceptive chemicals may kill a fertilized ovum (i.e. a potential person) is more germaine to a treatise on abortion, and will not be discussed here. Furthermore, such an argument is not applicable to most modern methods of contraception including the pill and intrauterine devices. The problem of eugenics and population control is as much a moral dilemma as it is a matter of social ethics.

The economic argument for contraception emphasizes that parents should only have the number of children they can support in an adequate fashion. This argument possesses its greatest strength and appeal when it is applied to large families with below average income. The fact that some good may be derived from contraception employed for economical reasons does not make such a practice morally right. In order that all children in a family be provided with adequate food, clothing, shelter and education, contraception may be no more morally

---

10. Fletcher, Y. "Contraception: Our Right to Control Parenthood," in *Morals & Medicine*, 1954. Princeton Univ. Press, pp. 65-99.
11. McFadden, C. Y. "Contraception," in *Medical Ethics*, 5th edit., 1961. Davis Publishers, Phila., pp. 65-92.

justified than robbery by the parents to provide for the needs of the children. Robbery and contraception are both immoral, although both might achieve a desirable outcome. The solution to the economic argument for contraception is a better organization of society, with sufficient work and distribution of wealth for all.

Medical indications for the use of contraceptive devices and methods are many and include diseases wherein pregnancy would result in a marked deterioration of the mother's health or even threaten her life. Such conditions are rheumatic heart disease, tuberculosis, certain kidney diseases, severe diabetes and others. However, to masquerade behind a medical indication, particularly psychiatric illness, where none exists, or where the risks are minimal, is certainly immoral.

It is sometimes asserted that the stability, or even the preservation, of a marriage depends upon the practice of contraception. Reasons may include the desire of a wife to continue working after marriage, the lure of a professional career, unwillingness to give up an active social life and reluctance to financially drain the marriage by having children. Such reasons, purely of convenience, for the use of contraceptives, are certainly immoral.

Eating and drinking should not be pure biological acts. They should be performed with the realization of the power which the Creator has bestowed upon us, namely, the preservation of one's life and health. In this sense, abusing the privilege of food and beverage would be considered immoral. So too, the use of man's reproductive powers is immoral when employed deliberately to circumvent G-d's commandment of *be fruitful and multiply* (Genesis 1:28).

Catholic Attitude Toward Contraception

The most thorough, scholarly, objective analysis of Catholic doctrine on birth control throughout history is the recently published work of John T. Noonan, Jr.[12] This book traces the development of the

---

12. Noonan, J. T., Jr. *Contraception: A History of its Treatment by the Catholic Theologians and Canonists.* Cambridge, Mass., Harvard Univ. Press, 1966, 561 pp.

CONTRACEPTION

Church's position on contraception, and analyzes the historical situations that influenced various Church decisions over the centuries from the year 50 C.E. until 1965.

The traditional Catholic viewpoint is to prohibit all forms of contraception, except the rhythm method. This position is based upon the doctrine that the primary purpose of marriage is procreation, not companionship. Any method of birth control which violates the "natural law" is thus prohibited. Birth control by natural means, that is using the rhythm method or abstinence, is not considered a violation of the "natural law."

Recent pronouncements by several Popes have reaffirmed the traditional Catholic teaching on this matter. In his famous 1930 Encyclical *Casti Connubii* (On Christian Marriage), Pope Pius XI solemnly restated the condemnation of contraception, but gave his approval to the rhythm method. This approval was repeated by Pope Pius XII in 1951 when he said, "We affirm the legitimacy and, at the same time, the limits—in truth very wide—of a regulation of offspring which, unlike so-called 'birth control,' is compatible with the law of G-d. One may even hope that science will succeed in providing this licit (rhythm) method with a sufficiently secure basis."[13]

In a second address in 1951 the Pope elaborated on the conditions under which Catholics may use the rhythm method and be exempt from the duty of procreation and parenthood. Examples are "serious reasons, such as those often provided in the so-called indications of the medical, eugenical, economic and social order."[13]

In an address to hematologists in 1958, Pope Pius XII approved the use of oral contraceptives for the treatment of disease, but condemned their use for birth control.

In 1966, a papal commission, appointed two years earlier to reexamine the Church's position on marriage and the family, submitted its report to Pope Paul VI. There were both minority and majority reports. The former recommended continued adherence to the tradi-

13. Guttmacher, A. *Birth Control and Love*. London, McMillan Co., 1969, 2nd edit., pp. 141-168.

tional beliefs, whereas the latter urged changes in past teachings to allow chemical and mechanical contraceptives. In July 1968, in his Encyclical *Humanae Vitae,* the Pope rejected the majority report and condemned the use of techniques other than abstinence or the rhythm method. Dissent within the Catholic hierarchy was considerable with progressive views being voiced by Catholic theologians and laymen alike. As a result, married Catholic couples are often caught in agonizing crises of conscience: they are faced with a conflict between their duty to obey the Pope's teachings, and their duty to maintain a healthy marriage. And there the matter rests.

PROTESTANT VIEWS ON CONTRACEPTION

Protestant churches are virtually unanimous in their endorsement of birth control as enunciated in the 1961 statement of the National Council of Churches, the federation of 32 major Protestant denominations. Such an endorsement stems from the view that the basic purposes of marriage include not only procreation but also the "nourishment of the mutual love and companionship of husband and wife and their service to society."[13] Attitudes toward contraception of Baptists, Episcopalians, Lutherans, Methodists, Presbyterians and other Protestant churches are summarized by Guttmacher.[13]

JEWISH ATTITUDE TOWARD CONTRACEPTION

The most extensive study of the principles of Judaism concerning contraception, based on a wealth of primary sources, is that of David Feldman.[14] In his book, Rabbi Feldman examines the relevant precepts of the Talmud, Codes, Commentaries and Rabbinic Responsa. Feldman's work is so exhaustive that more recent articles on the subject[15] add very little to the overall picture.

14. Feldman, D. *Birth Control in Jewish Law.* New York Univ. Press, 1968, 322 pp.
15. Levy, J. *Hagelulah Limeniyath Harayan* (The Pill for Contraception). *NOAM* Jerusalem, 1968, vol. 11, pp. 167-177 (Heb.).

Procreation:

A brief discussion of the Biblical commandment *be fruitful and multiply* as decreed first to Adam and Eve (Gen. 1:28) and later to Noah and his sons (Gen. 9:1 and 7) and to Jacob (Gen. 35:11) seems appropriate. The importance of this commandment is stated in the Babylonian Talmud (*Yevamoth* 63b):

> "Rabbi Eliezer stated: He who does not engage in propagation of the race is as though he sheds blood; for it is said, *Whoso sheddeth man's blood by man shall his blood be shed* (Gen. 9:6); and this is immediately followed by the text *And you, be ye fruitful and multiply* (Gen. 9:7). Rabbi Jacob said: As though he has diminished the Divine Image; since it is said, *For in the image of G-d made He man* (Gen. 9:6), and this is immediately followed by *And you, be ye fruitful and multiply* (Gen. 9:7). Ben 'Azzai said: As though he sheds blood *and* diminishes the Divine Image . . .".

The explanation of the commandment is provided by the *Mishnah* (*Yevamoth* 6,6) where it states:

> "A man shall not abstain from the performance of the duty of the propagation of the race unless he already has children. (As to the number), Beth Shammai ruled: two males, and Beth Hillel ruled: A male and a female, as it is written (Gen. 1:27 and 5:2); *male and female* created He them."

It is beyond the scope of the present essay to delve in depth into the Rabbinic ramifications of the commandment of procreation. Detailed discussions are available elsewhere.[14,16] Suffice it to say that "the moral obligation, if not the commandment, still rests upon the husband of propagating the race when he already has two children."[17] The role of the woman in procreation is described by Feldman[14] and

---

16. Jakobovits, I. *Jewish Medical Ethics.* New York, Bloch Publishers, 1959, 389 pp.

17. Hertz, J. H. quoted by Jakobovits, I. in his *Journal of a Rabbi,* New York, Living Books, 1966, p. 215.

summarized in a quote from the fourteenth century Talmudic Commentary of Rabbi Nissim (*Hiddushei Ran to Kiddushin* 41a):

> ". . . even though she is not personally commanded concerning procreation, she performs a *mitzvah* (meritorious act) in getting married because she thereby assists her husband in the fulfillment of his *mitzvah* (religious duty) of *be fruitful and multiply*."

In a Jewish marriage, over and above the question of procreation, there exist the conjugal rights of the wife, technically termed *onah*. Thus, non-procreative intercourse such as occurs if the wife is too young to bear children, or is barren, or is pregnant, or post menopausal, or following a hysterectomy, is not only allowed but required. Improper emission of seed (*hash-chatat zera*) is not involved, or is cancelled out so long as the intercourse is in the manner of procreation. Not only are such sexual activities permitted, but they are in fact required by Biblical law (based on Exodus 21:10). "Marriage and marital relations are both independent of procreation, achieving the many desiderata spoken of in Talmudic, Responsa and Mystic literatures."[14] Such goals include fulfilling the wife's desire, physical release of the husband's sexual pressures, and the maintenance of marital harmony and domestic peace.

A lengthy chapter in Feldman's book[14] is devoted to a discussion of the legitimacy of sexual pleasure in Judaism. He quotes Nachmanides who said that "sexual intercourse is holy and pure when carried on properly, in the proper time and with the proper intentions. No one should claim that it is ugly or unseemly. G-d forbid! . . ." In a similar vein, Rabbi Jacob Emden is cited as having said: ". . . to us the sexual act is worthy, good and beneficial even to the soul. No other human activity compares with it; when performed with pure and clean intention it is certainly holy. There is nothing impure or defective about it, rather much exaltation. . . ."

Thus, whereas Christian teaching promulgates that procreation is the sole purpose of marriage and sexual intercourse, Judaism feels that not only need procreation result from sex, but mutual pleasure is sufficient reason in the sex act.

Contraception: Methods Employed by the Man:

There are at least six methods of contraception mentioned in the Bible and Talmud. The first of these is "coitus interruptus" which is unequivocally prohibited as stated by Maimonides (*Mishneh Torah. Hilchoth Issurei Biyah* 21:18):

> "It is forbidden to expend semen to no purpose. Consequently, a man should not thresh within and ejaculate without.... As for masturbators, not only do they commit a strictly forbidden act, but they are also excommunicated. Concerning them it is written, *Your hands are full of blood* (Isaiah 1:15) and it is regarded as equivalent to killing a human being."

A similar prohibition is found in Asheri, known as *Rosh* (*T'shuvoth HaRosh* 33:3) and in Karo's *Shulchan Aruch* (*Even Ha'ezer* 23:5) as well as in other Codes of Jewish Law.

The Scriptural sources upon which is based the prohibition of improper emission of seed is not clear, although many consider the act of Er and Onan (Gen. 38:7-10) to be the classic case of coitus interruptus. The Talmud, however, (*Yevamoth* 34b) views the act of Er and Onan as unnatural intercourse. Er wanted to preserve his wife's beauty by avoiding her becoming pregnant, and Onan sought to frustrate the Levirate law. Therefore, argues Feldman, if this was Onan's sin, no clear Biblical prohibition of improper emission of seed can be derived from the story of Onan, because the circumstances of the Levirate marriage are special, and allow for no more than an intimation (*remez*) of the evil of this method of contraception.

Other possible Biblical sources outlawing emission of seed for naught have been suggested. The Decalogue's commandment against adultery (Exod. 20:13) is said to have wider application, perhaps to immorality in general. The generation destroyed by the great flood (Gen. 5:12ff) is thought to have been liquidated because of the sin of improper emission of seed. Others say that this cardinal sin is implied in the commandment of *be fruitful and multiply*. Finally, states Feldman, the injunction (in Leviticus 18:6) against incest, literally, "immorality with one's own flesh" (*ish ish el kol sh'er b'saro*) includes improper emission of seed.

Whether this offense is considered homicide or only immoral as self defilement is also a matter of argumentation. The *Zohar* apparently espouses both reasons. Bringing forth semen in vain would also be prohibited if a man were to use a condom during intercourse, even if the sex act were performed in the natural way. Procurement of sperm for medical reasons (i.e. not in vain) is permitted under certain circumstances, such as sterility testing. Abstinence as a contraceptive method is prohibited as a double destruction of seed. Not only is the seed prevented from fulfilling its function of procreation, but it also fails to fulfill the commandment of *Onah,* one of the wife's conjugal rights.

Since the commandment of procreation in Judaism rests primarily on the man, any contraceptive method employed by him such as coitus interruptus, the condom or abstinence, would be strictly prohibited because of the onanistic nature of these methods. Even in situations where contraception is permitted by Jewish law, such as for situations in which pregnancy might endanger the life of the mother, these methods are not allowable.

Contraception: Methods Employed by the Woman:

The Talmud discusses four methods and techniques employed by the woman to prevent conception: The safe period, twisting movements following cohabitation, an oral contraceptive, and the use of an absorbent material during intercourse. These will be discussed separately.

The Safe Period

The period of fertility of a woman is mentioned in the Talmud (*Niddah* 31b) as follows:

> "Rabbi Isaac... stated: A woman conceives only immediately before her menstrual period, for it is said *Behold, I was brought forth in iniquity* (Psalms 51,7). But Rabbi Yochanan stated: a

woman conceives only immediately after her ritual immersion for it is said *And in cleansing did my mother conceive me* (Psalms 51,7) ..."

Feldman[14] cites rabbinic Responsa that call attention to cycles of fertility and sterility as a possible method of contraception. He concludes that there is no impropriety in the use of this method when birth control is required, such as in situations of hazard to the mother. However, by its use, the commandment of procreation and the wife's conjugal rights (*Onah*) are both frustrated. Furthermore, the unreliability of this method makes it unacceptable in cases of danger to life.

Twisting Following Cohabitation

An ancient method of contraception is when the woman makes violent and twisting movements following cohabitation in order to spill her husband's seed. This method is described in the Talmud (*Kethuboth* 37a) by Rabbi Jose who is of the opinion that "a woman who plays harlot turns over in order to prevent conception." The Talmud (*ibid.* 72a) further entitles a woman to receive her marriage settlement (*Kethubah*) if the husband imposes a vow on her to produce violent movements immediately after intercourse to avoid conception.

Oral Contraceptives

Throughout the centuries, numerous recipes have been recommended for oral contraception, from Pliny the Elder's parsley and mint, to Dioscorides' willow leaves in water; from Soranes' opopanix with cyrenaiac sap, to the marjoram, parsley and thyme of medieval Germany. In the Talmud, there are at least two discussions of a "cup of roots" or sterility potion. In *Yevamoth* 65b we find the following:

> "... Judith, the wife of Rabbi Hiyya, having suffered agonizing pains of childbirth, changed her clothes (on recovery) and appeared (in her disguise) before Rabbi Hiyya. She asked 'Is a

woman commanded to propagate the race?' He replied, 'No.' And relying on this decision (literally: she went), she drank a sterilizing potion..."

Elsewhere the Talmud states (*Shabbath* 109b-110b) that a potion of roots may be imbibed on the Sabbath because it is a cure for jaundice and gonorrhea. However, the imbiber may become impotent thereby. Thus, a woman may drink a sterilizing (i.e. contraceptive) potion as a cure for jaundice. A smaller dose recommended to treat gonorrhea does not produce permanent sterility. The ingredients of this "cup of roots" are enumerated by Rabbi *Yochanan* (*ibid.* 110a) and include Alexandrian gum, liquid alum, and garden crocus, powdered and mixed with beer (for jaundice) or wine (for gonorrhea). The *Tosefta* (supplemental Talmud) in Tractate *Yevamoth* 8,2 specifically states that a man is not allowed to drink any potion in order not to be fertile, because he is commanded to propagate the race, whereas a woman is permitted to drink the potion in order not to conceive.

The latter ruling is codified by both Maimonides (*Hilchoth Issurei Biyah* 12,12) and Karo (*Shulchan Aruch Even Ha'ezer* 5,12) unconditionally. Later Rabbis, however, stipulate that there must be some medical indication as in the case of Rabbi Hiyya's wife (*vide supra*) to allow the use of the potion of roots. Furthermore, as pointed out by Feldman,[14] "the bulk of the legal discussion surrounding the cup of roots is based on the crucial assumption that the sterilizing effect of this potion is permanent," thus raising the problem of castration, an act prohibited by Jewish law (Talmud, Tractate *Shabbath* 110b-111a) and based upon the Biblical phrase *that which has its stones bruised or crushed or broken or cut, ye shall not offer unto the Lord; neither shall ye do thus in your land* (Levit. 22,24).

The oral contraceptive pill of today seems to embody within itself the Talmudic "cup of roots." It allows intercourse to proceed in a natural and unimpeded manner, thus allowing fulfillment of the wife's conjugal rights. Furthermore, whereas the effect of the "cup of roots" is permanent, the effect of "the pill" is temporary, thereby setting aside the question of castration. No improper emission of seed is involved in the use of "the pill" (*Responsa Iggroth Mosheh, Even Ha'ezer* #65, 1961; and *Responsa Tzitz Eliezer*, Vol. 9, #51, 1967). However, without medical indication it appears as if the oral contraceptives should not be employed prior to the fulfillment of the commandment of procreation (i.e. at least two children). Furthermore, the question of the safety of "the pill" is both of medical and Jewish legal concern. Certainly, women in whom medical contraindications make the use of oral contraceptives dangerous, would be prohibited by Jewish law from taking them. Other deleterious side effects discussed in an earlier section of this essay, must also be taken into consideration. However, at the moment, "the pill" seems to be the least objectionable method of birth control in Jewish law.

Absorbent (Tampon) As A Contraceptive

Virtually all rabbinic rulings on the subject of contraception are based upon a key Talmudic statement which has been called "The *Beraita* of the Three Women." It reads as follows (*Yevamoth* 12b):

> "Rabbi Bebai recited before Rabbi Nachman: Three (categories of) women may (or must) use an absorbent (Hebrew: *moch*) in their marital intercourse (to prevent conception): a minor, a pregnant woman and a nursing woman. The minor, because (otherwise) she might become pregnant and as a result might die. A pregnant woman because (otherwise) she might cause her fetus to become a *sandal* (a flat fish-shaped abortion due to superfetation). A nursing woman, because (otherwise) she might have to wean her child prematurely (owing to her second conception), and he would die. And what is a minor? From the age of eleven years and one day until the age of twelve years and one day. One who is under or over this age (when conception is not possible or where pregnancy involves no fatal outcome, respectively) carries on her marital intercourse in the usual manner. This is the opinion of Rabbi Meir. But the Sages say: The one as well as the other carries on her marital intercourse in the usual manner, and mercy be vouchsafed from

Heaven (to save her from danger), for Scripture says *The Lord preserveth the simple* (Psalms 116,6) . . ."

Rabbi Feldman[14] excels in the discussion of this important passage or *beraita*. The nature and the status of the absorbent (or *moch*) in Talmudic law is explored in an entire chapter of Feldman's book. Subsequent chapters are devoted to an in-depth consideration of the three categories of women in the *beraita*, the many levels of debate concerning the meaning of the *beraita*, including the Talmudic commentators *Rashi* and *Rabbenu Tam*, early post Talmudic authorities (*Rishonim*), the Codes of Maimonides, Alfasi, Asheri and Karo, and finally the Rabbinic Responsa literature of the past several centuries.

Does the *beraita* allow or require the three women to use the absorbent? *Rashi* states that Rabbi Meir means "may use" and the Sages mean "may not," whereas *Rabbenu Tam* reports that Rabbi Meir means "must" and the Sages mean "must not but may." A second level of debate is concerned with whether the absorbent is to be used before (i.e. during) or after coitus? The outcome of the argumentation in the interpretation of the *beraita* is summarized by Jakobovits,[16] as follows:

> ". . . several authorities assume that this dispute applies only to these particular cases (i.e. three women) where the danger of a conception is in any event rather remote; hence, they infer that, in cases of a more definite threat to the mother's life arising from a pregnancy, there would be no objection at all to the use of contraceptives. Others hold that the three women are mentioned to illustrate the attitude to cases of resultant danger to life in general; while yet others regards the entire sanction as limited to these three women only."

Jakobovits, Feldman and others express surprise at the omission of reference to the pivotal *beraita* by the major codes of Jewish law, Maimonides and Karo. Even the Codes which mention the *beraita* (Asheri and Alfasi) only relay it verbatim without deriving any legal ruling therefrom. To perhaps compensate for this silence, there is available an enormous Rabbinic Responsa literature dealing with contraception. The most lenient or permissive view is that of 16th century Rabbi Solomon Luria (*Yam Shel Shlomo, Yevamoth* 1,8) who allows the wife to apply a tampon before intercourse, if a conception and pregnancy would prove dangerous. Many subsequent writers including Rabbis Solomon Zalman of Posen (*Responsa Chemdath Shlomo, Even Ha'ezer* #46), Simchah Bunem Sofer (*Responsa Shevet Sofer, Even Ha'ezer* #2) Mordechai Horowitz (*Responsa Mattei Levy*, Vol. 2, #31), Chayim Ozer Grodzinsky (*Responsa Achiezer, Even Ha'ezer* #23), Sholem Mordechai Schwadron (*Responsa Maharsham*, Vol. 1, #58), David Hoffmann (*Responsa Melamed Leho'il, Even Ha'ezer* #18) and others agree with Luria.

On the other hand, there is a school of non-permissivists who do not allow any impediment to natural intercourse. The chief proponents of this school are Rabbis Akiba Eger (*Responsa Akiba Eger* #71 and 72), Jacob Ettlinger (*Responsa Binyan Tziyon* #137) and Moses Schreiber (*Responsa Chatam Sofer, Yoreh Deah* #172).

Other Contraceptive Methods

For situations of pregnancy hazard, the pessary or diaphragm is allowed by numerous authorities including Rabbis Joshua Baumohl (*Responsa Emek Halacha* #66), Sholom Mordechai Schwardon (*Responsa Maharsham*, Vol. 1, #58), Chayim Sofer (*Responsa Machaneh Chayim, Even Ha'ezer* #53), and Mosheh Feinstein (*Responsa Iggroth Moshe, Even Ha'ezer* #63). The reason is that the normal coital act is not interfered with. This is not the case with the condom which constitutes an improper interference and is strictly prohibited. Chemical spermicides and douches are other contraceptive methods which leave the sex act alone and are thus permitted by many responsa writers but only in a case of danger to the mother from pregnancy. As to whether spermicides are preferable to the use of a diaphragm or vice versa is also a matter of debate. On the one hand the occlusive diaphragm does in fact constitute a mechanical barrier. On the other hand, "spermicides destroy the seed immediately upon its entry into the canal" (Rabbi Eliezer Waldenberg, *Responsa Tzitz Eliezer*, Vol. 9, #51, 2,3).

As to the intrauterine contraceptive devices, recent medical evidence seems to indicate that these produce contraception by inhibiting proper implantation of the fertilized ovum in the wall of the uterus. If this is so, then their abortifacient action might prohibit their use.

Final Note

The Jewish attitude toward contraception by any method is a non-permissive one if no medical or psychiatric threat to the mother or child exists. The duty of procreation, which is primarily a commandment on men, coupled with the wife's conjugal rights in Jewish law, mitigates against the use of the condom, coitus interruptus or abstinence under any circumstances. Where pregnancy hazard exists, and where Rabbinic sanction for the use of birth control is obtained, a hierarchy of acceptability emerges from the Talmudic and Rabbinic sources. Most acceptable are contraceptive means that least interfere with the natural sex act and least interfere with the full mobility of the sperm and its natural course. "Oral contraception by pill enjoys preferred status as the least objectionable method of birth control."[14] Since many different factors must be brought to bear on the final decision, it is suggested that competent Rabbinic opinion be sought to adjucate any given case, such opinion to be based upon expert medical testimony.

Chapter IV

The Jewish Attitude Toward Abortion

INTRODUCTION

Abortion is defined as the expulsion of a fetus from the uterus by premature termination of pregnancy. It can occur spontaneously or it can be induced; it may be therapeutic in nature, or criminal.

Tremendous interest in this subject is evidenced by the flood of books,[1] articles[2] and editorials[3] in the medical literature as well as

---

1. See Smith, D. T., editor, *Abortion and the Law* (Cleveland: Western Reserve Univ. Press, 1967), and Calderone, M. S., editor, *Abortion in the United States — A Conference sponsored by the Planned Parenthood Federation of America, Inc.* at Arden Home and the New York Academy of Medicine (New York: Hoeber-Harper, 1958); Guttmacher, A. F., editor, *The Case for Legalized Abortion* (Berkeley: Diablo Press, 1967); Robinson, W. J., *The Law Against Abortion: Its Perniciousness Demonstrated and its Repeal Demanded* (New York: Eugenics Publishing Co., 1933); Rongy, A. J., *Abortion: Legal or Illegal* (New York: Vanguard Press, 1933); Bates, J. E. and Zawadzki, E. S., *Criminal Abortion: A Study in Medical Sociology* (Springfield: C. C. Thomas Co., 1964); Devereux, G., *A Study of Abortion in Primitive Societies. A typological, distributional and dynamic analysis of the prevention of birth in 400 preindustrial societies* (New York: Julian Press, 1955); Rosen, H., editor, *Therapeutic Abortion: Medical, Psychiatric, Legal, Anthropological and Religious Considerations* (New York: Julian Press, 1954); *Abortion in Britain*, Proceedings of a Conference held by the Family Planning Association at the University of London on April 22, 1966 (London: Pitman Med. Publishing Co., 1966); Gebhard, P. H., Pomeroy, W. B., Martin, C. E. and Christenson, C. U., *Pregnancy, Birth and Abortion* (New York: Hoeber-Harper, 1958).

2. See Culiner, A., "Some Medical Aspects of Abortion," *J. Forensic Med.*, 10(1):9-13 (Jan.-March 1963); Moore, J. G. and Randall, J. H., "Trends in Therapeutic Abortion. A Review of 137 Cases," *Amer. J. Obst. Gynec.*, 63(1):28-40 (Jan. 1952); Calderone, M. S., "Illegal Abortion as a Public Health Problem," *Amer. J. Public Health*, 50(7):948-954 (July 1960); Bolter, S., "The Psychiatrists' Role in the Therapeutic Abortion: The Unwitting Accomplice," *Amer. J. Psychiatry*, 119(4):312-316 (Oct. 1962); Russel, K. P., "Changing Indications for Therapeutic

writings in the lay press.[4] In addition, there is an abundance of papers and books in the legal, theological and social science literatures, enumeration of which is beyond the scope of this essay. One of the reasons for this flurry of interest in abortion is the changing moral and legal attitudes toward therapeutic abortion. Consequently, laws are revised to conform with these changing sets of values. Even the conservative American Medical Association has modernized its 1871 position on this matter and has published a new statement of policy[5] spelling out the indications for therapeutic abortion.

Abortion. Twenty Years' Experience at Los Angeles County Hospital," *J.A.M.A.,* 151(2):108-11 (Jan 10, 1953); Kummer, J. M. and Leavy, Z., "Therapeutic Abortion Law Confusion," *J.A.M.A.,* 195(2):96-100 (Jan. 10, 1965); Niswander, K. R., Klein, M. and Randall, C. L., "Changing Attitudes Toward Therapeutic Abortion," *J.A.M.A.,* 196(13):1140-1143 (June 27, 1966); Hellegers, A. E., "Abortion, the Law and the Common Good," *Med. Opinion and Review,* 3(5):76-93 (May 1967); Hardin, G., "Blueprints, DNA and Abortion: A Scientific and Ethical Analysis," *Med. Opinion and Review,* 3(2):74-85 (Feb. 1967); Lederberg, J., "A Geneticist Looks at Contraception and Abortion in the Changing Mores of Biomedical Research. A Colloquium on Ethical Dilemmas from Medical Advances," *Ann. Int. Med.,* 67 (III part 2): Suppl. 7:25-27 (Sept. 1967); Hall, R. E., "Therapeutic Abortion, Sterilization and Contraception," *Amer. J. Obst. Gynec.,* 91(4):518-532 (Feb. 15, 1965); Gold, E. M., Erhardt, C. L., Jacobziner, H., and Nelson, F. G., "Therapeutic Abortions in New York City: a 20-year Review," *Amer. J. Public Health,* 55(7):964-972 (July 1965); Page, I. H., editor, "Abortion: The Doctor's Dilemma," *Modern Medicine,* 35(9):12-32 (April 24, 1967).

3. Elkinton, J. R., "Abortion and the Doctor," *Annals Int. Med.,* 67(5):1111-1113 (Nov. 1967); Guttmacher, A. F., "Induced Abortion," *N. Y. State Journal of Medicine,* 63(16):2334-2335 (Aug. 15, 1963).

4. Ober, W. B., "We Should Legalize Abortions," *The Sat. Eve. Post,* (Oct. 8, 1966); Guttmacher, A. F., "The Law that Doctors Often Break," *Redbook Magazine,* (August, 1959).

5. AMA Policy on Therapeutic Abortion. *J.A.M.A.,* 201(7):544 (Aug. 14, 1967). "The American Medical Association is cognizant of the fact that there is no consensus among physicians regarding the medical indications for therapeutic abortion. However, the majority of physicians believe that, in the light of recent advances in scientific medical knowledge, there may be substantial medical evidence brought forth in the evaluation of an occasional obstetric patient which would warrant the institution of therapeutic abortion either to safeguard the health or life of the patient, or to prevent the birth of a severely crippled, deformed or abnormal infant.

ABORTION

Religious attitudes concerning abortion play a paramount role in shaping the thoughts, decrees and actions of various groups. The present article is an attempt to survey the Biblical, Talmudic, and Rabbinic literatures, and, from these sources, to describe in detail the Jewish attitude toward abortion. For comparative purposes, the Catholic and Protestant positions on abortion are briefly outlined.

The Problem

Of the estimated 1,000,000 abortions that occur yearly in the United States,[6] approximately two thirds are spontaneous, and at least 300,000

"Under these special circumstances, it is consistent with the policy of the American Medical Association for a licensed physician, in a hospital accredited by the Joint Commission on Accreditation of Hospitals, and in consultation with two other physicians chosen because of their recognized professional competence who have examined the patient and have concurred in writing, to be permitted to prescribe and administer treatment for his patient commensurate with sound medical judgment and currently established scientific knowledge. Prior to the institution of a therapeutic abortion, the patient and her family should be fully advised of the medical implications and the possible untoward emotional and physical sequelae of the procedure.

"In view of the above, and recognizing that there are many physicians who on moral or religious grounds oppose therapeutic abortion under any circumstances, the American Medical Association is opposed to induced abortion except when:

(1) There is documented medical evidence that continuance of the pregnancy may threaten the health or life of the mother, or
(2) There is documented medical evidence that the infant may be born with incapacitating physical deformity or mental deficiency, or
(3) There is documented medical evidence that continuance of a pregnancy, resulting from legally established statutory or forcible rape or incest may constitute a threat to the mental or physical health of the patient;
(4) Two other physicians chosen because of their recognized professional competence have examined the patient and have concurred in writing; and
(5) The procedure is performed in a hospital accredited by the Joint Commission on Accreditation of Hospitals.

"It is to be considered consistent with the principles of ethics of the American Medical Association for physicians to provide medical information to State Legislatures in their consideration of revision and/or the development of new legislation regarding therapeutic abortion."

6. Taussig, F. J., *Abortion, Spontaneous and Induced: Medical and Social Aspects* (St. Louis: C. V. Mosby, 1936).

criminal.[7] The latter figure, however, may be erroneously high.[8] Therapeutic abortions were carried out at the rate of 18,000 per year.[9] Indications for therapeutic abortions until recently have included various threats to the life of the mother such as psychiatric or organic medical disease. Medical illnesses in the mother necessitating premature termination of pregnancy are exemplified by cardiovascular disorders as rheumatic heart disease, renal diseases as pyelonephritis, gastro-intestinal disturbances as severe ulcerative colitis, neoplastic diseases as carcinoma of the breast or uterus, infections as tuberculosis, allergic disorders as advanced asthma, endocrine and metabolic conditions as thyrotoxicosis and uncontrolled diabetes and diseases of the central nervous system as multiple sclerosis or epilepsy. Prior to the recently enacted abortion reform laws, socio-economic or fetal factors were not acceptable as reasons to perform therapeutic abortions. Thus, women exposed to drugs as thalidomide, or viruses as rubella, or radiation or Rh diseases were denied abortion of the potentially defective fetus.

LEGAL STATUS OF THERAPEUTIC ABORTION IN THE UNITED STATES

Until April 1967, abortion was a crime in all fifty states. In forty-six states and the District of Columbia, an abortion was permissible if it were necessary to save the life of the mother.[10] The statutes, however, differed in regard to who is to perform the operation, who is to

---

7. Taylor, H. C., Jr., Chairman, *The Abortion Problem* — Proceedings of the Conference held under the auspices of the National Committee on Maternal Health, Inc. at the New York Academy of Medicine, June 19 and 20, 1952 (Baltimore: Williams and Wilkins Co., 1944).

8. Reppun, J. I. F., "Validity of Figures," *New Eng. J. Med.*, 278(3):168, (Jan. 18, 1968).

9. Hefferman, R. J. and Lynch, W. A., "What is the Status of Therapeutic Abortion in Modern Obstetrics?" *Amer. J. Obst., and Gynec.*, 66(2):335-345 (Aug. 1953).

10. George, B. J., Jr., "Current Abortion Laws: Proposals and Movements for Reform in Abortion and the Law," in *Abortion and the Law* (Cleveland: Western Reserve Univ. Press, 1967), pp. 1-36.

determine the necessity of the abortion and how many physicians must participate in such a decision.

The American Law Institute, in 1959, formulated a Model Penal Code (207-11) which states as follows: "A licensed physician is justified in terminating a pregnancy if:

(a) he believes there is substantial risk that continuance of the pregnancy would gravely impair the physical or mental health of the mother or that the child would be born with a grave physical or mental defect, or the pregnancy resulted from rape or from incest; and:

(b) two physicians, one of whom may be the person performing the abortion, have certified in writing their belief in the justifying circumstances and have filed such certificates prior to the abortion in the licensed hospital where it is to be performed, or in such other place as may be designated by law."

It is upon this Model Penal Code that the abortion reform laws and the new American Medical Association therapeutic abortion policy statement are based.

A major impetus to change the abortion laws in the United States came in 1962 with the celebrated case of a Phoenix, Arizona housewife who took thalidomide tablets early in pregnancy. This drug is known to produce birth defects such as congenital partial or complete absence of one or more limbs. Unable to obtain a legal abortion in this country, she finally had the operation performed in Sweden where it was confirmed that her fetus was severely malformed.

The nationwide German measles (rubella) epidemic in 1963 and 1964 provided further impetus for abortion law reform. During these two tragic years, 20,000 stillbirths and 30,000 congenitally abnormal babies were born to women who had contracted rubella during the first trimester of pregnancy.

With this background, Colorado, on April 25, 1967, became the first state to legalize abortion according to the guidelines set down by the Model Penal Code of the American Law Institute.

The Colorado statute authorizes an abortion whenever a pregnancy (a) results from rape or incest, (b) threatens the woman's physical or mental health or (c) is likely to produce a mentally deranged or physically deformed child. The Colorado law further specifies that the abortion must be approved by a panel of three physicians and the operation must be performed in an accredited hospital.

North Carolina enacted an abortion reform law a few weeks later, but excluded non-residents (less than four months). California followed with its abortion liberalization which was signed into law on June 15, 1967. The California bill does not, however, permit abortions where the child is likely to be deformed.

Georgia, early in 1968, became the fourth state to reform its abortion statute. Its bill is more restrictive in that it requires three separate physicians to examine the woman requesting the abortion. Each physician must certify in writing that the abortion is necessary and specify the reasons. Maryland followed with its abortion reform law on July 1, 1968, which permits abortions where the mother's physical or mental health is endangered, where there is substantial risk that the baby would be seriously deformed or retarded and where the pregnancy results from rape.

In many other state legislatures, abortion reform bills were introduced—some ended in defeat, others tabled for further consideration. Nonetheless it appears that more states will adopt abortion reforms similar to those in Colorado, North Carolina and California.

The initial fear that the above states will become "abortion meccas"[11] has proved unfounded. In the first three months after the signing of Colorado's new liberalized abortion law, only 25 therapeutic abortions were performed.[12] During the first eight months under the new law, 120 carefully selected and supervised abortions were performed in

---

11. Brody, J. E., "Abortion: Once a Whispered Problem, Now a Public Debate," *The New York Times* (January 8, 1968), 28.

12. *The American Medical Association News*, Volume 10, no. 73, (Sept. 11, 1967).

Colorado hospitals, 29 of them on women from other states.[13] (See addendum at the end of this chapter.)

LEGAL ATTITUDES TOWARD ABORTION IN OTHER COUNTRIES

In England, the Criminal Abortion (Offenses against Persons) Act of 1861 states[14] that it is an offense to procure or attempt to procure abortion and any person, including the pregnant woman herself, who attempts to do so by any means whatsoever (by the administration of drugs or injections or surgical intervention) is guilty of a felony. Nearly seven decades later, the Infant Life (Preservation) Act was enacted into law in 1929.[15] This statute specifices that the act of causing the death of the child (unborn fetus) must be done in good faith and only for preserving the life of the mother. A new law permitting abortion for social as well as medical reasons in England was recently passed by the House of Commons and became effective in April, 1968.

The new British law permits abortion when two physicians agree that continued pregnancy might threaten the mother's life or physical or mental health, or might result in the birth of a child with handicapping physical or mental abnormalities.

Another ground for abortion is the judgment that the child's birth might injure the physical or mental health of the woman's existing children. This so-called social clause, which goes far beyond the most liberal abortion laws in the United States, provoked bitter controversy in Parliament. It permits physicians to consider such factors as overcrowding, inadequate housing or the emotional tensions that might be produced by too large a family.

Leaders of the British Medical Association opposed this latter clause on the ground that it called for assessments beyond the physician's

---

13. *Medical World News*, 9(6):20 (Feb. 9, 1968).
14. Roques, F. W., "Therapeutic Abortion, or Miscarriage," in *Medical Ethics, A Guide to Students and Practitioners*, (London: Lloyd Luke, 1957) pp. 100-101.
15. "Sweeping British Law Eases Abortion," *Medical World News*. Vol. 8 (45):29, (Nov. 10, 1967).

area of competence. Supporters of the clause maintained that the law does not require an unwilling physician to perform any abortion.[15]

In Hungary, since 1950, legal abortion is allowed before the twelfth week of pregnancy, virtually at the request of the patient.[16]

In Japan, because of the population explosion and high incidence of criminal abortion, therapeutic abortion was legalized in 1948 for health and social reasons.[17]

In Sweden, the liberalized abortion laws are based upon the thesis that adoption is not considered an acceptable alternative to abortion[18] for care of unwanted children. The legal preconditions include danger to life or physical or mental health of the mother, the risk of giving birth to a defective or diseased child and pregnancies resulting from rape or incest. An additional provision in the Swedish law states that social circumstances shall be judged as part of the risk to the mother's health.

Liberalization of abortion laws for social reasons indicate the trend in Bulgaria, Poland, Czechoslovakia, Yugoslavia, and Hungary.[19] These countries followed the example of the Soviet Union which was the first country to legalize abortion in 1920. Other writings on the legal status of abortions are available.[20–21]

16. Beattie, J., "Therapeutic Procedures and the Sanctity of Life," in *Ethical Responsibility in Medicine, A Christian Approach*. V. Edmunds and S. C. Scorer, editors, (London: E. and S. Livingston Ltd., 1967), pp. 72-87.

17. *Ibid.*, pp. 72-87.

18. Geijerstam, G. K., "In Sweden, Abortion is the Last Resort," *Medical World News*, (Sept. 29, 1967) p. 53. For a discussion of abortion legislation in Denmark see Skalts, V. and Norgaard, M., "Abortion Legislation in Denmark," in *Abortion and the Law*, edited by D. T. Smith, pp. 144-178; Hoffmeyer, H., "Medical Aspects of the Danish Legislation on Abortion," in *Abortion and the Law*, edited by D. T. Smith, pp. 179-205.

19. Breitenecker, L. and Breitenecker, R., "Abortion in German-Speaking Countries of Europe," in *Abortion and the Law*, edited by D .T. Smith, pp. 206-223.

20. Guttmacher, M. S., "The Legal Status of Therapeutic Abortions," in *Therapeutic Abortion*, edited by H. Rosen, (New York: Julian Press, 1954), pp. 175-186.

21. Good, F. L. and Kelly, O. F., *Marriage, Morals and Medical Ethics*, (New York: P. T. Kennedy & Sons, 1951); Drinan, R. F., "The Inviolability of the Right to be Born," in *Abortion and the Law*, edited by D. T. Smith, pp. 107-123.

The AMA Policy on Therapeutic Abortion

Following an emotion filled debate before Reference Committee G of the House of Delegates of the American Medical Association at its meeting in Atlantic City in June 1967, a new policy statement on therapeutic abortion emerged to rescind the previous policy that stood immobile since 1871. The Committee on Human Reproduction had prepared the policy statement and unanimously recommended it to the Board of Trustees which in turn unanimously recommended it to the AMA membership. The latter adopted the new policy which no longer opposes therapeutic abortion if continued pregnancy threatened the health or life of the mother, if the child might be physically deformed or mentally deficient or if conception had resulted from rape or incest.[5]

Catholic Attitude Toward Therapeutic Abortion

The Catholic Church's attitude toward therapeutic abortion is that any direct attack on the fetus is considered murder, even if it is carried out with the best intentions. Neither man nor the state has the authority to destroy the life of an innocent person, and both criminal and therapeutic abortion involve a direct and deliberate destruction of an innocent life. The emphasis is on the word "innocent." The unborn child, from conception onward is considered a human being with all the rights of any other human person. Therefore, although a direct abortion would preserve the mother's life or health, it is not morally permissible.

On October 29, 1951, Pope Pius XII delivered an address on morality in marriage in which he stated:[22]

> "Every human being, even the infant in the mother's womb, has the right to life immediately from G-d, not from the parents or from any human society or authority. Therefore, there is no

---

22. McFadden, C. J., *Medical Ethics* (Philadelphia: F. A. Davis Co., 5th edit., 1961), pp. 140-141.

man, no human authority, no science, no medical, eugenic, social, economic or moral indication, that can show or give a valid juridical title for direct deliberate disposition concerning an innocent life. . . . Thus, for example, to save the life of the mother is a most noble end, but the direct killing of the child as a means to this end is not licit . . ."

Further reasons for Catholic opposition to abortion include the teaching that all unbaptized fetuses and infants are forever excluded from participation in G-d's divinity and in the Beatific Vision reserved for those who have been baptized. No one has the right to exclude an unborn infant from such participation.[23]

The penalty for performing an abortion is stated in Canon 2350 of the Church's Code of Canon Law: "Persons who procure abortion, the mother not excepted, automatically incur excommunication." The same penalty is incurred by all those who assist in procuring the abortion.

From the standpoint of the Catholic Church, there seem to be neither psychiatric nor medical indications for terminating a pregnancy.

Protestant Attitudes Towards Therapeutic Abortion

The Baptists consider abortion to be primarily "a medical problem and that the theological implications can be trusted to our Omniscient Heavenly Father."[24] Similarly, the Methodist Church considers abortion a scientific, medical matter on which only competent medical opinion has any value.

The attitude of the Lutheran Church is very similar to that of the Catholics in that "the use of abortifacients and of medicines designed to produce sterility is condemned."[25] The American Lutheran Con-

---

23. Healy, E. F., *Medical Ethics* (Chicago: Loyola Univ. Press, 1956), pp. 357-358; Marshall, J., *The Ethics of Medical Practice* (London: Darton, Longman & Todd, 1960), pp. 152-153.

24. Curran, F. J., "Religious Implications," in *Therapeutic Abortion, Medical, Psychiatric, Legal, Anthropological and Religious Considerations,* edited by H. Rosen (New York: Julian Press, 1954), pp. 153-174.

25. *Ibid.*, pp. 153-174.

ference, however, at its biennial meeting in 1952 pronounced a statement part of which reads as follows: "Abortion must be regarded as the destruction of a living being, and, except as a medical measure to save the mother's life, will not be used by a Christian to avoid an unwanted birth. ..."

The Presbyterian Church believes the life of the mother would receive first consideration. Ministers and members are allowed to follow "enlightened conscience with regard to this matter."[26] The Episcopalians also permit individual clergymen to make the decision.

The Unitarian Church states that "judgment regarding therapeutic abortions rests upon the principle of preserving and extending human life and that this decision must be the patient's and the physician's—not the Church's or any other institution's."[27]

Jewish Attitude Toward Abortion

The question of intentional abortion is not raised directly in the Bible. We deduce the status of the fetus from the following relevant passages.

An unborn fetus in Jewish law is not considered a person (Hebrew: *nefesh*, meaning soul) until it has been born. The fetus is regarded as a part of the mother's body and not a separate being until it begins to egress from the womb during parturition. In fact, until forty days after conception, the fertilized egg is considered as "mere fluid." These facts form the basis for the present day Jewish legal views on abortion. Biblical, Talmudic and Rabbinic support for these statements will now be presented.

In Exodus (21:22-23) we find the following: "When men fight and one of them pushes a pregnant woman and a miscarriage results, but no other misfortune ensues, the one responsible shall be fined as the woman's husband may exact from him, the payment to be based

26. *Ibid.*, pp. 153-174.
27. *Ibid.*, pp. 153-174.

on judges' reckoning. But if other misfortune ensues, the penalty shall be life for life. . . ."

Rashi quotes the *Mechilta* which interprets "no other misfortune" to mean no fatal injury to the woman following her miscarriage. In that case, the attacker pays only compensation for the loss of the fetus. Most other Jewish Bible commentators including *Ramban, Ibn Ezra, Malbim, Torah Temimah,* Hirsch, and Hertz agree with Rashi's interpretation. We thus see that when the mother is unharmed following trauma to her abdomen and only the fetus is aborted, our major, if not only, concern is to have the one responsible pay damages to the husband since the fetus is his property. No prohibition is evident from this Scriptural passage against destroying the unborn child.

Based upon this Biblical statement Maimonides in his code asserts as follows: "If one assaults a woman, even unintentionally, and her child is born prematurely, he must pay the value of the child to her husband and the compensation for injury and pain to the woman."[28] Maimonides continues with statements regarding how these compensations are computed. A similar declaration is found in Karo's *Shulchan Aruch*.[29] No concern is expressed by either Maimonides or Karo regarding the status of the miscarried fetus. It is part of the mother and belongs jointly to her and her husband and thus damages must be paid for its premature death. However, the one who was responsible is not culpable for murder since the unborn fetus is not considered a person.

Murder in Jewish law is based upon Exodus 21:12 where it is written: "He that smiteth a man so that he dieth shall surely be put to death." The word "man" is interpreted by the Sages to mean a man but not a fetus.[30] Thus, the destruction of an unborn fetus is not considered murder.

Another pertinent Scriptural passage is Leviticus 24:17 where it states: "And he that smiteth any person mortally shall surely be put to

---

28. Code of Maimonides (*Mishneh Torah*). "Laws of Wounding and Damaging," (*Hilchoth Chovel Umazik*), Chapter 4, Paragraph 1.
29. *Shulchan Arukh, Choshen Mishpat,* Chapter 423, par. 1.
30. *Tractate Sanhedrin* 84b.

death." However, an unborn fetus is not considered a person or *nefesh* and, therefore, its destruction does not incur the death penalty.

Turning to Talmudic sources, the *Mishnah* in *Tractate Oholoth* 7:6 asserts the following: "If a woman is having difficulty in giving birth (and her life is in danger), one cuts up the fetus within her womb and extracts it limb by limb, because her life takes precedence over that of the fetus. But if the greater part was already born, one may not touch it, for one may not set aside one person's life for that of another."

Tosafot Yom Tov, in his commentary on this *Mishnah,* explains that the fetus is not considered a *nefesh* until it has egressed into the air of the world and, therefore, one is permitted to destroy it to save the mother's life. Similar reasoning is found in Rashi's commentary on the Talmudic discussion of this *Mishnah* where Rashi states that as long as the child did not come out into the world, it is not called a living being, *i.e. nefesh.*[31] Once the head of the child has come out, the child may not be harmed because it is considered as fully born, and one life may not be taken to save another.

The *Mishnah* in *Tractate Arachin* 1:4 states: "If a pregnant woman is taken out to be executed, one does not wait for her to give birth; but if her pains of parturition had already begun, (literally: she had already sat on the birth stool), one waits for her until she gives birth. . . ." One may conclude from this *Mishnah* that one does not delay the execution of the mother in order to save the life of the fetus because we wish to avoid causing grief to the mother.

The Talmud explains[32] that the embryo is part of the mother's body and has no identity of its own since it is dependent for its life upon the body of the woman. However, as soon as it starts to move from the womb, it is considered an autonomous being (*nefesh*) and thus unaffected by the mother's state. This concept of the embryo being considered part of the mother and not a separate being recurs through-

---

31. *Tractate Sanhedrin* 72b.
32. *Tractate Arachin* 7a.

out the Talmud[33] and Rabbinic writings.[34] The Talmud continues[32]: "Rab Judah said in the name of Samuel: If a (pregnant) woman is about to be executed, one strikes her against her womb so that the child may die first, to avoid her being disgraced." Rashi explains that if the child escaped death and came forth after the mother's execution, it would cause vaginal bleeding and disgrace the executed mother. Thus we have evidence that an unborn fetus does not have the status of a living being and destroying it to save the mother embarrassment is permissible if it is going to die anyway.

A very difficult and bizarre *Tosefot* states that "it is permissible to kill an unborn fetus."[35] Some authorities[36] consider these words of *Tosefot* verbatim whereas others are of the opinion that *Tosefot* should not be interpreted literally.[37] Yet others state that these words of *Tosefot* are erroneous.[38]

Prior to forty days after conception, a fertilized egg is considered nothing more than "mere fluid"[39] and one "need not take into consideration the possibility of a valid childbirth."[40] However, after 40 days have elapsed, fashioning or formation of the fetus is deemed to have occurred. Laws of ritual uncleanliness must be observed for

---

33. *Tractates Chullin* 58a, *Gittin* 23b, *Nazir* 51a, *Baba Kamma* 88b, *Temura* 31a.

34. *Responsa Maharit*: Section 1, no. 97 and no. 99; *Responsa Chavat Ya'ir*, no. 31; *Responsa Noda Biyehuda*: *Choshen Mishpat*, no. 59; *Chidushei Ramban on Niddah* 44b; *Peri Megadim*: *Orach Chayim* 328:7:1; *Me'iri on Sanhedrin* 72b; *Ha-Eshkol*: "Laws of Circumcision," no. 36; *Responsa Torat Chesed*: *Even Ha'ezer*, no. 42-32; *Responsa She'elath Ya'avetz*, Vol. 1, no. 43; *Responsa Beth Shlomoh*: *Choshen Mishpat*, no. 132; *Responsa Tzitz Eliezer*, Vol. 9, no. 51:3 and numerous others.

35. *Tractate Niddah* 44b.

36. *Responsa Tzitz Eliezer*, **Vol. 9, no.** 51:3 by Rabbi Eliezer Waldenberg, present Chief Justice of the Rabbinic High Court in Jerusalem; *Responsa Chavath Ya'ir*, no. 31 by Rabbi Ya'ir Bacharach (1639-1702).

37. Unterman, I. Y., *Be'inyan Peekuach Nefesh Shel Ubar* (Regarding danger to life of the fetus). NOAM (Jerusalem), Vol. 6, 1-11, 1963; *Responsa She'elat Yaavetz*, Vol. 1, no. 43 by Rabbi Jacob Emden.

38. *Responsa Bet Yitzchak, Yoreh Deah*, Part 2, no. 162.

39. *Tractates Yevamot* 69b; *Niddah* 30b; *Mishnah Keritoth* 1.

40. *Mishnah Niddah* 3:7.

abortuses older than 40 days.[41] This period of uncleanliness is similar to that prescribed following the birth of a child and is not the same as that for a menstruant woman. Furthermore, a woman who aborts after the 40th day following conception is required to bring an offering just as if she had given birth to a live child.[42] These laws of ritual impurity and offerings apply even where the abortus "resembles cattle, a wild beast or a bird" or a "shapeless piece of flesh." These facts imply that the unborn fetus, although not considered a living person (*nefesh*), still has some status. Nowhere, however, does it state that killing this fetus by premature artificial termination of pregnancy is prohibited.

Based upon these Talmudic sources as well as the Scriptural passages cited earlier, one may again ask why do most Rabbinic authorities prohibit abortion, except in certain situations, as a serious moral offense even though it is not considered murder? Distinguished Jewish physicians of ancient and more recent times also admonished against abortion. Denunciations of the practice of abortion are recorded in the medical oaths and prayers of Asaf Judaeus[43] in the seventh century, Amatus Lusitanus[44] in the sixteenth century and Jacob Zahalon[45] in the seventeenth century. What are the objections to abortion in the opinion of these Jewish physicians in view of the fact that an unborn fetus does not have the status of a person (*nefesh*) in Jewish law? If abortion is not considered murder, on what legal basis is it prohibited?

This question will be answered by establishing the time that a fetus becomes equal to an adult human being. We have referred to the

41. *Mishnah Niddah* 3:2-6.
42. *Mishnah Keritoth* 1:3-6.
43. Rosner, F. and Muntner, S., "The Oath of Asaph," *Annals Int. Med.*, 63(2):317-320 (August 1965).
44. Friedenwald, H., "The Oath of Amatus," in *The Jews and Medicine* (Baltimore: Johns Hopkins Press, 1944), pp. 368-370.
45. Savitz, H., "Jacob Zahalon and his book, 'The Treasure of Life.'" *New England J. of Med.*, 213:167-176 (1935); Simon, I., "La Prière des Médecins, 'Tephilat Harofim,'" de Jacob Zahalon, Médicin et Rabbin en Italie (1630-1693), *Rev. Hist. Méd. Hebr.*, 8:38-51, (1955); Friedenwald, H., "The Physician's Prayer of Jacob Zahalon of Rome," in *The Jews and Medicine* (Baltimore: Johns Hopkins Press, 1944), pp. 273-279.

Mishnah in *Tractate Oholoth* 7:6 upon which the Jewish legal attitude toward therapeutic abortion is based. The *Mishnah* states in part that if the "greater part was already born, one may not touch it, for one may not set aside one person's life for that of another." Thus the act of birth changes the status of the fetus from a non-person to a person (*nefesh*). Killing the newborn after this point is infanticide. Many Talmudic sources[46] and commentators on the *Talmud*[47] substitute the word "head" for "greater part" in the above *Mishnah*. Others[48] maintain the "greater part" verbatim. Maimonides[49] and Karo[50] also consider the extrusion of the head to indicate birth. They both further state that by Rabbinic decree, even if only one limb of the fetus was extruded and then retracted, childbirth is considered to have occurred.[51]

Not only is the precise time of the birth of paramount importance in adjucating whether aborting the fetus is permissible to save the mother's life, but the viability of the fetus must also be taken into account. The newborn child is not considered fully viable until it has survived thirty days following birth as it is stated in the *Talmud*[52]: "Rabban Simeon ben Gamliel said: Any human being who lives thirty days is not a *nephel* (abortus) because it is stated (Num. 18:16): 'And those that are to be redeemed of them from a month old shalt thou redeem,' since prior to 30 days it is not certain that he will survive." Further support for the necessity of a 30 day *post partum* viability period for adjucating various Jewish legal matters pertaining

---

46. *Mishnah Niddah* 3:5; *Tractates Sanhedrin* 72b; *Niddah* 29a; *Tosefta Yevamot* 9:9.

47. Commentaries of *Bertinoro* (Rabbi Obadiah ben Abraham of Bertinoro, Italy, 15th Century); *Rosh* (Asher ben Yechiel, 1250-1327) and *Rishon Letzion* (Rabbi Isaiah Berlin of Breslau) on the *Mishnah* in *Oholoth* 7:2, and the commentaries of *Rashi* on *Tractate Sanhedrin* 72b and *Tosefot* on *Tractate Sanhedrin* 59a.

48. Jerusalem or Palestinian Talmud, *Tractates Shabbat* 14:4 and *Avodah Zarah* 2:2.

49. *Mishneh Torah, Hilchoth Essurey Biyah*, Chapter 10, Par. 3.

50. *Shulchan Arukh, Choshen Mishpat*, Chapter 425, Par. 2.

51. *Shulchan Arukh, Yoreh Deah*, Chapter 194, Par. 10 and ref. 49.

52. *Tractate Shabbat* 135b.

to the newborn comes from Maimonides who asserts[53]: "Whether one kills an adult or a day-old child, a male or a female, he must be put to death if he kills deliberately . . . provided that the child is born after a full term pregnancy. But, if it is born before the end of nine months, it is regarded as an abortion until it has lived for 30 days, and if one kills it during these 30 days, one is not put to death on its account."

Thus, although the newborn infant reaches the status of a person or *nefesh* which it didn't have prior to birth, it still does not enjoy all the legal rights of an adult until it has survived for 30 days *post partum*. One is not liable for the death penalty if one kills such a child until it has established its viability but it is certainly prohibited because "one may not set aside one person's life for that of another."[54]

The permissibility to kill the unborn fetus to save the mother's life rests upon the fact that such an embryo is not considered a person (*nefesh*) until it is born. Maimonides[55] and Karo[56] present a second reason for allowing abortion or embryotomy prior to birth where the mother's life is endangered and that is the argument of "pursuit" whereby the fetus is "pursuing" the mother. The argument of pursuit is based upon two passages in the Pentateuch:

(1) Deut. 25:11-12 "When men strive together one with another, and the wife of one draws near to save her husband from the hand of the one that smiteth him, and she puts her hand and taketh hold of his genitals, then you shall cut off her hand, your eye shalt have no pity."

(2) Leviticus 19:16 "Thou shalt not stand idly by the blood of thy neighbor."

In the former case, the woman is pursuing the man by maiming him and she should be stopped. The latter case is interpreted by Rashi and most other commentators to mean that one should not stand idly

---

53. *Mishneh Torah, Hilchoth Rotzeach Ushemirath Hanefesh*, Chapter 2, Par. 6.
54. *Mishnah Oholot* 7:3.
55. *Mishneh Torah, ibid.*, Chapter 1, Par. 9.
56. *Shulchan Arukh, Choshen Mishpat*, Chapter 425, Par. 2.

by without attempting to rescue one's fellow man whose life is threatened by robbers, drowning or wild beasts. Based upon these Biblical passages, the *Mishnah* states[57]: "These may be delivered at the cost of their lives: he that pursues after his fellow man to kill him...." The *Talmud*[58] follows with a lengthy discussion asserting that it is one's duty to disable or even take the life of the assailant to protect the life of one's fellow man.

This discussion prompted Maimonides to state: ... "Consequently, the Sages have ruled that if a pregnant woman is having difficulty in giving birth, the child inside her may be excised, either by drugs or manually (i.e. surgery) because it is regarded as pursuing her in order to kill her. But, if it's head has been born, it must not be touched for one may not set aside one human life for that of another, and this happening is the course of nature" (i.e. an act of G-d, that is, the mother is pursued by Heaven, not the fetus). An identical statement is found in Karo's Code.

Many Rabbinic authorities[59] pose the following question to Maimonides. How can the argument of pursuit be invoked here since, if it were applicable, then killing the fetus even after the head or greater part is born should be permissible? *Tifereth Israel*[60] states that the argument of pursuit is totally inappropriate because the child endangering the mother's life is an act of G-d. The child does not intend to kill the mother. It is a case of Heavenly pursuit. This concept of Heavenly pursuit is discussed in the *Talmud* and mentioned by both Maimonides and Karo. Jakobovits[61] amplifies the problem. He states

---

57. *Sanhedrin* 8:7.
58. *Sanhedrin* 72b and 73a.
59. Zweig, M. Y. H., *Al Hapalah Melachutit* (Regarding Therapeutic Abortion), NOAM (Jerusalem), Vol. 7:36-56, (1964); *Commentary on Tosefot Rabbi Akiba Eger* 1761-1837) on the *Mishnah Oholot* 7:6; *Responsa Noda Biyehudah* Part 2, *Choshen Mishpat* no. 59 by Rabbi Ezekiel Landau (1737-1793) and ref. 36.
60. Commentary of Rabbi Israel Lipschutz (1782-1860) on the *Mishnah Oholoth* 7:6.
61. Jakobovits, I., "Abortion and Embryotomy," in *Jewish Medical Ethics* (New York: Bloch Publlishing Co., 1959), pp. 170-191.

ABORTION

that a contradictory ruling seems to be emerging. On the one hand, we invoke the argument of pursuit to allow therapeutic abortion and on the other hand, the validity of this argument is dismissed because nature and not the child pursues the mother.

The problem is resolved by several Rabbis[36,37,59,60] whose separate Responsa state that the non-person status of the fetus prior to birth is not sufficient to warrant the embryo's destruction since this would still constitute a serious moral offense, even if it is not a penal crime. Thus one must invoke the additional argument of pursuit. After the baby's head has emerged, however, the fetus attains the status of a *nefesh*, even prior to proved 30 day *post partum* viability and the "weak" argument of pursuit no longer justifies killing the child even if the mother's life is threatened since it is a case of Heavenly pursuit. However, even after egress of the head, if *both* lives are threatened one may kill the fetus to save the mother. The reason is that the mother's life is a certainty without the fetal threat whereas the viability of the fetus is in doubt until 30 days have elapsed following birth. This viewpoint is also subscribed to by Rabbi Moses Schick[62] and Rabbi David Hoffman.[63] Others[64] dispute this ruling.

We now return to the original question. If the unborn child is not considered a *nefesh*, why should its destruction not be allowed under all circumstances? Why is only a threat to the mother's life or health an acceptable reason for therapeutic abortion?

One answer is given by Rabbi Ya'ir Bacharach who, contrary to the *Mishnah* in Tractate *Arachin* 1:4, states that one waits for a condemned pregnant woman to give birth because a potential human being can arise from each drop of human seed (sperm). Interference with this pregnancy would constitute expulsion of semen for naught, an act akin to coitus interruptus as practiced originally by Er and Onan[65] and

62. *Responsa Maharam Schik, Yoreh Deah* no. 155.
63. *Responsa Melamed Leho'il, Yoreh Deah* no. 69.
64. Rabbi Chayim Sofer in his *Responsa Machanay Chayim, Choshen Mishpat* no. 50; Rabbi Mayir Ashkenazi Eisenstadt in his *Responsa Panim Me'iroth*, Part 3, no. 8.
65. Genesis 38:9.

strictly prohibited by Jewish law. The reason for prohibiting therapeutic abortion upon demand is also subscribed to by others.[66]

A second reason for not allowing abortion without specific indication is that the unborn fetus, although not a person, does have some status. This is evident from the laws regarding ritual impurity and offerings that a woman who aborts after 40 days of conception must adhere to. These requirements are similar to those prescribed following the live birth of a child. Thus the fetus may be considered as a "partial person."[67]

A third reason for prohibiting abortion on demand is that one is not permitted to wound oneself[68] and thus a woman undergoing vaginal abortion by manipulative means is considered as intentionally wounding herself. At least two Rabbinic authorities adhere to this viewpoint.[69]

A fourth reason for prohibiting abortion without maternal danger, is asserted by at least one Rabbi[70] who states that the operative intervention entails danger. One is prohibited by Jewish law from placing oneself in danger based upon Deuteronomy 4:15: "Take ye therefore good heed unto yourselves . . ."

Another reason for prohibiting therapeutic abortion in cases where no threat to the mother exists is stated by the present Chief Rabbi of Israel, Issur Yehuda Unterman. He states that one may desecrate the Sabbath to save the life or preserve the health of an unborn fetus in order that the child may observe many Sabbaths later.[71] As a result, destroying the fetus, although not legally murder, is nevertheless forbidden because of an appurtenance to murder. Rabbi Bacharach, who permits abortion prior to 40 days of pregnancy because the fetus has no status at all but is considered mere fluid, is taken to task by

---

66. *Responsa Ateret Chachamin, Ehven Ha'ezer* no. 1; *Repsonsa She'elat Yaavetz*, Vol. 1, no. 43 by Rabbi Jacob Emden.
67. *Responsa Tzofnat Paneach*, Vol. 1, no. 49.
68. *Baba Kamma* 91b; *Mishneh Torah, Hilkot Chovel Umazik*, Chapter 5, Par. 1.
69. *Responsa Maharit*, Vol. 1, no. 99 by Rabbi Joseph Trani; Zweig, M. Y. H. See ref. 59.
70. *Responsa Beth Shlomoh, Choshen Mishpat* no. 132.
71. *Ramban on Niddah* 44b.

Rabbi Unterman who states that even prior to 40 days there is an appurtenance to murder.

Another argument of Rabbi Unterman is that a fetus, even less than 40 days after conception, is considered a potential (literally: questionable) human being which, by nature alone, without interference, will become an actual human being. Thus a potential person (*sofek nefesh*) has enough status to prohibit its own destruction.

A final argument of Rabbi Unterman comes from the interpretation of R. Ishmael for the Scriptural verse[72]: "Whoso Sheddeth man's blood, by man shall his blood be shed, for in the image of G-d did He make man." This can be translated "whoso sheddeth the blood of man in man, his blood shall be shed. . . ." The "man in man" is interpreted to mean a fetus.[73] This Noachidic prohibition of killing a fetus applies also to Israelites even though the Jewish legal consequences might differ.

A final reason for prohibiting abortion on demand in Jewish law is suggested by the present Chief Rabbi of the British Commonwealth, Immanuel Jakobovits[74] and Belgian Rabbi Moshe Yonah Zweig, among others. They point to the *Mishnah* in *Tractate Oholoth* 7:6 which permits abortion prior to birth of the child only when the mother's life is endangered. The implication is that when the mother's life is not at stake, it would be prohibited to kill the unborn fetus.

SUMMARY OF RABBINIC OPINION REGARDING THERAPEUTIC ABORTION

A small minority of Rabbinic Responsa is of the opinion that prior to forty days after conception, the fetus has no status at all and is not a *nefesh* and abortion at this stage might be permissible for the

---

72. Genesis 9:6.
73. *Sanhedrin* 57b.
74. Jakobovits, L., "Jewish Views on Abortion,' in *Abortion and the Law*, edited by D. T. Smith, pp. 124-143; Jakobovits, I., "Artificial Insemination, Birth Control and Abortion," *Hebrew Med. J.* (*Harofe Haivri*), Vol. 2, pp. 183-169, Eng. ed. and pp. 114-129, Hebrew ed.; Jakobovits, I., *Jewish Law Faces Modern Problems* (New York: Yeshiva University Studies in Torah Judaism Series, 1965), pp. 74-79.

slightest reason. According to these few Rabbis, such a reason might be the fear that a deformed child may be born, due to exposure of the mother early in pregnancy to German measles or a teratogenic drug such as thalidomide or possibly even for socio-economic reasons or family planning. Such rulings are vigorously denounced by others who prohibit therapeutic abortion both in the case where the mother was exposed to German measles[75] or where the mother ingested thalidomide early in pregnancy.[76] Most Rabbinic authorities permit therapeutic abortion where the health or life of the mother is threatened. Some are more stringent and require the mother's life to be in danger, however remote such danger[77] whereas other authorities permit abortion for a threat to the mother's health.[78] Such dangers to maternal health may include deafness,[79] cancer, pain or psychiatric disease.[80] Psychiatric indication for abortion would be acceptable only if some grave danger to the mother is in fact anticipated to result from her fears or nervous condition, as certified by competent medical opinion, and only on the basis of previous experiences of mental strain by the mother.[81]

Some authorities extend the permissibility to perform therapeutic abortion to any maternal need.[82] This would include cases of incest or

75. Unterman, I. Y., *Be'inyan Peekuach Nefesh Shel Ubar*, NOAM, Vol. 6, pp. 1-11, 1963.
76. Jakobovits, I., "Deformed Babies and Thalidomide Babies," in *Journal of a Rabbi* (New York: Living Books, 1966), pp. 262-266.
77. *Respoonsa Aryeh Debey Eelaye: Yoreh Deah* no. 19; *Responsa Peri Hasadeh*, Vol. 4, no. 50; *Responsa Bet Shlomoh: Choshen Mishpat* no. 132; *Responsa Binyan David* no. 47; *Responsa Levushei Mordechai: Choshen Mishpat* no. 39; *Responsa Ko'ach Schor* no. 21; *Responsa Tzur Yaakov* no. 141; *Responsa Avnei Tzedek: Choshen Mishpat* no. 19.
78. *Responsa Rav Pa'alim*, Vol. 1, *Even Ha'ezer* no. 4; *Sdei Chemed Pe'at Hasadeh*, Vol. 1, no. 52.
79. *Responsa Mishpetei Uziel*, Part 3, no. 46, 47 by Rabbi Z. Uziel, late Chief Rabbi of the Sephardic Community in Israel.
80. *Responsa Peri Ha'aretz, Yoreh Deah* no. 21 by Rabbi Israel Meir Mizrachi; *Responsa Netzer Mata'ai*, Part 1, no. 8 by Rabbi Nathan Zvi Friedman.
81. Jakobovits, I., *Personal Communication*, May 24, 1968.
82. *Responsa Torat Chesed: Even Ha'ezer* no. 42:32; *Responsa Tzitz Eliezer*, Vol. 9, no. 51:3.

rape[83] where shame or embarrassment to the mother in the continuance of the pregnancy are considered threats to the mother's health. This, however, is a minority viewpoint. Only a very small group of Rabbinic Responsa regard the possibility of a deformed child being born to prey so much on the mother's mind as to constitute impairment of her health. This "maternal" indication is not acceptable to most Rabbinic opinions.

If the mother becomes pregnant while nursing a child and the pregnancy changes her milk so that the suckling's life is endangered, then considerable Rabbinic opinion would permit abortion in this case.[84]

Malformed Babies and Monster Births

The Talmud[85] contains the following quotation: "In the case of a birth given to a creature which possesses a double back or a double spine, Rab said: If it was a woman (who miscarried), it is not regarded as an offspring . . .", that is, the laws concerning a birth are not observed. However, this creature, once it has been born, has the status of a person and killing it would be considered infanticide which is prohibited.

The thirteenth century *Sefer Chasidim*[86] describes the case of a child born with teeth and a tail. It was said that the end will be that people will eat him, therefore it is better to kill him. The reply by the author was that one should remove the teeth in the front and tail from below so that the infant will be like a human body and he will not be able to do any harm. Thus we see that the killing of monster births is prohibited.

83. *Responsa She'elat Yaavetz*, Vol. 1, no. 43.
84. *Responsa Chayim Ve shalom*, Vol. 1, no. 40; *Responsa Bet Yehuda: Even Ha'ezer* no. 14; *Responsa She'eilot Yitzchak* no. 69; *Responsa Tzitz Eliezer*, Vol. 9, no. 51:3.
85. *Tractate Bekhorot* 43b.
86. Authored by Rabbi Judah ben Samuel the Pious. Reprinted in Buenos Aires in 1952, no. 186, p. 568.

An early Rabbinic responsum relating to a malformed child is that of Rabbi Elazar Fleckeles in the nineteenth century.[87] His ruling is that once a child is born of a human mother and survives, it is a living human being in all respects and may not be destroyed. Starving it to death is considered homicide.

The problem of malformed babies usually born without one or more limbs or with seal-like limbs to mothers who ingested the teratogenic drug thalidomide early in pregnancy is discussed by two recent Rabbinic Responsa. Rabbi Moshe Jonah Halevi Zweig of Antwerp, Belgium writing in a Hebrew periodical[59] condemns the killing of the thalidomide deformed baby which resulted in the famous Liège, Belgium trial involving parents, relatives and a physician charged with the murder of this drug-damaged child.[88] Rabbi Zweig's lengthy dissertation, however, deals primarily with abortion (i.e. antenatal) and not infanticide (i.e. postnatal).

Rabbi Immanuel Jakobovits, writing in a London journal[89] concludes as follows: a physically or mentally abnormal child has the same claim to life as a normal child because it is considered a person (*nefesh*). Furthermore, while only the killing of a born and viable child constitutes murder in Jewish law, the destruction of the fetus, too, is a moral offense and cannot be justified except out of consideration for the mother's life or health. Consequently, the fear that a child may or will be deformed is not in itself a legitimate indication for its abortion, particularly since there is usually a chance that the child might turn out to be quite normal. Killing a cripple is similarly prohibited.

Once a malformed child has been born, one cannot use the argument of euthanasia or mercy killing to sanction its destruction. This act is positively prohibited by Jewish law as nothing less than murder (in-

---

87. *Responsa Teshuva Me-Ahavah*, Part 1, no. 53.
88. Colebrook, L., "The Liège Trial and the Problem of Voluntary Euthanasia," *Lancet* 2:1225, (1962).
89. *The Jewish Review* (London), November 14, 1962.

fanticide). The Jewish attitude toward euthansia in general is discussed at length elsewhere,[90] and in another chapter of this book.

Conclusion

Prior to forty days following conception, the fertilized egg is considered by some Rabbinic authorities as nothing more than "mere fluid." From forty days until birth, the fetus is not considered a living person (*nefesh*) but is regarded as part of the mother's flesh and aborting it might not be legally considered murder. However, the destruction of an unborn fetus without sufficiently strong indication is still condemned for a variety of reasons. Abortion is permitted by most Rabbinic authorities where a medical or psychiatric threat to the mother's life exists. Many authorities permit abortion not only if her life is in danger but even if her health may deteriorate by continuation of the pregnancy. A small minority of Rabbinic opinion allows therapeutic abortion for reasons such as incest, rape and fear that a malformed child may be born. Justification for this position rests on the grounds of concern for the mother, i.e. that such a birth would adversely affect her mental or physical health by causing her anguish, shame or embarrassment. This latter viewpoint is not subscribed to by most Rabbinic authorities, however.

After the head or greater part of the body of the infant is born, only a threat to BOTH lives would allow sacrifice of the child to save the mother because the mother's life is a certainty without the fetal threat, whereas the fetus has not proved its viability until thirty days *post partum* have elapsed. After thirty days of life, every human being, whether deformed, crippled or otherwise deficient has rights equal to every other adult human being.

Since many important legal and moral considerations which cannot be spelled out in the presentation of general principles may weigh upon the verdict in any given case, it seems advisable to submit every

90. Rosner, F., "Jewish Attitude Toward Euthanasia," *New York State J. of Medicine*, 67(18):2499-2506 (Sept. 15, 1967).

individual case to Rabbinic judgment in the light of the prevailing medical and other circumstances.

ADDENDUM TO CHAPTER 4

Since this article was published, abortion reform laws or total repeal were passed in ten more states: in 1969 in New Mexico, Arkansas, Delaware, Oregon and Kansas, and in 1970, in New York, Hawaii, Virginia, South Carolina and Alaska. Federal and local courts in the same two-year period have declared abortion laws in 5 states to be unconstitutional: Texas, California, Wisconsin, Illinois and the District of Columbia. Legislation to legalize abortion on a nationwide basis was introduced in the United States Senate by the Senator from Oregon. It is likely that by the time the above appears in print, it will already be outdated. Such is the rapidly changing legal situation concerning abortion in this country.

Chapter V

The Morality of Abortion

INTRODUCTION

There are two extreme viewpoints in the abortion controversy. One says that there is no moral justification for abortion. The other proclaims that it is a woman's right to have an abortion on demand. In the last few years, the debate has become heated and sometimes even borders on fist fights. "Reform" or "repeal" are the words of today's abortion discussions.

Prior to 1967, induced abortion in every state of the Union was considered a crime unless performed to save the mother's life. Why did three states (Colorado, North Carolina, and California) reform their abortion laws in 1967? Why did Georgia and Maryland follow suit in 1968? Why did five additional states in 1969 (New Mexico, Arkansas, Delaware, Oregon, Kansas) and five more in 1970 (New York, Hawaii, Virginia, South Carolina, and Alaska) reform their abortion laws? These fifteen states now allow abortion for pregnancy resulting from rape or incest, or where the fetus may be born malformed phyically, or deficient mentally, or where the mother's life or health are threatened. Why have federal and local courts in the past two years declared the abortion laws in five states (Texas, California, Wisconsin, Illinois, and the District of Columbia) unconstitutional? Why does it appear as if many other states will soon either reform or repeal their abortion laws? Legislation to legalize abortion on a nationwide basis has been introduced in the United States Senate by Sen. Robert Packwood (Democrat) of Oregon.

Why is the abortion controversy and movement for reform or repeal only a few years old? The past few years seem to have heralded a time for change. Why? What has happened in the United States to move even the ultra-conservative American Medical Association (AMA) to twice modify its archaic 1871 position which sanctioned abortion only to save the mother's life? In 1967, the AMA House of Delegates adopted a resolution stating that it is not opposed to abortion if

1. there is documented medical evidence that continuance of the pregnancy may threaten the health or life of the mother, or

2. there is documented medical evidence that the infant may be born with incapacitating physical deformity, or mental deficiency, or,

3. there is documented evidence that continuance of a pregnancy, resulting from legally established statutory or forcible rape or incest, may constitute a threat to the mental or physical health of the patient.

In 1970, the AMA adopted another resolution which is interpreted by many to indicate that the AMA favors abortion on demand. In fact, the resolution, which is a substantial liberalization over the 1967 AMA position, places abortion in the position of being a decision between the patient and her physician. In addition, it safeguards physicians who object to abortion. The resolution's exact wording follows:

Whereas, abortion, like any other medical procedure, should not be performed when contrary to the best interests of the patient since good medical practice requires due consideration for the patient's demands; and

Whereas, the standards of sound clinical judgment, which, together with informed consent, should be determinative according to the merits of each individual case; therefore be it

Resolved, That abortion is a medical procedure and should be performed only by a duly licensed physician and surgeon in an accredited hospital acting only after consultation with two other physicians chosen because of their professional competency and in conformance with standards of good medical practice and the Medical Practice Act of his State; and be it furhter

Resolved, That no physician or other professional personnel shall be compelled to perform any act which violates his good medical judgment. Neither physician, hospital, nor hospital personnel shall be required to perform any act violative of personally held moral principles. In these circumstances good medical practice requires only that the physician or other professional personnel withdraw from the case so long as the withdrawal is consistent with good medical practice.

Reasons for Abortion Reform

Is there a new moral climate in our society, as some people claim, that has caused all the above changes? Why has our moral code been altered? By whom? Is there increased premarital sex leading to more pregnancies, as some statistics seem to indicate? Are there more contraceptive failures with increased numbers of unwanted pregnancies? Numerous reasons put forth by protagonists of abortion reform have in fact been applicable for several decades, rather than just for several years. For example, population control, women's rights, and the ending of illegal abortions by putting abortionists out of business, are points of controversy that have been debated for many, many years.

Major impetus for abortion reform in the various state legislatures followed two incidents that occurred in the United States in the early 1960's. In 1962, an Arizona housewife, Mrs. Sherri Finkbine of Phoenix, early in pregnancy, took a tranquilizing pill called thalidomide. This drug had produced approximately seven thousand deformed babies, usually born without arms or legs, in women who took this medication during the first few months of pregnancy. Mrs. Finkbine, denied an abortion in her own state of Arizona and in several other states, finally went to Sweden where an abortion verified the fact that her baby would have been born with only stumps instead of arms and legs.

Two years later, in 1964, a major German measles epidemic in the United States resulted in the birth of many thousands of physically and mentally deformed babies as well as many other thousands of stillborn infants, over and above the expected number for a comparable period. Thus, the thalidomide and German measles tragedies, occurring in rapid succession, provided the stimulus for Colorado to become the first state to reform its abortion law on April 25, 1967.

Although the legal status of abortion in this country and abroad has drastically changed in the past few years, the Jewish viewpoint toward abortion, as governed by Halachah (Jewish law), remains unchanged. For a detailed discussion of the Jewish attitude toward abortion and abortion in Halachic literature, the reader is referred to Chapter 4 of this book. The remainder of this chapter examines the morality of abortion from the Jewish viewpoint.

We ask the reader to consider the various reasons for abortion requests by the mother: the physical (thalidomide or German measles infection), the emotional (the unwed mother or the accidental pregnancy), the social (the unwed mother), and the economic (impoverished or overpopulated families). It would appear that the physical reason would statistically be the least likely to be given. The major thrust of our thesis, therefore, will be directed to those women, physicians, legislators, and other interested parties who would cite emotional, social, or economic reasons.

The Morality of Abortion

The destruction of the unborn fetus, although Halachically not considered murder, can be considered to constitute "moral murder." The unborn baby has a heartbeat, a brain, arms, legs, and nearly everything with which a healthy newborn baby is endowed. Thus, killing the unborn fetus, according to Chief Rabbi Unterman of Israel, is an "appurtenance of murder" and strictly prohibited although, because of a legal technicality, such an act is not considered murder for which the death penalty is imposed.

The major Biblical citation dealing with abortion, a passage in *Shemoth* (Exodus 21:22-23), concerns accidental abortion, not intentional or induced abortion, a deed initiated at the outset (*lechatchilah*). Therefore, one can argue that premeditated interruption of pregnancy is not allowed except perhaps to save the life or preserve the health (mental or physical) of the mother. Though some may cite Jewish law which may not impose a death penalty upon the mother or the person performing the abortion, there may, however, prevail a Rabbinic concept of a non-penalized but prohibited act (*potur avol ossur*).

The concept of time seems all important. If one destroys a baby five minutes *after* birth, it is considered murder, legally and Halachically; yet if one destroys the fetus five minutes *before* it is born, such an act is not murder. Why not? What is the difference? Certainly it is moral murder, although perhaps not legal murder. The same principle applies if one destroys a baby five hours, five days, or five months before and after birth. To some people, abortion is acceptable if done prior to the time the fetus might be expected to live. How then is life defined? Must there be a heartbeat? Limbs? Is not the fertilized zygote already alive? Does life mean that which is able to duplicate itself in the biological sense? Does life refer to the stage of fetal development when physical movement is first detected? Or is life the "breath of life" instilled in a newborn infant immediately after the birth process? The recent era of heart transplantation forced society, the medical community particularly, to re-examine the definition of death. The present abortion controversy and the question of legal murder versus moral murder seems to demand a re-examination of the definition of life.

The next moral issue is the question of potentiality. The unborn fetus, if left alone, may turn out to be a genius. Or he may just be a person of normal intelligence. Or, if physically deformed, he may still make a positive contribution to society. In the secular world, should we not cite the contributions made by such handicapped or deformed human beings as Helen Keller, Ludwig von Beethoven, and Henri de Toulouse Lautrec? Or in our religious experience, should we not marvel at the learned and soul-rending contributions made by the blind Talmudic scholars Rav Sheshes and Rav Yosef, the unsightly Rabbi Yehoshua ben Chananyah, and the limbless Rabbi Amnon of Mayence (author of the renowned *Unethaneh Tokef* prayer recited on the High Holy Days)? The potential of an unborn infant is unknown.

However, as Chief Rabbi Unterman points out, the potential human being, i.e., the unborn fetus, if left alone, will develop into an actual human being. Hence, this potential person (*sofek nefesh*) has enough status to prohibit its destruction. Jewish law also allows, and in fact requires, that one desecrate the Sabbath to save the life or health of the unborn fetus in order that the fetus may observe many Sabbaths later, after it is born.

The Talmud compares the unborn fetus to an extra appendage of the mother (*ubar yerech imo hu*), destruction or damage to which requires that financial retribution be paid to the mother for pain, shame, anguish, medical bills, inability to work, and the like. However, how can one compare the unborn fetus to a finger of the mother? If one destroys a finger, the woman has lost a finger which would never have become anything other than a finger. The unborn fetus, if left alone, would have developed into a full and complete human being.

Philosophical-moral arguments against abortion are also very potent. If a woman become pregnant, then certainly Almighty G-d so willed it. How dare we interfere? Even if the child might be born physically deformed, this too is the will of G-d. One is reminded of the encounter between King Hezekiah and the Prophet Isaiah as described in the Talmud (*Berachoth* 10a):

> The Holy One, Blessed be He, brought sufferings upon Hezekiah and then said to Isaiah: Go visit the sick, For it is written: *In those days Hezekiah was sick unto death, and Isaiah, the prophet, son of Amoz, came to him and said unto him, Thus saith the Lord, set your house in order, for you shall die and not live, etc.* (Isaiah 38:1). What is the meaning of *you shall die and not live?* You shall die in this world and not live in the World-to-Come. [Hezekiah] said to [Isaiah]: Why so bad? [Isaiah] replied: Because you did not try to have children. [Hezekiah] said: The reason was because I saw by the holy spirit that the children issuing from me would not be virtuous. [Isaiah] said to [Hezekiah]: What have you to do with the secrets of the All-Merciful? You should have done what you were commanded, and let the Holy One, blessed be He, do that which

pleases Him . . . (Although this defiance of G-d's will by Hezekiah was punished, the outcome of the story is a happy one: Hezekiah was healed and lived another fifteen years.)

King Hezekiah apparently knew that his children would be morally corrupt so he put aside the "first" commandment of the Torah which states: "be fruitful and multiply," and he did not take a wife. However, Isaiah charges him with lacking faith. In a similar vein, is not the faith in the Almighty's future being challenged by the mother who requests abortion because she can see no way of solving her future social or economic difficulty?

A further philosophical argument against abortion contends that throughout the ages, millions of Jews have perished at the hands of their enemies. Are we today to kill even more by performing indiscriminate abortion? Certainly not! The State of Israel needs Jews. Yet, according to a report by Britain's Chief Rabbi Dr. Immanuel Jakobovits, 50,000 induced abortions yearly may be performed in Israel. Since the birth of the State of Israel in 1948, over 1,000,000 potential Jews may have thus been "aborted." Such facts and figures, as shocking as they seem, may nevertheless be true.

Let us turn to some of the possible consequences of liberalized abortion laws. If abortion on demand becomes a nationwide practice, will legal infanticide follow? Legal genocide? Legal extermination of social misfits as Hitler proposed? Legal euthanasia? Where does the trend end? What about psychological consequences to the mother? After the abortion is over, she cannot change her mind. The deed is done.

The next area to be discussed is the decision-making process. Who decides whether an abortion is to be performed? Why only the mother? How about the father? Has he nothing to say? Why not? Why should not the boy-friend be consulted if an unwed pregnant girl seeks an abortion? How about the siblings of the unborn fetus? Should they have a say in this matter? Furthermore, to use a "Catholic" argument, who speaks for the fetus? We have a Society for the Prevention of Cruelty Against Animals, a Society for the Prevention of Cruelty

Against Children, yet there is no Society for the Prevention of Cruelty Against Fetuses. Theoretically, if we could communicate with the fetus and ask it whether it would still choose life if it knew that it would be born without arms or legs, the answer would doubtless be a resounding "Yes." If the fetus were told he would be the twelfth child in a very poor family living in a very small apartment, he would still probably choose life. So who speaks for the fetus in the decision-making process concerning an abortion? Why is the mother the major, if not the only, determining factor? Why should we, society, not speak for the fetus? In divorce proceedings, the courts decide the disposition of the involved children, if any. Why should not the courts have a say about the continued life of the fetus?

The woman, as all human beings, was created in the image of G-d, and thus is not the sole owner of her body and soul, to treat as she pleases. She has no right to take her own life, i.e., to commit suicide, for the same reason. G-d wills it that we live, and live by the Torah.

Turning to the unwed girl who is pregnant, the dilemma is severe indeed. Which is better, to have the baby and to give it away, or to destroy it before it is born? How would she feel in giving her child away for adoption to a foster mother? How would she feel in aborting her pregnancy? The argument that this unfortunate girl should not have become pregnant is no consolation to her present predicament. Should this mother-to-be be permitted to extinguish the life of what will probably be a healthy human being in order to avert her personal shame or a socially unpleasant situation?

Let us now briefly examine the moral issues involved in the various social reasons proposed for liberalizing abortion. Practically everyone loyal to Jewish law would subscribe to the proposition that to sacrifice a potential life to save an actual living person is permissible, if there is danger to the latter. But even if abortion in thalidomide and German measles cases were allowed, should abortion for social reasons, or abortion on demand, be permitted? In such a situation (i.e., poverty, inadequate housing, accidental pregnancy, etc.), one is sacrificing a potential life solely for the convenience or happiness of an adult, either mother or father, or both.

If one is told to kill somebody or to be killed, one is not allowed to kill because one may not set aside one person's life for that of another. True, the unborn fetus is only a potential life, but why should the mother be able to spill her unborn baby's blood? Why is her convenience more valuable than a potential life?

If a woman seeks an abortion for social reasons, might not the social conditions change? Perhaps the family's financial situation will improve. Perhaps larger living quarters will be provided to the family. Is not the abortion for social reasons a denial of one's faith in G-d and His ability to provide sustenance? There are alternatives to the mother of eleven children seeking an abortion because she cannot afford or has no room for another child, or is emotionally drained by the present eleven children. Jewish foster homes are available. An Israeli kibbutz might be the answer for some. At a time when Israel appeals for increased immigration and population growth, shouldn't these unborn souls be given an opportunity for fulfillment in a homeland which begs for increased manpower? Society should help to see the implementation of such solutions, rather than help to see the implementation and spread of liberalized abortion.

There are other reasons, moral and otherwise, which speak against legalized abortion. When a married woman or an unwed girl has an abortion, what guarantee does she have that she can ever become pregnant again? Is she so certain that the Divine mystery of conception will be hers again? Should she not pause and ask herself, "Will I ever regret denying myself this ultimate of feminine fulfillment, if I should never conceive again?"

Might it not happen that an abortion is contra-indicated for medical or psychiatric reasons? If a physician can reject a woman for abortion because of such a contra-indication, why should the abortion request not be rejected by the physician or society because of a moral contra-indication? If induced abortion becomes commonplace, will there not be an undermining or subversion of the ethics of medical practice? Will there be a shift from the "healer" physician to the "exterminator" physician?

A totally new moral issue has been recently raised by a report from England which claims that aborted fetuses are being sold for medical research. Who should have the say regarding the disposal of the fetus? The woman? The father? The gynecologist? The pathologist? Society? Who? Jewish morality and law require burial not only for a dead body but for removed human organs (for example, as a result of an operation or an accidental amputation) as well. Our Sages refer to the human body and its parts as "vessels which contain the human soul." How coarse, therefore, are those who would deal with, and profit from, the sale of the fetus, this potential "soul container."

Concluding Note

The Halachic, legal, medical, theological, psychiatric, and other aspects of abortion have been presented in great detail in numerous books, pamphlets, articles, and television and radio discussions. This essay has attempted to raise some of the moral issues involved in the abortion controversy. More questions are posed than answers given. Intimately related topics such as procreation and birth control are not even mentioned, because these topics are beyond the scope of the present discussion. I would like to leave the reader with the ancient pronouncement: "He who maintains one life of the people of Israel is as if he has maintained an entire world." A single life, in Jewish teaching, is equivalent to a whole world.

Chapter VI

Artificial Insemination in Jewish Law

DEFINITION AND INTRODUCTION

Artificial insemination is the instrumental deposition of semen into the female genital tract without sexual intercourse. There are two types of insemination, and they are frequently referred to by their abbreviations which are, respectively, A.I.H. (artificial insemination, husband) and A.I.D. (artificial insemination, donor). One can also use a mixture of semen obtained from husband and donor. Results of artificial insemination employing the husband's semen are good if the indication for the procedure is an anatomical defect, but fair to poor if there is moderate infertility in the male. Women can conceive two or more times from donor insemination.[1]

Artificial insemination has been practiced in animals for many years, primarily to increase the usefulness of the best male animals. For example, a single prize bull can provide enough semen to inseminate and impregnate 500 cows. In the human, John Hunter is known to have artificially inseminated a woman in London in 1790, although earlier accounts are described, while in the United States, J. Marion Sims is credited with the first insemination in 1866. Today, there are an estimated 250,000 people in this country who are the offspring of such inseminations, thousands of which are performed annually.

These days, there is much writing—books, articles, reviews and monographs—in the medical and lay press, concerning this subject

---

1. D. P. Murphy and E. F. Torrano, "The Day of Conception: A Study of 48 Women Having 2 or More Conceptions by Donor Insemination," *Fertility and Sterility*, 14:410-415, 1963.

from the moral, legal, religious, medical, psychological, sociological, genetic and other standpoints. The present paper deals primarily with the Jewish religious viewpoint.

Since many moral, legal and religious problems may arise from artificial insemination, one might well ask why a barren couple should not simplify matters and adopt a baby? The psychological stress on women who consider themselves adulteresses following A.I.D. would be bypassed if adoption were resorted to, and, similarly, the emotional strains on some husbands, perhaps due to feelings of inadequate masculinity, might vanish if an adopted child, rather than one conceived from A.I.D., became part of the family.

There are, however, numerous reasons why a woman prefers to carry and give birth to her own child. First, her emotional craving to be pregnant is fulfilled; she has proven her femininity. Second, both the husband and the wife are part of the conception, the antenatal care, the whole pregnancy and the delivery, whereas an adopted child is usually not granted until it is several months old. Third, the child physically resembles the siblings and the father, if A.I.H. is resorted to; with an adopted child this resemblance is impossible. Fourth, the adopted child's new parents always fear the appearance of the real mother, a fear which does not exist with a child born following artificial insemination. Finally, since two-thirds of the adopted infants are born to unwed mothers and the other third are unwanted babies, the genetic background of these children may be poor and less desirable to the couple wishing to acquire a child, whereas semen from donors is frequently obtained from college and graduate students.

Around the major parties who may be involved in artificial insemination, namely the husband, the wife, the child, the physician, the donor and the donor's wife, any number of legal questions may arise. Can the husband sue for divorce on the grounds of adultery following A.I.D. if he can prove that he is sterile? Can the physician and/or donor also be implicated as having participated in the adultery? Would the question of adultery vanish if the husband made the injection? Is the doctor responsible if a defective child is born? Is the doctor guilty of perjury when he signs the birth certificate, since he knows that the true father is not the one named on the birth certificate? Is the child considered legitimate? What are his rights concerning inheritance, support and custody? Can he sue for the donor's estate? Can the mother sue the donor for support of the child? Can the donor sue for custody of the child? Should the husband legally adopt the child when his wife gives birth? How do adoption laws apply here, if at all? If insemination is performed without the woman's consent, it is considered rape? If so, by whom—the physician, the donor or the husband?

Surprisingly, with only one exception, artificial insemination does not exist in the law books of any state in the union. Only Oklahoma, in 1967, passed a statute which resolves the legitimacy, support, custody and inheritance rights of a child born of A.I.D.

JEWISH VIEWPOINT

Ancient Sources

Before entering into Jewish legal discussions in the Rabbinic Responsa literature dealing with artificial insemination, it might be useful to cite three major ancient sources in the Talmud and the Codes of Jewish law upon which these discussions are based. They are a passage of the Babylon Talmud, a pronouncement in the 13th century by Rabbi Peretz ben Elijah of Corbeil, and the Midrashic legend of Ben Sira.

In the Talmud we find: ". . . Ben Zoma was asked: may a High Priest marry a maiden who has become pregnant (yet who claims she is still a virgin)? Do we take into consideration Samuel's statement, for Samuel said: I can have repeated sexual connections without (causing) bleeding (i.e., without the woman losing her virginity) or is the case of Samuel rare? He replied: The case of Samuel is rare, but we do consider (the possibility) that she may have conceived in a bath (into which a male has discharged semen) . . ."[2]

From this 5th century Talmudic passage we see that generation

---

2. Babylonian Talmud—Tractate *Hagigah,* 14b.

sine concubito was recognized as possible by the Sages of old. Though Rabbi Judah Rozanes of Constantinople, the renowned commentator on Maimonides' *Mishneh Torah*, expresses doubt that impregnation through bathing in water into which a man had previously discharged semen can occur,[3] many authorities, including Rabbi Chaim Joseph David Azulai,[4] Rabbi Jonathan Eybeschütz[5] and Rabbi Jacob Ettlinger[6] differ with him and interpret the Talmudic passage literally. Others,[7] however, agree with Rabbi Rozanes.

The second major ancient sources indicating the possibility of pregnancy without sexual intercourse is by Rabbi Peretz ben Elijah of Corbeil in his work *Hagahot Smak*, who states: ". . . a woman may lie on her husband's sheets but should be careful not to lie on sheets upon which another man slept lest she become impregnated from his sperm. Why are we not afraid that she become pregnant from her husband's sperm and the child will be conceived of a *niddah* (menstruating female)? The answer is that since there is no forbidden intercourse, the child is completely legitimate (literally: kosher) even from the sperm of another just as Ben Sira was legitimate. However, we are concerned about the sperm of another man because the child may eventually marry his sister. . . ."[8]

Several things emerge from this statement. First, generation *sine concubito* was recognized. Second, the offspring is considered legitimate.

---

3. J. Rozanes, "*Hilkhot Ishut*," Commentary—*Mishnah L'melekh* on Maimonides' Code, Chapter 15:4.
4. Quoted by I. Jakobovits in "Artificial Insemination, Birth Control and Abortion," *Harofé Haivri* 2:169-183 (Eng.) and 114-129 (Heb.), 1953.
5. J. Eybeschütz, "*Hilkhot Ishut*," Commentary—*Bnei Ahuvah* on Maimonides' Code, Chapter 15:6.
6. J. Ettlinger, Commentary *Arukh L'ner* on Tractate *Yevamot*, 12b.
7. Moshe Schick (known as Maharam Shick), *Taryag Mitzvot*, Chapter 1; Solomon Schick, "*Even Haezer*," *Responsa Rashbam*, Chapter 8.
8. Quoted by Rabbi Joel Sirkes, known as the *Bah* or *Bet Hadash*, in his commentary on Rabbi Jacob ben Asher's *Tur Shulchan Arukh*, Section *Yoreh Deah*, Chapter 195. Also quoted by Rabbi David ben Samuel Halewy, known as the *Taz* or *Turei Zahav*, in his commentary on Rabbi Joseph Karo's *Shulchan Arukh*, Section *Yoreh Deah*, Chapter 195:7.

Third, no prohibition is mentioned concerning cohabitation of the woman with her husband afterwards, even if she has become pregnant from another. The only reason for her to avoid contact with the linen upon which another has lain is to prevent incest at a later date, i.e., the child marrying its own sibling. Finally, only forbidden intercourse would make her forbidden to her husband, whether or not she has lost her virginity, and irrespective of whether or not her male partner has emitted sperm into her genital tract during the forbidden sexual act.

The third ancient source for artificial insemination is the legend of Ben Sira, first mentioned by Rabbi Jacob Molin Segal (1365-1427) in his work entitled *Likutei Maharil*. This Midrashic legend relates that Ben Sira was conceived without sexual intercourse by the prophet Jeremiah's daughter, in a bath, the father having been Jeremiah himself who, coerced by a group of wicked men, emitted semen into the water.[9] The legend has since been quoted many times in medical literature[10] as well as in nearly all of the Rabbinic Responsa dealing with artificial insemination.

Some authorities, notably Rabbi David Gans,[11] deny the legend of Ben Sira's birth having followed a conception *sine concubito*. Rabbi Gans claims that he could not find the legend of Ben Sira in either the Talmud or the Midrash, and quotes Rabbi Solomon Ibn Verga who says that Ben Sira was the son of the daughter of Joshua ben Yehozadak, the High Priest mentioned in the book of Ezra.[12]

Recent Rulings

Since there is a vast Rabbinic literature which addresses itself to the question of artificial insemination, and since the problem is so complex

---

9. I. D. Eisenstein, "*Alpha Betha de ben Sira,*" in *Otzar Midrashim*. (New York, 1928), p. 43.
10. J. Preuss, *Biblisch-Talmudische Medizin* (Berlin, S. Karger, 1923), p. 541; H. Friedenwald, *The Jews and Medicine* (Baltimore, Johns Hopkins Press, 1944), Vol. I, p. 386; I. Jakobovits, *Jewish Medical Ethics* (New York, Bloch Publishers, 1959), Appendix on "Artificial Insemination," pp. 244-250.
11. D. Gans, *Zemah David* (Offenbach, 1768), 1:1:441, p. 14b.
12. S. Verga, *Shevet Yehudah* (Lemberg, 1846).

from the Jewish legal viewpoint, it seems desirable to subdivide the discussion into the major questions involved. Some of these are: Is the woman prohibited to her husband following an artificial insemination? Is it considered an act of adultery? What is the status of the child? Is the child a *mamzer* (illegitimate)? Is artificial insemination permitted at all? Is it permissible to use the sperm of the husband, or a donor, or a gentile? Does the donor fulfill the commandment of procreation? Is the offspring considered the child of the donor? Is the woman considered to be the pregnant or nursing wife of another and prohibited to marry again for a certain interval if her husband should die or divorce her? Is the husband permitted to provide his sperm for analysis and subsequent insemination if it is found suitable? How should one obtain the sperm from husband or donor? If artificial insemination is permitted, may it be performed during the woman's unclean period (menstruation and the ritual cleansing period thereafter)?

Is the Woman Prohibited to her Husband Following A.I.D.?—The question obviously does not apply to A.I.H. since the problem of possible adultery arises only with the semen of a man other than the husband. The case in the Talmud of the High Priest marrying a pregnant maiden who claims to be a virgin, as cited above, concludes that Samuel's capacity to impregate a woman without producing bleeding or loss of virginity is extremely rare. Thus, the maiden is permitted to marry the High Priest as she is deemed trustworthy when she claims to be a virgin despite having been impregnated in a bath into which a man had previously discharged semen. It would seem from this Talmudic passage that only the act of sexual intercourse makes a maiden ineligible to marry a High Priest.

The analogy between these situations can, however, be invalidated. The case of a High Priest requires only that the girl's virginity be preserved to comply with the Biblical commandment (Levit. 21:14) ... "but a virgin (*betulah*) of his own people shall he take to wife." Thus, if she becomes pregnant *sine concubito* or if she cohabits with a man without her virginity being lost, as in the case of Samuel, she is still permitted to a High Priest. However, to prohibit a woman to her husband requires only a sexual union between the woman and another (*be'ulat ba'al*) as enunciated in Deut. 22:22. Therefore, even without the loss of virginity, she is considered an adulteress.

The question remains: Does A.I.D. constitute an adulterous act or not? Rabbi Judah Rozanes states that even without loss of virginity the sexual act makes a maiden prohibited to marry a High Priest.[13]

Rabbi Hananel ben Kusiel (11th century), in his commentary on the Talmud, interprets the discussion of the maiden and the High Priest entirely differently. He states that the whole question revolves around the requirement of the pregnant maiden to bring a sacrifice to purify herself from the ritual impurity of birth. Does the Biblical phrase "if a woman conceive seed and bear a man child, then she shall be unclean for seven days" (Levit. 12:2) apply only to a woman who has become pregnant as a result of sexual intercourse, or is it also applicable for conception *sine concubito*? This, says Rabbi Hananel, is the major question discussed in the Talmud and the problem of the maiden's permissibility to a High Priest is only coincidental.

Thus, whether or not we subscribe to Rabbi Hananel's interpretation of the Talmudic passage, it seems difficult, if not impossible, from this source to resolve the question as to whether A.I.D. constitutes an act of adultery which would prohibit the woman to her husband.

We then turn to another ancient source, namely the pronouncement of Rabbi Peretz ben Elijah of Corbeil, who doubts the feasibility of conception *sine concubito* and specifically states that a married woman who becomes impregnated in a bathouse is not forbidden to her husband because there has been no prohibited intercourse involved.

In our times, Rabbi Benzion Uziel also states that no adultery or incest can occur unless there is a physical union of man and woman.[14] Rabbi Moses Feinstein agrees that, without an act of sexual intercourse, the woman is not prohibited to her husband even if she has been inseminated with the semen of another without the husband's consent.

---

13. J. Rozanes, *"Hilkhot Issurei Biyah"* (Laws of Forbidden Sexual Connections), op. cit., Chapter 17:13.

14. B. Uziel, *"Even Haezer,"* *Responsa Mishpatei Uziel*. (Tel Aviv, 1935), No. 19.

The law of an adulteress, says Rabbi Feinstein, applies only for the sexual act and is involved even if there is no emission of sperm or even if the act is performed in an unnatural manner, i.e. sodomy.[15] Other authorities, such as Rabbi Sholom Mordecai Schwadron,[16] Rabbi Yehoshua Baumol[17] and Rabbi Aaron Wolkin[18] also permit the woman to her husband if no sexual contact has occurred between her and the donor of the semen.

Others disagree vehemently. Rabbi Judah Leib Zirelsohn looks upon A.I.D. as adultery, plain and simple.[19] The same view is held by Rabbi Abraham Lurie of South Africa[20] and Rabbi Obadya Hedaya.[21] Rabbi Eliezer Yehuda Waldenberg of Jerusalem is of the opinion that A.I.D. is akin to adultery, and cites numerous Rabbinic Responsa to support his viewpoint.[22] He dismisses the Talmudic passage and the pronouncement of Rabbi Peretz ben Elijah, stating that in both instances impregnation of the woman occurred passively and as an accident. On the other hand, A.I.D. entails the active participation of woman, physician and donor and thus constitutes a prohibited act. The husband, continues Rabbi Waldenberg, is entitled to divorce his wife on these grounds and she forfeits the monetary settlement written into the marriage contract (*ketubah*).

What is the status of the child? Is it illegitimate (mamzer)?—Here there is marked difference of opinion in the Rabbinic literature. Rabbis Zirelsohn, Lurie, Hedaya, Mordecai Jacob Breisch[23] and others consider

---

15. M. Feinstein, *"Even Haezer," Responsa Iggrot Moshe.* (New York, 1961), No. 10.
16. S. M. Schwadron, *Responsa Maharsham* (Brezany, 1910), Vol. 3, No. 268.
17. Y. Baumol, *Responsa Emek Halakhah*, (New York, 1934), No. 68.
18. A. Wolkin, *"Even Haezer," Responsa Zoken Aharon*, (New York, 1951), Part 2, No. 97.
19. J. L. Zirelsohn, *Responsa Ma'arkhei Lev* (Kishinev, 1932), No. 73.
20. A. Lurie, *Haposek* (Tel Aviv, [Heshvan-Kislev 5710] 1949).
21. O. Hedaya, *"Hazra'a Melakhutit"* (Artificial Insemination), *Noam*, Vol. 1, 1958 (5718), pp. 130-137.
22. E. Y. Waldenberg, *Responsa Tzitz Eliezer* (Jerusalem, 1967), Vol. 9, No. 51, Section 4.
23. M. J. Breisch, *Responsa Helkat Yd'akov* (Jerusalem, 1951), No. 24.

the child to be a *mamzer*, while Rabbi Waldenberg and others consider the child a questionable or possible *mamzer* (Hebrew: *sofek mamzer*). On the other hand, Rabbis Uziel, Weinberg, Feinstein, Baumohl, Wolkin, Joseph Saul Nathanson,[24] Menachem Kirshbaum,[25] Raphael Pladi,[26] Abraham Y. Neemrok[27] and Shlomo Zalman Auerbach,[28] as well as others, are of the opinion that the child is perfectly legitimate and not a *mamzer*.

Is Artificial Insemination from a Donor Permissible?—The previous questions dealt with the result of A.I.D., but the question as to whether A.I.D. is permitted at all has not yet been definitively answered. Rabbi Waldenberg categorically prohibits it as an utter abomination, and cites Rashi's comment on a Talmudic passage. Rashi interprets the Biblical phrase "'... to be a G-d unto thee and to thy seed after thee" (Genesis 17:7) to mean that G-d favors only those whose genealogy (i.e., paternity) is known.[29] The phrase in the Talmud itself reads "to distinguish between the seed of the first (husband) and the seed of the second." Thus, Rabbi Waldenberg prohibits A.I.D. because the genealogy of the child is unknown. Another reason given by Rabbi Waldenberg and in many other responsa is "lest he marry his sister" as mentioned in the Talmud. Therefore, avoidance of possible incest would interdict A.I.D. A third reason for prohibiting it is that after the "proxy" father's death, his other children may "steal" the portion of inheritance belonging to the child produced by A.I.D. Alternatively, the child may wrongly receive inheritance from his mother's husband

24. J. S. Nathanson, *Responsa Shoel U'meshiv* (Lemberg, 1868), Part 3, Vol. 3, No. 132.
25. M. Kirshbaum, *Responsa Menahem Umeshiv*. Quoted by D. B. Kranzer in "*Hazrd'a Melakhutit*" (Artificial Insemination). *Noam*, Vol. 1, 1958 (5718), pp. 111-123.
26. R. Pladi, *Responsa Yad Rama*. Quoted by D. B. Kranzer, *loc. cit.*
27. A. Y. Neemrok, "*Kashruth Hayilod*" (The Legitimacy of the Offspring), *Noam*, Vol. 1, 1958 (5718), pp. 143-144.
28. S. Z. Auerbach, "*Hazrd'a Melakhutit*" (Artificial Insemination), *Noam*, Vol. 1, 1958 (5718), pp. 145-166.
29. Commentary of Rashi in *Tractate Yevamot*, 42a.

upon the latter's death. Therefore, the question of stealing an inheritance makes A.I.D. forbidden.

Even if the donor's identity is known, continues Rabbi Waldenberg, A.I.D. is still prohibited, one reason being that the Scriptural phrase "And thou shalt not lie carnally with thy neighbor's wife to defile thyself with her" (Levit. 18:20) includes the prohibition of having one's semen enter another's wife even without the sexual act. There is, generally, strong Rabbinic opinion, including that of Jakobovits, that A.I.D. should be condemned as "an act of hideousness" or "an abomination" or "human stud farming." Although, technically, A.I.D. does not produce an illegitimate offspring, according to most viewpoints, it should be outlawed lest it pave the way to increased promiscuity. Only under situations of extreme need does Rabbinic opinion, as stated by Schwadron and Baumol, permit A.I.D.

Does the Donor Fulfill the Commandment of Procreation? Is the Child Considered the Child of the Donor?—Again, there are differing viewpoints on this problem. The specific question is asked by Rabbi Moshe of Brisk in his commentary on Karo's code as follows:

> ". . . one may raise the question, in the case of a woman who became pregnant in a bathhouse, whether the father has fulfilled (the precept) of 'be fruitful and multiply' (Gen. 1:28; 9:1 and 9:7) and if the child is considered his son in all respects. And in the *Likutei Maharil* we find that Ben Sira was the son of Jeremiah who washed in the bathhouse because Sira numerically equals Jeremiah . . ." i.e., the arithmetical sum of the Hebrew letters of the name Sira is identical with that of Jeremiah.[30]

Another commentary on Karo's code, that of Rabbi Samuel ben Uri, answers that the child is considered the man's son in all respects.[31] He bases his answer on the pronouncement of Rabbi Peretz ben Elijah (*Hagahot Smak*) quoted above. Rabbi Rozanes quotes both Rabbi Moshe of Brisk and Rabbi Samuel ben Uri and states that he agrees

---

30. Commentary *Helkat Mehokek* on *"Even Haezer," Shulchan Arukh*, 1:6.
31. Commentary *Beth Shmuel* on *"Even Haezer," Shulchan Arukh*, 1:6.

with them. Others, such as Rabbis Jacob ben Samuel,[32] Yisroel Zev Mintzberg,[33] Simon ben Zemach Duran[34] and Jacob Ettlinger[35] also subscribe to this viewpoint. Some, such as Rabbis Jacob Embden[36] and Moshe Schick disagree, and claim that although the child is considered the son of the donor, the donor has not fulfilled the precept of procreation because there has been no sexual act involved. Yet others, such as Rabbis Hedaya and Moshe Aryeh Leb Shapiro state that the child is neither his nor has he fulfilled the commandment of procreation.[37]

One might argue that if the case of impregnation in the bathhouse, where there was no intent on the part of the true father to impregnate the woman, results in a child considered to be his son in all respects and he has fulfilled the commandment of procreation (according to most authorities), then certainly *a fortiori* the same results should pertain to A.I.D. where at least the doctor and the woman intentionally seek a pregnancy. This argument can be countered by the fact that anonymous donors provide their sperm to semen banks without intention as to their use for a specific woman, but on the other hand, there is the intent on the part of the donor that his sperm be utilized for the purpose of artificial insemination. Thus, the argument of intent seems to have little if any validity or applicability to the problem under discussion.

Is the Woman Following A.I.D. Considered to be the Pregnant or Nursing Wife of Another? — Should the woman's husband die or divorce her following A.I.D., is she allowed to remarry while she is still pregnant or, following delivery, while she is still nursing? A Talmudic pronouncement states that a man should not marry the

32. Jacob Ben Samuel, *Responsa Beit Ya'akov* (Dyrenfurth, 1696), No. 122.
33. Y. A. Mintzberg, *Noam*, Vol. 1, 1958 (5718), p. 129.
34. S. Duran, *Responsa Tashbatz* (Amsterdam, 1739), Part 3, No. 263.
35. J. Ettlinger, Commentary *Arukh L'ner on Tractate Yevamot* (Pietrkow, 1914), p. 10.
36. J. Embden, *Responsa Shee'lat Ya'avetz* (Altona, 1739), Part 2, No. 96.
37. M. A. L. Shapiro, "*Hazra'a Melakhutit*" (Artificial Insemination), *Noam*, Vol. 1, 1958 (5718), pp. 138-142.

pregnant wife of another or the nursing wife of another, even though she has been divorced or widowed, until after the child is born or until she stops nursing, respectively.[38] Three reasons are given. First, we are concerned lest the woman conceive again while she is pregnant, thus making it impossible to identify which part of the child is the offspring of the first husband and which is the offspring of the second. Whether a woman can conceive by two different men and produce one child has been stated as fact by some[39] and denied by others.[40] Second, there may be danger to the fetus from abdominal pressure from sexual relations with the new husband, who might not be as careful to avoid harming the unborn fetus as would the true father. Third, if the woman conceives during the nursing period, her milk would become turbid and the nursing baby might die of starvation.

This rule has been codified by Maimonides who states: "And the Sages also ordained that a man not marry the pregnant wife of another or the nursing wife of another even though (in the former case), the owner of the seed which made her pregnant is known—lest the fetus be harmed during intercourse because he is not careful with the child of another. And (in the case of) a nursing woman lest her milk become turbid and he does not pay attention to heal the milk with things which improve turbid milk."[41]

Rabbi Jacob ben Asher and Rabbi Joseph Karo in their Codes also state that "the Sages decreed that a person should not marry nor betroth the pregnant wife of another or the nursing wife of another . . .".[42]

With this discussion as background, Rabbi Waldenberg ponders whether the decree against a man marrying the pregnant or nursing

---

38. Babylonian Talmud, *Yevamot*, 36b and 42a.
39. *Tosafot* (various French and German authors of the 12th and 13th centuries). Commentary on Tractate *Sotah*, 42b s.v., *"Me'ah Pappi"*; Jerusalem Talmud, *Yevamot*, 4:2.
40. Rashi, Commentary on Tractate *Sotah*, 42b s.v., *"Bar Me'ah Pappi."*
41. M. Maimonides, *"Hilkhot Gerushin"* (Laws Pertaining to Divorce), *Mishneh Torah*, Chapter 11:25.
42. Jacob ben Asher, *"Even Haezer," Tur Shulchan Arukh*, 13:11; J. Karo, *"Even Haezer," Shulchan Arukh*, 13:11.

wife of another is applicable to the husband whose wife has undergone A.I.D. He concludes in the affirmative and the new husband must, as a result, abstain from cohabitation with his wife until after she stops nursing. Some Rabbis, such as Malchiel Zvi Halevy Tanenbaum,[43] Zirelsohn and Uziel agree with Waldenberg, whereas others, such as Chayim Joseph David Azulay,[44] are in doubt whether the decree applies to A.I.D.

Artificial Insemination Using the Husband's Semen — Using the husband's sperm to inseminate the woman would eliminate many of the objections raised regarding A.I.D., such as possible adultery, the offspring possibly marrying a sibling, "stealing" of an inheritance and licentiousness, among others. Is then A.I.H. permissible? Difference of opinion exists on this question in the Responsa literature. Rabbis Feinstein, Schwadron, Wolkin, Zvi Pesach Frank and others state that A.I.H. is permissible.[45] Others, such as Rabbis Tannenbaum and Waldenberg frown upon it, stating it is permissible only in extreme situations. The Rabbis who normally forbid A.I.H. claim that Rabbi Elijah ben Peretz' pronouncement allowing a woman to lie on sheets upon which her husband has lain (and possibly emitted sperm) is because impregnation in that situation is extremely rare. However, A.I.H. commonly leads to pregnancy. Furthermore, in the case described by Rabbi Elijah, pregnancy occurred passively and by accident, whereas in A.I.H. the physician, the donor and the woman are active participants. Furthermore, claim the Rabbis who object to A.I.H., if A.I.H. were permitted, the physician might be tempted to add foreign semen to that of the husband in order to facilitate conception, thus performing A.I.D., which is certainly prohibited. Even the Rabbis who

---

43. M. Z. Tanenbaum, *Responsa Divrei Malkiel* (Vilna, 1901), Part 4, Nos. 107 and 108.
44. C. J. D. Azulay, Commentary *Birkei Joseph* — quoted by Waldenberg, see ref. 19.
45. M. Feinstein, *"Even Ha'ezer" Responsa Iggrot Moshe*, Part 2, No. 18 (New York, 1963), Supplement to *Hoshen Mishpat*; A. Wolkin, *"Even Haezer," Responsa Zaken Aharon*, Part 2, No. 97; Pesach Zvi Frank, as quoted by Waldenberg; *Responsa Yabeeya Omer*, Part 2, No. 1, as quoted by Feinstein.

permit A.I.H. would prohibit the use of a mixture of the husband's and another man's sperm. Thus, Rabbi Feinstein states that such an admixture of semens is a trick to overcome the weakness of the husband's sperm and is, therefore, considered like A.I.D. and is not A.I.H. Rabbis Waldenberg, Henkin and others agree. One must be sure that only the husband's sperm is employed and only trustworthy physicians must be sought.

Insemination While the Woman is Ritually Unclean (Niddah)—If we follow the permissive ruling regarding A.I.H., then the question arises as to whether it is allowed to perform artificial insemination on a woman during the period of her ritual uncleanliness.

Rabbi Abraham Isaiah Karelitz, known as the *Hazon Ish*, in his book *Haish Vehazono*, relates that he was asked about a woman who had very short menstrual cycles so that her fertile periods always occurred during her counting of the "seven clean days." Physicians recommended that A.I.H. be performed during this period prior to the woman's *tevilah* (ritual immersion for purification), and Rabbi Karelitz answered that she should abbreviate her unclean period to four days but that she should not be inseminated while ritually unclean prior to *tevilah*.

Rabbis Schwadron, Waldenberg, Hedaya, Tannenbaum and others permit A.I.H. but not while the woman is ritually unclean, whereas Rabbis Feinstein, Wolkin, Auerbach and others permit A.I.H. even during this period if no other way proves successful.

An additional requirement before A.I.H. can be performed is an interval of time after the wedding during which pregnancy has been attempted in the usual manner of cohabitation, but without results. This interval must be ten years, according to Rabbi Jacob Yitschak Weiss,[46] five years in the opinion of Rabbi Feinstein,[47] two years

---

46. J. Y. Weiss, *Responsa Minhat Yitzhak* (London, 1955).
47. M. Feinstein, "*Even Haezer,*" *Responsa Iggrot Moshe*, (New York, 1963), Part 2, No. 16. Supplement to *Hoshen Mishpat*.

according to Rabbi Karelitz and long enough to establish the medical necessity for A.I.H., in the opinion of Rabbi Waldenberg.

Procurement of Semen for Artificial Insemination — Since most Rabbinic opinion sanctions A.I.H. under circumstances where pregnancy can be achieved in no other way, the question arises as to how to obtain the semen for the insemination without transgressing the prohibition of improper emission of seed or emission of semen for naught. This was the sin of Er and Onan (Genesis 38:7-10). This subject alone is of such broad dimensions as to require a separate essay and the interested reader is referred to extensive discussions elsewhere.[48]

In brief, most Rabbis (Frank, Feinstein, Waldenberg, Schwadron, Wolkin, Shapiro, Auerbach, Mintzberg, Baumohl) state that procurement of semen by acceptable means from the husband for insemination into his wife is permissible and does not constitute emission of seed for naught, since the semen will be used to fulfill the commandment of procreation. Some, like Rabbis Tannenbaum, Uziel, Hedaya and Breisch disagree, but they are in the minority. Two methods of obtaining the sperm are mentioned in the Talmud where we find a discussion concerning a Priest who is wounded in his testicles (*petzuah dakkah*) or whose membrum is cut off (*kerut shafkhah*):

> ". . . Rabbi Judah stated in the name of Samuel: If it (the membrum) had a small perforation which was closed up, the man is deemed to be unfit if the wound re-opens when semen is emitted, but if it does not reopen the man is regarded as fit. . . . Raba, the son of Rabbah, sent to Rabbi Joseph: Will our Master instruct us how to proceed (to test whether the semen will reopen the closed perforation). The other replied: Warm barley bread is procured and placed upon the man's anus. Thereby the

---

48. D. M. Feldman, "Improper Emission of Generative Seed" in *Birth Control in Jewish Law*, (New York University, Press, 1968), pp. 109-169; L. M. Epstein, "Wasting Nature," *Sex Laws and Customs in Judaism* (New York, Ktav Publishing House, 1967), pp. 144-147; S. J. Zevin, "Hashhatat Zera," *Talmudic Encyclopedia* (Jerusalem, 1965), Vol. 11, pp. 129-141.

flow of semen sets in, and the effect can be observed . . . said Abaye, colored (women's) garments are dangled before him (exciting his passions thus causing semen emission). . . ."[49]

Both of these two methods, as well as others, are perfectly acceptable, according to Rabbi Feinstein.[50] In addition, it is permissible to think of a woman in order to excite the emotions and to cause semen emission for the purpose of artificial insemination into one's wife. The least objectionable method is the procurement of sperm from coitus interruptus, or, if this is unsatisfactory for any reason, a condom may be applied on the male membrum prior to coitus. These latter two procedures involve the natural sex act and are, therefore, most acceptable to Jewish law. Masturbation to obtain sperm is strongly condemned by Rabbi Feinstein, based upon the following Talmudic passage: ". . . Rabbi Eleazer stated: Who are referred to in the Scriptural text *'Your hands are full of blood'* (Isaiah 1:15)? Those that commit masturbation with their hands. It was taught at the school of Rabbi Ishmael *'Thou shalt not commit adultery'* (Exod. 20:13) implies that thou shalt not practice masturbation either with hand or with foot...".[51]

To have sexual intercourse in the physician's office and for the physician to retrieve the sperm from the vagina of the woman to combine several ejaculates for subsequent insemination is considered licentious and improper, according to Rabbi Feinstein, although Rabbi Waldenberg allows this practice.[52] Rabbi Waldenberg also permits masturbation to obtain semen if all the other methods cannot be employed. He states that, if possible, the physician should perform the masturbation but, if that is not feasible, the husband can do it. Rabbi Waldenberg further states that one is permitted to extract semen directly from the testicle.

---

49. Tractate *Yevamot*, 76a.

50. M. Feinstein, *"Even Haezer," Responsa Iggrot Moshe* (New York, 1961), No. 70.

51. Tractate *Niddah*, 13b.

52. E. Y. Waldenberg, Op. cit., Section 1, Chapter 2.

Conclusions

Artificial insemination using the semen of a donor other than the husband is considered by most Rabbinic opinion to be an abomination and strictly prohibited for a variety of reasons, including the possibility of incest, lack of genealogy and the problems of inheritance. Some authorities regard A.I.D. as adultery, requiring the husband to divorce his wife and her forfeiture of the *ketubah,* and even the physician and the donor are guilty when involved in this act akin to adultery. Some Rabbinic opinion, however, states that without a sexual act involved, the woman is not guilty of adultery and is not prohibited to cohabit with her husband.

Regarding the status of the child, Rabbinic opinion is divided. Most consider the offspring to be legitimate as was Ben Sira, the product of conception *sine concubito,* a small minority of Rabbis consider the child illegitimate, and at least two authorities take a middle view and label the child a *sofek mamzer.* Considerable Rabbinic opinion regards the child (legitimate or illegitimate) to be the son of the donor in all respects (i.e., inheritance, support, custody, incest, Levirate marriage, and the like). Some regard the child to be the donor's son only in some respects but not others. Some Rabbis state that although the child is considered the donor's son in all respects, the donor has not fulfilled the commandment of procreation. A minority of Rabbinic authority asserts that the child is not considered the donor's son at all.

The woman, following A.I.D. or A.I.H., is considered to be the nursing or pregnant wife of another and, if her husband dies or divorces her, she cannot remarry another until after she has finished nursing the child. Several Rabbis also invoke this rule to prohibit a man to cohabit with his pregnant or nursing wife following A.I.D.

There is near unanimity of opinion that the use of semen from the husband is permissible if no other method is possible for the wife to become pregnant. However, certain qualifications exist. There must have been a reasonable period of waiting since marriage (2, 5 or 10 years or until medical proof of the absolute necessity for A.I.H.), and, according to many authorities, the insemination may not be performed during the wife's period of ritual impurity.

It is permitted by most Rabbis to obtain sperm from the husband both for analysis and for insemination, but difference of opinion exists as to the method to be used in the procurement of it. Masturbation should be avoided if at all possible and *coitus interruptus* or the use of a condom seem to be the preferred methods.

Since many important legal and moral considerations which cannot be enunciated in the presentation of general principles may weigh heavily upon the verdict in any given situation it seems advisable to submit each individual case to Rabbinic judgment which, in turn, will be based upon expert medical advice and other prevailing circumstances.

Chapter VII

Jewish Attitude Toward Euthanasia*

The word euthanasia is derived from the Greek "eu" meaning well, good, or pleasant and "thanatos" meaning death. Webster's dictionary defines euthanasia as the mode or act of inducing death painlessly or as a relief from pain. The popular expression for euthanasia is mercy killing. Perusal of the medical literature of the last two decades reveals a host of books,[1-3] articles,[4-33] editorials,[34-38] and letters to editors of journals[39-41] dealing with this subject. This is exclusive of the legal, theologic, psychologic, and social literatures. Even the lay press is replete with writings on euthanasia[42] dating back to February, 1873, when both the *Fortnightly Review* and the *Spectator* carried feature articles on the subject.[8] A recent lead article in the *Times* of London on the acquittals of parents, relatives, and a physician charged with murdering a thalidomide-damaged child raised such interest from readers that 42 of the numerous letters written to the *Times* in response to the article were published in a subsequent issue.[40]

There is thus little doubt as to the tremendous interest in euthanasia today. The present report is an attempt to review briefly the subject of euthanasia by providing classification and terminology, citing selected examples, describing the legal attitude toward euthanasia in various countries, discussing the arguments put forth for and against euthanasia, briefly mentioning the Catholic and Protestant viewpoints on euthanasia, and finally presenting in detail the Jewish attitude toward euthanasia.

CLASSIFICATION AND TERMINOLOGY

As already stated, euthanasia is popularly spoken of as "mercy killing." A less painful term used by euthanasia societies is "merciful

---

* See footnotes at end of chapter, p. 121.

release"[32] or "liberating euthanasia."[24] Some people classify euthanasia into three types: eugenic, medical, and preventive.[24,28] A more meaningful classification speaks of eugenic, active medical, and passive medical euthanasia.[32] Eugenic euthanasia would encompass the "merciful release" of birth monsters and socially undesirable individuals such as the mentally retarded and psychiatrically disturbed. Perhaps an extreme example of this method of exterminiation was the Nazi killing of all the socially unacceptable or socially unfit. To many, this German practice as well as all eugenic euthanasia is considered nothing less than murder, and thus there are very few proponents of this type of euthanasia.

Active medical euthanasia is exemplified by the case where a drug or other treatment is administered, and death is thereby hastened. This type of euthanasia may be voluntary or involuntary, that is, with or without the patient's consent.

Passive medical euthanasia is defined as the situation in which therapy is withheld so that death is hastened by omission of treatment. This type of euthanasia has also been called automathanasia[30] meaning automatic death, such as without therapeutic heroics. This passive form of euthanasia can also be voluntary or involuntary.

A new term, antidysthanasia, has been put forth by one of the most outspoken proponents of euthanasia in this country, the Anglican minister Joseph Fletcher.[43] This new words seems only to add to the confusion.

Exemplification of the Problem

Many a physician has had to wrestle with the problem of an incurably ill, suffering patient. Such physicians fully realize that "whereas life is lengthened, man's period of usefulness is not always lengthened."[25] Some are of the opinion that advanced medicine should "serve only to improve the condition of human life as it increases the life span and not the useless prolongation of human suffering."[25] Thus, on December 4, 1949, H. N. Sander, M.D., a general practitioner in Manchester, New Hampshire, ended a cancer patient's suffering by injecting into the patient a substantial quantity of air intravenously.

He was acquitted.[24] On March 9, 1950, Miss C. A. Paight of Stamford, Connecticut, shot and killed her father who was dying of incurable cancer. She was acquitted.[24]

The problem is far from localized to the shores of the United States. In December, 1961, Giuseppe Faita, having settled in France, was struck with an incurable disease. He summoned his brother Luigi and convinced the latter to kill him, which Luigi did. The jury acquitted Luigi.[27]

One of the most famous instances exemplifying many of the problems surrounding euthanasia is the case of Maurice Millard, M.D., son of the founder of the British Euthanasia Society. Dr. Millard told a Rotary meeting: "To keep her from pain . . . I gave her an injection to make her sleep."[25] His objective as specifically stated was to relieve pain, not to put an end to the patient's life. An outcry in the British press followed, labeling the incident "a mercy killing." Even the British Euthanasia Society admitted that from a strictly legal sense mercy killing is murder, but it backed Dr. Millard by insisting that "every doctor must be guided by his own conscience." Many physicians disagreed, saying euthanasia is only legalized murder. Others cited the Hippocratic oath which states: "I will give no deadly medicine to anyone if asked, nor suggest any such counsel." Still others were of the opinion that the Hippocratic oath refers only to premeditated murder. The medical council refused to act against Dr. Millard unless the family of the deceased lodged a formal complaint. However, the family consented to Dr. Millard's actions. Thus, all the ingredients to emphasize the problem of euthanasia are present in this case: the incurable patient in great pain, the request for euthanasia by patient and family, and the physician's acquiescence and participation.

The list of examples one could cite is endless. The aforementioned illustrative cases serve as background for the ensuing discussion.

Legal Attitude Toward Euthanasia

Although suicide is not legally a crime in most American jurisdictions, aiding and abetting suicide is murder.[16] Euthanasia in the United

States, even at the patient's request, is legally murder. In England the Suicide Act enacted into law in 1961 states that it is no longer a criminal offense for a person, whether in sickness or in health, to take his own life or to attempt to do so. However, any individual who helps him to do so becomes liable to a charge of manslaughter.[44] Euthanasia per se does not exist in the law books of France and Belgium, and in both countries it is considered premeditated homicide.[27,28,30] However, a bill to legalize euthanasia for some "damaged" children came before the Belgian government on November 26, 1962, following the famous Liège trial involving parents, relatives, and a physician charged with murdering a thalidomide-damaged child.[40]

In Italy, euthanasia is only a crime if the victim is under eighteen years of age, mentally retarded, or menaced or under the effect of fear.[28] More tolerant attitudes also exist in Denmark, Holland, Yugoslavia, and even Catholic Spain.[28] In Russia, euthanasia is considered "murder under extenuating circumstances" and punishable with three to eight years in prison.[24] Switzerland seems to have the most lenient legislation.[28] The Swiss penal code was revamped in 1951 and distinguishes between killing with bad intentions, that is, murder, and killing with good intentions, that is, euthanasia.[24] In addition, in 1964 in Sweden, passive euthanasia was legalized.[45]

Even in the countries where euthanasia is legally murder, "the sympathies of juries towards mercy killings often cause the law to be circumvented by various methods, making for great inequities of the legal system."[16] In the several sample cases cited here, the defendants were all acquitted. Although judges and juries are usually very lenient, a recent case of euthanasia is described from Perth, Australia, in which the death penalty was imposed.[30]

In 1935 the first Euthanasia Society was founded in England by C. Killick Millard M.D., for the purpose of promoting legislation which would seek to "make the act of dying more gentle."[44] In 1936, one year after the founding of the Society, a bill was introduced into the House of Lords which sought to permit voluntary euthanasia in certain circumstances and with certain safeguards. Following a rather heated debate, it was decided that "in view of the emergence of so many controversial issues, it would be best to leave the matter for the time being to the discretion of individual medical men ... the bill was rejected by 35 votes to 14."[44] The Euthanasia Society of England is quite active today under the presidency of the Earl of Listowel and the chairmanship of Leonard Colebrook, M.D., and its goal is to see implemented a "Plan for Voluntary Euthanasia which would permit an adult person of sound mind, whose life is ending with much suffering to choose between an easy death and a hard one; and to obtain medical aid in implementing that choice."[44]

In 1938, three years after the inception of the British group, the Euthanasia Society of America, Inc., was founded by Charles Frances Potter. This nonsectarian, voluntary organization currently presided over by Rev. Donald W. McKinney, rather than seeking to have legislation enacted to legalize euthanasia, is attempting to achieve a more enlightened public understanding of euthanasia through dissemination of information. This goal is being strived for through discussions of euthanasia in medical societies and other professional groups, research studies and opinion polls, dissemination of literature, a speaker's bureau, and other responsible media of communication.[46]

Other euthanasia societies have cropped up in Sweden and Japan. Support for these societies and their work comes from various other groups such as the American Humanist Association and the Ethical Culture Society.[45] Opposition to euthanasia is also strong, however. Thus, the Academy of Moral and Political Sciences of Paris voted on a motion completely outlawing, forbidding, and rejecting euthanasia in all its forms.[24] In addition, the Council of the World Medical Association, meeting in Copenhagen in April, 1950, recommended that the practice of euthanasia be condemned.[1] The debate continues, and some of the arguments presented by proponents and opponents of euthanasia will be presented here.

The problem has been well stated by Filbey[32]: "When a tortured man asks: 'For G-d's sake, doctor, let me die, just put me to sleep,' we have yet to find the answer as to whether to comply is for G-d's sake, the patient's sake, our own, or possibly all three." Even if the moral issue of euthanasia could be circumvented, other questions of logistics would immediately arise: Who is to initiate euthanasia proceedings? The patient? The family? The physician? Who is to make the final decision? The physician? A group of physicians? The courts? Who is to carry out the decision if it is affirmative? The physician? Others?[26]

Pros and Cons

Arguments in favor and against euthanasia are numerous, have and continue to be heatedly debated in many circles, and will be only briefly summarized here.

Opponents of euthanasia say that if voluntary, it is suicide. Although by British law suicide is no longer a crime,[44] Christian and Jewish religious teachings certainly outlaw suicide. The answer offered to this argument is that martyrdom, a form of suicide, is condoned under certain conditions. However, the martyr seeks not to end his life primarily but to accomplish a goal, death being an undesired side product. Thus, martyrdom and suicide do not seem comparable.

It is also said that euthanasia, if voluntary, is murder. As one writer so aptly put it: "Euthanasia must be defined within the knife's edge area between suicide and murder."[29] Murder, however, usually connotes premeditated evil. The motives of the person administering euthanasia are far from evil. On the contrary, such motives are commendable and praiseworthy, although the methods may be unacceptable.

A closely related objection to euthanasia says that it transgresses the Biblical injunction "Thou shalt not kill." To overcome this argument, some modern Biblical translators substitute "Thou shalt not commit murder" and, as just mentioned, murder usually represents "violent killing for purposes of gain, or treachery or vendetta"[44] and is totally dissimilar to the "merciful release" of euthanasia.

That G-d alone gives and takes life as it is written in Deut. 32:39: "I kill and I make alive" and Ezekial 18:4: "Behold, all souls are Mine" and that one's life span is divinely predetermined, is not denied by the proponents of euthanasia. The difficulty with this point, however, seems to be the question of definition as to whether euthanasia represents shortening of life or shortening of the act of dying.

To complete the religious argumentation, it is said that suffering is part of the divine plan with which man has no right to tamper. This phase of faith remains a mystery and is best exemplified by the story of Job.

It is further argued by opponents of euthanasia that since physicians are only human beings, they are liable to error. There is no infallibility in a physician's diagnosis of an incurably ill patient, and mistakes have been made. Rabinowitch and MacDermot,[7] in an address on the subject of euthanasia delivered before the Medical Undergraduates Society of McGill University on March 21, 1950, quote Rabinowitch's own case. Eighteen years earlier a diagnosis of carcinoma of the esophagus had been made, yet Dr. Rabinowitch was very much alive when he spoke at McGill University eighteen years later. Such mistaken diagnoses are exceedingly rare, but they do occur. The same is true of spontaneous remission of cancer: It has been reported, but only in very rare instances.

The need for euthanasia today is minimized by some because the availability of hypnotics, narcotics, anesthetics, and other analgesic means is sufficient to keep any patient's pain and distress at a tolerable level. This fact, in general, may be true, but occasional patients develop severe pain which is refractory to all drugs and requires surgical interruption of the nerve pathways for relief.

The Hippocratic oath or a similar vow which all physicians swear to on graduation from medical school is conflicting. On the one hand, it states that a physician's duty is to relieve suffering yet, on the other hand, it also states that the physician must preserve and protect life. This oath is used as an argument by both proponents and opponents of euthanasia.

A very valid point of debate is the suggestion that if euthanasia for incurably ill, suffering cancer patients were legalized, then extension of such legislation to the grossly deformed, psychotic, or senile patients might follow. A recent editorial stated: "If euthanasia is granted to the first class, can it long be denied to the second? . . . Each step is so short; the slope so slippery; our values in this age, so uncertain and unstable . . ."[35]

Further debatable questions are the sincerity of patient and/or family in requesting euthanasia. A patient racked with pain may make an impulsive but ill-considered request for merciful release which he will not be able to retract or regret after the *fait accompli*. The patient's family may not be completely sincere in its desire to relieve the patient's suffering. The family also wishes to relieve its own suffering.[30] Enemies or heirs of the patient may request hastening of the patient's death for ulterior motives.[1] These and further arguments both for and against euthanasia are discussed at greater length by Fletcher,[1] Sperry,[2] and others.[22,24]

Ideally, euthanasia should not be necessary if medicine had all the answers to the problems of presently incurable disease. This thesis was well enunciated by a recent writer who stated: "Let us hope that with the advances of medical science, the requests for euthanasia would be few and far between, for each request represents a failure in our present methods of providing adequate relief . . ."[41]

Catholic Attitude Toward Euthanasia

The New Testament in at least five places (Matthew 5:21, Matthew 19:18, Mark 10:19, Luke 18:20, Romans 13:9) contains the Biblical admonition "Thou shalt not kill." Based on this, the attitude of the Catholic Church in this matter is cited as follows:

> . . . The teaching of the Church is unequivocal that G-d is the supreme master of life and death and that no human being is allowed to usurp His dominion so as deliberately to put an end to life, either his own or any one else's without authorization . . . and the only authorizations the Church recognizes are a nation engaged in war, execution of criminals by a Government, killing in self defense . . . The Church has never allowed and never will allow the killing of individuals on grounds of private expediency; for instance . . . putting an end to prolonged suffering or hopeless sickness . . .[7]

Thus we see a blanket condemnation of active euthanasia by the Catholic Church as murder and, therefore, a mortal sin. The reasons behind this teaching include the inviolability of human life or the supreme dominion of G-d over His creatures and the purposefulness of human suffering.[22] Man suffers as penance for his sins, perhaps an earthly purgatory; man endures pain for the spiritual good of his fellow man; suffering teaches humility and helps the Catholic identify with his crucified Lord.

Passive medical euthanasia is treated quite differently. The Church distinguishes between "ordinary" and extraordinary" measures employed by physicians when certain death and suffering lie ahead. In this day of auxiliary hearts, artificial kidneys, respirators, pacemakers, defibrillators, and similar instruments, the definition of "extraordinary" is unclear and nebulous. Pope Pius XII, in the last year of his life, issued an encyclical not requiring physicians to use heroic measures in such circumstances.[27,29,33] Thus, passive euthanasia is sanctioned by the Catholic Church. In an address to the congress of Italian anesthetists on February 24, 1957, the Pope further stated: "Even if narcotics may shorten life while they relieve pain, it is permissible."[27]

Protestant Attitude Toward Euthanasia

In the Protestant Church there are "all possible colors in the spectrum of attitudes toward euthanasia."[22] Some condemn it, some favor it, and many are in between, advocating judgment of each case individually. Perhaps the greatest Protestant advocate of legalized euthanasia is the Anglican minister Joseph Fletcher. His three main reasons are the following: (1) Suffering is purposeless, demoralizing, and degrading; (2) human personality is of greater worth than life per se; and (3) the phrase "Blessed are the merciful, for they shall obtain mercy" is as important as "Thou shalt not kill."

Jewish Attitude Toward Euthanasia

Before tracing the Jewish attitude toward euthanasia through Rabbinic sources, it would seem appropriate to cite Biblical references to this matter. In the book of Genesis, (Genesis 9:6), we find "whoso sheddeth man's blood, by man shall his blood be shed . . ." In the second book of the Pentateuch, (Exodus 20:13), it is stated: "Thou shalt not murder" and further in the next chapter, (Exodus 21:14), is the following sentence: "And if a man come presumptuously upon his neighbor, to slay him with guile: thou shalt take him from Mine altar, that he may die." In Leviticus, (Leviticus 24:17), is the phrase "And he that smiteth any man mortally shall surely be put to death" and four sentences later we find again ". . . And he that killeth a man shall be put to death." In the book of Numbers it is stated (Numbers 35:30): "Whoso killeth any person, the murderer shall be slain at the mouth of witnesses . . ." Finally, in Deuteronomy, the sixth commandment of the decalogue is repeated (Deuteronomy 5:17): "Thou shalt not murder." Thus, in every book of the Pentateuch, we find at least one reference to murder or killing. Accidental death or homicide is dealt with seperately in the Bible and represents another subject entirely.

Probably the first recorded instance of euthanasia concerns the death of King Saul in the year 1013 B.C. Thus at the end of the first book of Samuel, (Chapter 31:1-6), we find the following:

> Now the Philistines fought against Israel, and the men of Israel fled from before the Philistines and fell down slain in Mount Gilboa. And the Philistines pursued hard upon Saul and upon his sons; and the Philistines slew Jonathan and Abinadab and Malchishua, the sons of Saul. And the battle went sore against Saul and the archers overtook him and he was greatly afraid by reason of the archers. There said Saul to his armor-bearer: "Draw thy sword, and thrust me through therewith, lest these uncircumsized come and thrust me through and make a mock of me." But his armor-bearer would not; for he was sore afraid. Therefore, Saul took his sword and fell upon it. And when the armor-bearer saw that Saul was dead, he likewise fell upon his sword and died with him. So Saul died and his 3 sons, and his armor-bearer, and all his men, that same day together.

From this passage it would appear as if Saul committed suicide. However, at the beginning of the second book of Samuel when David is informed of Saul's death, we find the following (Chapter 1:5-10):

And David said unto the young man that told him: "How
knowest thou that Saul and Jonathan his son are dead?" And the
young man that told him said: "As I happened by chance upon
Mount Gilboa, behold Saul leaned upon his spear; and lo, the
chariots and the horsemen pressed hard upon him. And when he
looked behind him, he saw me, and called unto me. And I
answered: Here am I. And he said unto me: Who art thou?
And I answered him: I am an Amalekite. And he said unto me:
Stand, I pray thee, beside me, and slay me, for the agony hath
taken hold of me; because my life is just yet in me. So I stood
beside him, and slew him, because I was sure that he would not
live after that he was fallen. . . ."

Many commentators consider this a case of euthanasia. *Radak*
(Rabbi David Kimchi 1160 to 1235) specifically states that Saul did
not die immediately on falling on his sword but was mortally wounded
and in his death throes asked the Amalekite to hasten his death.
Ralbag (Rabbi Levi ben Gershon 1288 to 1344) and *Rashi* (Rabbi
Solomon ben Isaac 1040 to 1105) also support this viewpoint, as does
Metzudath David (Rabbi David Altschul, seventeenth century). Some
modern scholars think that the story of the Amalekite was a complete
fabrication.

The Mishnah or compilation of oral law dating approximately to
the second century states as follows (Tractate *Semachot* 1:1): "One
who is in a dying condition (Hebrew: *gosses*) is regarded as a living
person in all respects." This rule is reiterated by later codifiers of
Jewish law including Maimonides and Karo as described here. The
Mishnah continues (Tractate *Semachot* 1:2 to 4):

One may not bind his jaws, nor stop up his openings, nor place
a metallic vessel or any cooling object on his navel until such
time that he dies as it is written (Ecclesiastes 12:6): "Before the
silver cord (Midrash interprets this as the spinal cord) is snapped
asunder."

One may not move him nor may one place him on sand nor
on salt until he dies.

> One may not close the eyes of the dying person. He who touches them or moves them is shedding blood because Rabbi Meir used to say: this can be compared to a flickering flame. As soon as a person touches it, it becomes extinguished. So too, whosoever closes the eyes of the dying is considered to have taken his soul.

Other laws pertaining to a "gosses" or dying person such as the preparation of a coffin, inheritance, marriage, and so forth are then cited. These latter laws are not pertinent to our discussion of euthanasia and will not be further commented on here.

The fifth century Babylonian Talmud (Tractate *Sabbath* 151b) mentions as follows: "He who closes the eyes of a dying person while the soul is departing is a murderer (literally, he sheds blood). This may be compared to a lamp that is going out. If a man places his finger upon it, it is immediately extinguished." *Rashi* (Rabbi Solomon ben Isaac 1040 to 1105) explains that this small effort of closing the eyes may slightly hasten death.

The twelfth century Code of Maimonides (book of Judges, laws of mourning, Chapter 4:5) treats our subject matter as follows:

> One who is in a dying condition is regarded as a living person in all respects. It is not permitted to bind his jaws, to stop up the organs of the lower extremities, or to place metallic or cooling vessels upon his navel in order to prevent swelling. He is not to be rubbed or washed, nor is sand or salt to be put upon him until he expires. He who touches him is guilty of shedding blood. To what may he be compared? To a flickering flame, which is extinguished as soon as one touches it. Whoever closes the eyes of the dying while the soul is about to depart is shedding blood. One should wait a while; perhaps he is only in a swoon . . .

Thus, we again note the prohibition of doing anything that might hasten death. Maimonides does not specifically forbid moving such a patient as does the Mishnah, but such a prohibition is implied in Maimonides' text. Maimonides also forbids rubbing and washing a dying person, acts which are not mentioned in the Mishnah. Finally,

Maimonides raises the problelm of the recognition of death. This problem is becoming more pronounced as scientific medicine improves the methods for supporting respiration and heart function.

The sixteenth century code of Jewish law, the *Shulchan Aruch,* compiled in 1564 by Rabbi Joseph Karo (1488 to 1575) devotes an entire chapter (Section *Yoreh Deah,* Chapter 339) to the laws of the dying patient. The individual in whom death is imminent is referred to as a "gosses." Karo's code begins, as do Maimonides and the Mishnah, with the phrase: "a gosses is considered as a living person in all respects," and then Karo enumerates various acts that are prohibited. All the commentaries explain these prohibitions "lest they hasten the patient's death." One of the forbidden acts not mentioned by Maimonides or the Mishnah is the removal of the pillow from beneath the patient's head. This act had already been prohibited two centuries earlier by the *Tur* (Rabbi Jacob ben Asher about 1269 to 1343) in his code (*Tur Yoreh Deah,* Chapter 339). Karo's text is nearly identical to that of the *Tur.* The *Tur,* however, has the additional general explanation: "the rule in this matter is that any act performed in relation to death should not be carried out until the soul has departed." Thus, not only are physical acts on the patient such as described forbidden, but one should also not provide a coffin or prepare a grave or make other funeral or related arrangements lest the patient hear of this and his death be hastened. Even psychological stress is prohibited.

On the other hand, Rabbi Judah ben Samuel, the Pious (died 1217), author of the thirteenth century work *Sefer Chasidim,* reprinted in Buenos Aires, Argentina, in 1952, states in number 723, page 173: "... if a person is dying and someone near his house is chopping wood so that the soul cannot depart then one should remove the (wood) chopper from there ..."

Based on the *Sefer Chasidim,* the *Ramah* (Rabbi Moses Isserles 1510 to 1572) states (*Shulchan Aruch,* Section *Yoreh Deah,* Chapter 339:1) that

> if there is anything which causes a hindrance to the departure of the soul such as the presence near the patient's house of a knock-

ing noise such as wood chopping or if there is salt on the patient's tongue; and these hinder the soul's departure, then it is permissible to remove them from there because there is no act involved in this at all but only the removal of the impediment.

Furthermore, Rabbi Solomon Eger, known as the *Gilyon Maharsha*, in his commentary on Karo's code (*Yoreh Deah*, Chapter 339:1) quotes another Rabbinic authority (*Beth Yaakov* number 59) who states "it is forbidden to hinder the departure of the soul by the use of medicine." Other Rabbinic authorities, however, (*Shebuth Yaakov*, part 3:13) disagree with this latter view. The *Shiltei Gibborim* (Rabbi Joshua Boaz Baruch), a sixteenth century Italian commentary on Alfasi (Rabbi Isaac Alfasi 1013 to 1103), pleads at the end of Chapter 3 of Tractate *Moed Katan* for the abolition of the custom of those who removed the pillow from below the dying person's head following the popular belief that bird feathers contained in the pillow prevent the soul from departing. He further states that Rabbi Nathan of Igra specifically permitted this act. The *Shiltei Gibborim* continues: "after many years I found in the *Sefer Chasidim* number 723 support for my contentions as it is written there that if a person is dying but cannot die until he is put in a different place, he should not be moved." This law is not contradictory to the earlier statement of the *Sefer Chasidim* as both the *Shiltei Gibborim* and the *Ramah* (using the pen name *Darchei Moshe* in his commentary on the *Tur Yoreh Deah* 339) explain: to do an act which prevents easy death such as chopping wood is forbidden and on the contrary, such impediments to death should be removed. On the other hand, it is definitely forbidden to perform any act which hastens death such as moving the dying person from one place to another.

A more extensive discussion and bibliography of sources dealing with these and other aspects of a dying person according to Jewish law is found in the fifth volume of the monumental *Talmudic Encyclopedia*.[47]

The sum total of this discussion of the Jewish attitude toward euthanasia seems to indicate, as expressed by Jacobovits[3,23] that "... any form of active euthanasia is strictly prohibited and condemned as plain murder . . . anyone who kills a dying person is liable to the death penalty as a common murderer. At the same time, Jewish law sanctions the withdrawal of any factor—whether extraneous to the patient himself or not—which may artificially delay his demise in the final phase." Jacobovits is quick to point out, however, that all the Jewish sources refer to an individual in whom death is expected to be imminent, three days or less in Rabbinic references. Thus, passive euthanasia in a patient who may yet live for weeks or months may not necessarily be condoned. Furthermore, in the case of an incurably ill person in severe pain, agony, or distress, the removal of an impediment which hinders his soul's departure, although permitted by Jewish law (as described by Isserles), may not be analogous to the withholding of medical therapy that is perhaps sustaining the patient's life unnaturally. The impediments spoken of in the code of Jewish law, whether far removed from the patient as exemplified by the noise of wood chopping, or in physical contact with him such as the case of salt on the patient's tongue, do no constitute any part of the therapeutic armamentarium employed in the medical management of this patient. For this reason, these impediments may be removed. However, the discontinuation of instrumentation and machinery which is specifically designed and utilized in the treatment of incurably ill patients might only be permissible if one is certain that in doing so one is shortening the act of dying and not interrupting life. Yet who can make the fine distinction between prolonging life and prolonging the act of dying? The former comes within the physician's reference, the latter does not.

REFERENCES

1. Fletcher, J., "Euthanasia: Our Right to Die," in *Morals and Medicine*, Princeton, New Jersey, Princeton University Press, 1954, Chap. 6, p. 172.
2. Sperry, W. L., "The Prolongation of Life, Euthanasia-Pro and Euthanasia-Con," in *The Ethical Basis of Medical Practice*, New York, Medical Dept., Paul B. Hoeber, Inc., 1950, Chaps. 10 to 12, p. 124.
3. Jakobovits, I., "The Dying and Their Treatment. Preparation for Death and Euthanasia," in *Jewish Medical Ethics*. A Comparative and Historical Study of the Jewish Religious Attitude to Medicine and Its Practice, New York, Block Publishers, 1959, Chap. 11, p. 119.

4. Horder, T. J., "Signs and Symptoms of Impending Death," *Practitioner,* 161:73 (1948).
5. Barber, H., "The Act of Dying," *ibid.* 161:76 (1948).
6. Leak, W. N., "The Care of the Dying," *ibid.* 161:80 (1948).
7. Rabinowitch, I. M., and MacDermot, H. E., "Euthanasia," *McGill M. J.,* 19:160 (1950).
8. Banks, A. L., "Euthanasia," *Bull. New York Acad. Med.* 26:297 (1950).
9. Davis, E., "Should We Prolong Suffering?", *Nebraska M. J.* 35:310 (1950).
10. Hebb, F., "The Care of the Dying," *Canad. M.A.J.,* 65:261 (1951).
11. Alvarez, W. C., "Care of the Dying," *J.A.M.A.,* 150:86 (1952).
12. Rud, F., "Euthanasia," *J. Clin. & Exper. Psychopath.,* 14:1 (1953).
13. "Symposium on Euthanasia," *Maryland M.J.,* 2:120 (1953).
14. Rudd, T. N., "Family Doctor at the Deathbed; Medical Classics Reconsidered," *Med. World,* 85:50 (1956).
15. Mitchison, N., "The Right To Die," *ibid.,* 85:159 (1956).
16. Friedman, G. A., "Suicide, Euthanasia, and the Law," *M. Times,* 85:681 (1957).
17. Ogilvie, H., "Journey's End," *Practitioner,* 179:584 (1957).
18. Farrell, J. J., "The Right of a Patient to Die," *J. South Carolina M.A.,* 54:221 (1958).
19. Rynearson, E. H., "You Are Standing at the Bedside of a Patient Dying of Untreatable Cancer," *C.A.,* 9:85 (1959).
20. Karnofsky, D. A., "Why Prolong the Life of a Patient with Advanced Cancer?", *ibid.,* 10:25 (1960).
21. Betowski, E. P. S. J., "Prolongation of Life in Terminal Illness," *ibid.,* 10:25 (1960).
22. Torrey, E. F., "Euthanasia: A Problem in Medical Ethics," *McGill M.J.,* 30:127 (1961).
23. Jacobovits, I., "The Dying and Their Treatment in Jewish Law. Preparation for Death and Euthanasia," *Hebrew M.J.,* 2:251 (1961).
24. Delhaye, C. P., "Euthanasia or Death by Pity," *Union méd. Canada,* 90:613 (1961) (Fr.).
25. Levisohn, A. A., "Voluntary Mercy Deaths. Socio-Legal Aspects of Euthanasia," *J. Forensic Med.,* 8:57 (1961).
26. Jones, K. S., "Death and Doctors," *M.J. Australia,* 49:329 (1962).
27. Archambault, P. R., "The Problem of Euthanasia Considered by a Catholic Physician," *Union méd. Canada,* 91:543 (1962) (Fr.).
28. Crinquette, J., "L'Euthanasie," *J. sc. méd. Lille,* 81:522 (1963).
29. McClanahan, J. H., "The Patient's Right to Die. Moral and Spiritual Aspects of Euthanasia," *Memphis M.J.,* 38:303 (1963).
30. Monnerot-Dumaine, "Les Notions D'Euthanasie et D'Automathasie," *Presse méd.,* 72:1458 (1964).
31. Picha, E., "Gedanken über die Euthanasie missgebildeter Neugeborener," *Wien Med. Wchschr.,* 114:779 (1964).

32. Filbey, E. E., "Some Overtones of Euthanasia," *Hosp. Topics,* 43:55 (Sept.) 1965.
33. Hofling, C. K., "Terminal Decisions," *Med. Opinion & Review,* 2:40 (Oct.) 1966.
34. Long, P. H., "On the Quantity and Quality of Life," *M. Times,* 88:613 (1960).
35. "Euthanasia," editorial, *Lancet,* 2:351 (1961).
36. "Prolongation of Dying," editorial, *ibid.,* 2:1205 (1962).
37. Bordet, F., "Euthanasia," *Presse méd.,* 70:2022 (1962) (Fr.).
38. Farrar, C. B., "Euthanasia," *Am. J. Psychiat.,* 119:1104 (1963).
39. "Symposium on Terminal Care" (thirty-nine letters to the editor in regard to allowing the suffering, incurable, moribund patient to die quietly without the annoyance of radical procedures for short-period extension of life), *C.A.,* 10:12 (1960).
40. Colebrook, L., "The Liège Trial and the Problem of Voluntary Euthanasia," *Lancet,* 2:1225 (1962).
41. Gillison, T. H., "Prolongation of Dying," *ibid.,* 2:1327 (1962).
42. Readers Digest, December, 1960; Harpers Magazine, October, 1960; Saturday Evening Post, May 26, 1962, and September 10, 1966.
43. Fletcher, J. F., "Anti-Dysthanasia: The Problem of Prolonging Death," address read at the annual meeting of the Euthanasia Society of America, New York, February 26, 1962.
44. *A Plan for Voluntary Euthanasia,* London, The Euthanasia Society, 1962, p. 28.
45. Mamis, J. F., executive secretary of the Euthanasia Society of America, Inc., Personal communication, October 20, 1966.
46. *The Right to Die?,* New York, The Euthanasia of America, Inc.
47. Zevin, S. J., Ed., "A Digest of Halachic Literature and Jewish Law from the Tannaitic Period to the Present Time Alphabetically Arranged," in *Talmudic Encyclopedia,* Jerusalem, Talmudic Encyclopedia Publishing Ltd., 1963, vol. 5, p. 393.

Chapter VIII

The Definition of Death in Jewish Law

Introduction

Recent heart transplant operations have raised moral, religious, ethical and legal problems relating to life and death and have been discussed at length in medical[1] and lay[2] journals. The ascertainment of the death of the donor is a major problem confronting heart transplants. When exactly is the donor dead so that his heart or other organ may be removed for transplantation?

Medico-Legal Definition of Death

Medical and legal definitions of death, while similar in certain respects, differ in others.[3] Even among various physicians or medical

---

1. Wolstenholme, G. E. W. and O'Connor, M. Editors. Ciba Foundation Symposium. *Ethics in Medical Progress: With Special Reference to Transplantation.* Boston. Little, Brown & Co., 1966. 257 pp.
Ladimer, I. and Newman, R. W. Editors. *Clinical Investigation in Medicine: Legal, Ethical and Moral Aspects.* Boston Univ. Law-Medicine Research Instit. 1963. 517 pp.
Elkinton, J. R. "Moral Problems in the Use of Borrowed Organs, Artificial and Transplanted," (Editorial) *Annals Int. Med.,* 60:309-313, (Feb.) 1964.
Statement Prepared by the Board on Medicine of the National Academy of Sciences. "Cardiac Transplantation in Man," *J.A.M.A.,* 204:805-806, (May 27), 1968.
Beecher, H. K. "Ethical Problems Created by the Hopelessly Unconscious Patient," *New Eng. J. Med.,* 278:1425-1430, (June 27), 1968.
2. Yates, V. H. "Transplantation: Today and Tomorrow," *Today's Health,* 46:33-37, (April), 1968.
Lear, J. A. "Realistic Look at Heart Transplants," *Saturday Review,* Feb. 3, 1968, pp. 53-60.
3. Halley, M. M. and Harvey, W. F. "Medical vs. Legal Definitions of Death," *J.A.M.A.,* 204:423-425, (May 6th), 1968.

groups there is no unanimity of opinion nor uniformity in defining death, and religious definition may be at variance with either those of the medical or legal professions.

The criteria for defining death acceptable to many physicians include[4] bilateral, pupillary dilatation with no reaction to local constricting stimuli, complete abolition of reflexes, complete cessation of spontaneous respiration, absence of measurable blood pressure and a flat electro-encephalogram.

One neurologist[5] requires that

> ... there can be no induced or spontaneous purposeful movements, and reflex responses should be consistent with a decorticate or decerebrate state. Pupillary light responses should be absent and dilation present. The electroencephalogram should be isoelectric, or flat, indicating no cortical potentials are being produced. To further substantiate the degree of central nervous system damage, and its irreversability, the neurovegetative reaction of respiration should be absent as evidenced by the lack of spontaneous respiration for at least two minutes. Finally these observations of the brain and lower nervous system functions should be consistently present for a minimum of two or three days, after resolution of the process which induced cerebral death ...

These criteria may seem quite strict. However, they are not much less rigid than the criteria proposed by a special commission consisting of surgeons, neurosurgeons, anesthesiologists and medicolegal experts formed by the German Society of Surgery. This commission proposed that

> ... if the patient is unconscious for at least 12 hours and if spontaneous respiration ceases, bilateral mydriasis sets in, pupils do not react to light, all reflexes are extinct, and the encephalographic tracing shows an isoelectric line for at least one hour

---

4. Appel, J. Z. "Ethical and Legal Questions Posed by Recent Advances in Medicine," *J.A.M.A.*, 205:513-516, (Aug. 12th), 1968.
5. McCutchen, J. J. "A Neurologist Looks at Death," *J.A.M.A.*, 204·1;97-1198, (June 24th), 1968.

without interruption, then the patient can be considered dead notwithstanding the fact that the heart may still respond to artificial stimulation . . ."[6]

At the recent 1968 national meeting of the American Medical Association, guidelines for organ transplants were approved by the House of Delegates. One of the major guidelines states:[7]

> When a vital single organ is to be transplanted, the death of the donor shall have been determined by at least one physician other than the recipient's physician. Death shall be determined by the clinical judgment of the physician. In making this determination, the ethical physician will use all available, currently accepted scientific tests.

How does one ascertain the irreversibility of the process of life? The Ad Hoc Committee of the Harvard Medical School to Examine the Definition of Brain Death has recently arrived at a definition of irreversible coma.[8] The Canadian Medical Association had named its own committee of experts to come up with a legal and ethical definition of death before the 1969 convention.

At what point need a physician no longer attempt to resuscitate? The 22nd World Medical Association meeting in Australia on August 8, 1968 adopted a statement, known as the Declaration of Sydney, which states in part that a physician's determination of death "should be based on clinical judgment, supplemented if necessary by diagnostic aids, of which the electroencephalograph is the current most helpful single one." Drafters of the statement admitted its indefiniteness and stressed that there are no precise scientific criteria nor a definition for what is the moment of death.

---

6. "International Comments. When is a Person Dead?", *J.A.M.A.*, 203:998 (March 11th), 1968.

7. "Ethical Guidelines for Organ Transplantation," *J.A.M.A.*, 205:341-342, (Aug. 5th), 1968.

8. "A Definition of Irreversible Coma. Report of the Ad Hoc Committee of the Harvard Medical School to Examine the Definition of Brain Death," *J.A.M.A.*, 205:337-340, (Aug. 5th), 1968.

When is the dying patient beyond help? When is the physician guilty of a grave moral and religious sin by not doing everything possible to "maintain" his patient? Just as one cannot properly define health as the absence of disease, it seems totally inappropriate to define death as the absence of life. While society in general and the medical and legal professions in particular are struggling to come up with an acceptable definition of death, it is desirable to review some of the religious attitudes toward death.

Religious Definition of Death

The Catholic Church is on record[9] as not requiring a physician to use "extraordinary" means to prolong the life of a hopelessly ill patient. The term "extraordinary" is not defined, however. The Church is also opposed to the removal of hearts from persons certainly not dead.[10] The Church requires "clear and reasonable" evidence for death before a heart can be removed for transplantation. However, "clear and reasonable" remain to be defined.

Definition of Death in Jewish Law

Jewish law requires the physician to do everything in his power to prolong life[11] but prohibits the use of measures which prolong the act of dying.

The definition of death in Jewish law is first mentioned in the fifth century Babylonian Talmud. The Mishnah in *Yoma* 8:6-7 enumerates circumstances under which one may desecrate the Sabbath:

> . . . every danger to human life suspends the [laws of the] Sabbath. If debris [of a collapsing building] falls on someone

---

9. "The Pope Speaks Prolongation of Life," *Osservatore Romano*, 4:393:398, 1957.
10. Msgr. F. Lambruschini. Quoted in the *New York Times*, January 25, 1968.
11. Rosner, F., "Jewish Attitude Toward Euthanasia," *N. Y. State J. Med.*, 67:2499-2506, (Sept. 15th), 1967.

and it is doubtful whether he is there or whether he is not there, or if it is doubtful whether he is alive or whether he is dead or if it is doubtful whether he is an Israelite or a heathen, one must probe the heap of the debris for his sake [even on the Sabbath]. If one finds him alive, one should remove the debris but if he is dead, one leaves him there [until after the Sabbath].

The Talmud (*Yoma* 85a), commenting on the above Mishnah, states as follows:

> ... How far does one search [to ascertain whether he is dead or alive]? Until [one reaches] his nose. Some say: Up to his heart ... life manifests itself primarily through the nose as it is written "In whose nostrils was the breath of the spirit of life" [Genesis 7:22] ...

The renowned Biblical and Talmudic commentator Rashi explains that if no air emanates from his nostrils, he is certainly dead. Rashi further explains that some people suggest the heart be examined for signs of life, but the respiration test is considered of greatest import.

The Palestinian Talmud (*Yoma* 8:5) quotes certain authorities who require "until one reaches the navel" but this is a minority viewpoint.

The above rule from the Mishnah is codified by Maimonides as follows:[12]

> If upon examination no sign of breathing can be detected at the nose, the victim must be left where he is [until after the Sabbath] because he is already dead ...

The *Shulchan Aruch* states:[13]

> Even if the victim was found so severely injured that he cannot live for more than a short while, one must probe [the debris] until one reaches his nose. If one cannot detect signs of respiration

---

12. Maimonides, M., *Mishneh Torah, Book of Seasons* (Sefer Zemanim). *Laws of the Sabbath.* Chapter 2:19.
13. Karo, J., *Shulkhan Arukh.* Orach Chayim, *Laws of the Sabbath.* Chapter 329:4.

at the nose, then he is certainly dead whether the head was uncovered first or whether the feet were uncovered first.

Neither Maimonides nor Karo seem to require examination of the heart or navel, both mentioned as minority opinions in the Babylonian and Palestinian Talmuds respectively. Cessation of respiration seems to be the determining physical sign for the ascertainment of death.

Another pertinent passage found in Karo's Code[14] states as follows:

> If a woman is sitting on the birthstool [i.e., about to give birth] and she dies, one brings a knife on the Sabbath, even through a public domain, and one incises her womb and removes the fetus since one might find it alive.

Rabbi Moses Isserles adds to this statement:

> However, today we do not conduct ourselves according to this [rule] even during the week [i.e., even *not* on the Sabbath] because we are not competent to recognize precisely the moment of maternal death...

Several commentators explain that Isserles is concerned that perhaps the mother only fainted and incising her abdomen might kill her. Maimonides, five centuries earlier,[15] had already raised the problem of fainting complicating the recognition of death when he stated:

> ... whosoever closes the eyes of the dying while the soul is about to depart is shedding blood. One should wait a while; perhaps he is only in a swoon...

Both Maimonides and Isserles, however, agree that the Talmudic description of death for all practical purposes is the absence or cessation of respiration. We are not primarily concerned with the extremely rare case of someone recovering from what appears to be the deceased state. Such an example is described in *Semachot* 8:1. Rather, Jewish

---

14. *Ibid.* Chapter 330:5.
15. Maimonides, M., *Mishneh Torah. Book of Judges. Laws of Mourning.* Chapter 4:5.

law follows the rule of the majority. Rabbinic Responsa on the definition of death are summarized by Rabbi Eliezer Waldenberg,[16] chief judge in the Jerusalem Rabbinic court. In brief, all agree that death is established when respiration ceases. Absence of breathing is thought to be a direct result of cessation of cardiac action. However, some Rabbis also require a 20 minute to half hour wait after respiration has stopped in order for all doubts to be set aside. This is in compliance with the ruling of Maimonides that one should wait a while after death is thought to have occurred to make sure the patient didn't just faint. However, continues Rabbi Waldenberg, if any bodily movement or pulsation is noted, then the cessation of respiration is no longer a reliable indicator of death and other means must be employed in such an unusual instance.

The Chief Rabbi of Israel, Isaac Yehuda Unterman, addressing the Eleventh Congress on Jewish Law in August 1968, stated that by Jewish law one is dead when one has stopped breathing. Thus, most Talmudic and post Talmudic Sages agree that the absence of spontaneous respiration is the only sign needed to ascertain death. A minority would also require cessation of heart action. Thus a patient who has stopped breathing and whose heart is not beating is considered dead by Jewish law.

These classic sources and rulings may be insufficient to meet the entirely new need for the most precise definition of death arising from the recourse to organ transplantations. However, the tentative conclusion of the Chief Rabbi of the British Commonwealth,[17] based in part on the judgments of several leading Jewish Sages in various parts of the world is as follows: "the classic definition of death as given in the Talmud and Codes is acceptable today and correct. However, this would be set aside in cases where competent medical opinion deems any prospects of resuscitation, however remote, at all feasible." To

16. Waldenberg, E., *Responsa Tzitz Eliezer*. Vol. 9. Jerusalem 1967. Responsum No. 46, pp. 185-189.

17. Jakobovits, I., Personal Communication. August 1, 1968.

further cone down on the precise definition of death in Jewish law, an Institute of Judaism and Medicine has been established and commissioned, as its first assignment, to assemble the relevant medical and Jewish legal material on the determination of death.[18]

ADDENDUM TO CHAPTER 8

A recent article by Reb Chaim Zimmerman entitled "Life as a Relative Concept in Halakha" provides a comprehensive definition of life and death that establishes a continuance between *Psak Halakha* and scientific fact (INTERCOM, Vol. XI, No. 1, pp. 3-5, Shevat 5730 or January 1970. Published by the Association of Orthodox Jewish Scientists, New York City).

Another recent lengthy article, co-authored by a prominent Rabbi and an orthodox Jewish physician, discusses the halachic definition of death in the light of medical knowledge. (Rabinowitz, Gedaliah Aharon and Koenigsberg, Mordechai. *Hagedorath Hamaveth Ukeviyath Zemano Le'or Hahalacha*. HADAROM, No. 32, pp. 59-76, Tishri 5731. Published by the Rabbinical Council of America, New York City.)

---

18. *Ibid.*

Chapter IX

Autopsy in Jewish Law and the Israeli Autopsy Controversy

The purpose of postmortem examination—autopsy—is to modify, elaborate, confirm or reject antemortem diagnoses, thus aiding the medical profession in understanding human illness. It is performed to correlate the clinical aspects of disease for diagnostic and therapeutic evaluations, to determine the cause of death, to evaluate incompletely known disorders or discover new disease, to serve an educational function through demonstration of tissue alterations as they relate to pathogenesis and to the therapeutically altered or natural courses of disease, and to collect data for statistical analysis of disease incidence.[1]

---

1. The medical literature on autopsies is voluminous. The Committee on Necropsies of the American Society of Clinical Pathologists, in its bibliography on necropsies covering only a four year period, listed 158 articles. The following represents a list of the articles, textbooks and editorials on autopsies:
   Hazard, J. B., "The Autopsy," *J.A.M.A.*, 193: pp. 805-806, 1965. Rosahn, P. D., "The Autopsy," (Editorial). *Amer. J. of Clin. Path.*, 31: pp. 348-349, 1959. Angrist, A. A., "What Remedies for the Ailing Autopsy?", *J.A.M.A.*, 193: pp. 806-808, 1965. Angrist, A. A., "A Plea for Grant Support of the Autopsy," *AMA Archives of Path.*, 63: pp. 318-321, 1957. Davidsohn, I., Helwig, A., Saphir, O. and Warwick, M., Bibliography on Necropsies, 1931 to 1934. *Amer. J. Clin. Path.*, 7: pp. 199-208, 1937. Saphir, O., *Autopsy, Diagnosis and Technic.*, New York, Hoeber-Harper, 1958, 4th edit. Farber, S., *The Post Mortem Examination*, Springfield, Illinois, Charles Thomas, 1937. "Symposium on the Autopsy," *J.A.M.A.*, 193: pp. 805-814, 1965. "Medicine and the Law, Autopsy," *J.A.M.A.*, 165:697-699, 1957. Camps, F., "Post-mortem Examination from the Medicolegal Viewpoint," *Postgraduate Med.*, 35: pp. 47-51, 1964. Bowden, K. M., "Medico-legal Problems Based on Experience at the Morgue," *Med. J. of Austral.*, 1: pp. 12-15, 1949. Davis, J. H., "Hospitals and the Autopsy: Legal and Social Elements," *Hospitals*, 33: pp. 57-58, 1959. Hershey, N.,

In Paris in a study of 1,000 autopsies,[2] 85 percent were classified as useful and 15 percent as useless. A similar study of autopsies done in

"Who May Authorize an Autopsy?", *Amer. J. Nursing*, 63: pp. 103-105, 1963. Cahal, M. F. and Cady, E. L., "Invasion of Rights in Dead Bodies," *G. P.*, 27: pp. 183-184, 1963. Abeshouse, B. J. "The Problem of Autopsies on Orthodox Jewish Patients," *Sinai Hosp. J.* (Balt.), 6: pp. 76-98, April, 1957. Belford, J. L., "Religious Views of Autopsies," *Long Island Med. J.*, 9: p. 484, 1915. Gottlieb, J., "A Review of Jewish Opinions Regarding Postmortem Examinations," *Boston Med. & Surg. J.*, 196: pp. 726-728, 1929. Joslin, E. P., "Autopsies Upon Jews and Gentiles," *Boston Med. & Surg. J.*, 196: pp. 728-729, 1929. Kottler, A., "The Jewish Attitude on Autopsy," *New York State J. Med.*, 57: pp 1649-1650, 1957. Gordon, H. L., "Autopsies According to the Jewish Religious Laws," *The Hebrew Physician (Harofe Haivri)*, 1: pp. 203-201 Eng. & 130-141 (Heb.), 1937. Levinson, S. A., "The Dead Teacheth the Living," *Hospitals*, 35: pp. 81-92, August 15, 1961. Spivak, C. D., "Post Mortem Examination Among Jews," *New York Med. J.*, 99:1185, June 13, 1914. Plotz, M., "The Jewish Attitude Toward Autopsies," *Modern Hospital*, 45: pp. 67-68, November, 1935. Saphir, O., "Religious Aspects of the Autopsy," *Hospitals*, 12: pp. 50-55, July, 1938. Ribner, H., "Jewish Law, Social Prejudice and Autopsy," *Bull. Maryland Univ. School of Med.*, 44: pp. 21-25, Jan., 1959. Figon, G. and Pequignot, H., *"Nouvelles Dispositions Sur Les Autopsies et Leur Intérêt Pour la Recherche et la Thérapeutique,"* Sem. Hop. Paris, 24: pp. 193-194, 1948. Wolff, G., "Leichen-Besichtigung Und-Untersuhung Bis Zur Carolina Als Vorstufe Gerichtlicher Sektion," *Janus*, 42: pp. 225-286, 1938. Ackerknecht, E. H., "Primitive Autopsies and the History of Anatomy," *Bull. Inst. Hist. Med.*, 13: pp. 334-339, 1943. Schmeisser, H. C. and Scianni, J. L., "Autopsy and Museum Technique: The History of the Autopsy," *J. Tech. Meth. & Bull. Intern. Ass. Med. Museums*, 15: pp. 26-33, 1936. Rabl, R., *Die Wertung der Sektionen im Wandel der Zeiten. Eine Kulturgeschichtliche Betrachtung,"* Virch. Arch. Path. Anat., 321: pp. 142-162, 1952. Krumbhaar, E. B., "History of the Autopsy and Its Relations to the Development of Modern Medicine," *Hospitals*, 12: pp. 68-74, 1938. Chavarria, A. P. and Shipley, P. G., "The Siamese Twins of Espanola. The First Known Post-Mortem Examination in the New World," *Annals Med. Hist.*, 6: pp. 297-302, 1924. Ehrhardt, H., *"Sektionsbericht und Amtsarztliches Gutachten aus dem Jahre 1722."* Mediz. Welt, 8: pp. 426-427, 1934. Sporlein, G. and Glanz, H., *"Originalberichte Uber die Obduktion von zwei Wurzburger Furstbischofem aus den Jahren 1749 und 1754,* Virch. Arch., 283: pp. 513-539, 1932. Ficarra, B. J., "Eleven Famous Autopsies in History," *Annals Med. Hist.* (3rd series) 4: pp. 504-520, 1942.

2. Justin-Besançon, L., Chrétien, J. and Delavierre, P., *"Intérêt Clinique Des Autopsies Systématiques en Milieu Hospitaliér.* Sem. Hop. Paris. 40: pp. 531-534, 1964. Useful was defined as confirming (55.4 percent), contradicting (6 percent) or completing (23.5 percent) the clinical diagnosis.

London[3] revealed that the clinical diagnosis was completely right in 53 percent of patients; the clinical diagnosis was wrong or missed in 25 percent of patients; one diagnosis was right, another wrong or missed in 15 percent of patients; and the clinical diagnosis was completely wrong in 7 percent of patients. There is little doubt that autopsies sometimes are a revelation to the physician, sometimes of the expected, at other times of unanticipated disease. Cases where autopsy disclosed unexpected findings are well documented periodically in the medical literature.[4] There is also no dispute concerning the value of autopsy as an essential component of medical education.[5] These and other overwhelming reasons for the performing of autopsies, however, still leave many questions unanswered. How many autopsies are "needed"? How should they be done? Who should do them?[6] It is incorrect to assume that since autopsies are good, we must have more of them. It is also fallacious to presume that the more autopsies we perform the better quality medicine we have. Dr. Lester King, senior editor of the American Medical Association *Journal* refutes this assumption when he states:[7]

> It is a pernicious misconception that the mere performance of postmortem dissection leads to progress in medical science, or the discovery of new diseases, or the advancement of medical frontiers. We lose sight of the fact that progress depends not on the autopsy, but on the person who is examining the material, Those who believe that the more autopsies we perform, the more medi-

3. Wilson, R. R., "In Defense of the Autopsy," *J.A.M.A.*, 196: pp. 1011-1012, 1966.
4. Shaw, R. E. and Deadman, W. J., "The Clinical Value of Autopsies," *Canad. Med. Assn. J.* (new series) 42: pp. 168-171, 1940. Collis, J. S., "Permission for Autopsy—Granted," *Cleveland Clin. Quart.*, 28: pp. 105-108, 1961. Marx, G. F., "Value of Autopsy," *N.Y. State J. Med.*, 68: pp. 950-952, 1968. Frumin, M. J., and Fine, E., "Post Mortem or Post Hoc. The Necessity for Autopsy," *J.A.M.A.*, 208: pp. 519-520, 1969.
5. Angrist, A. A., "Effective Use of Autopsy in Medical Education," *J.A.M.A.*, 161: pp. 303-309, 1956.
6. Madden, S. C., "How Many Autopsies?", *J.A.M.A.*, 193: pp. 812-813, 1965.
7. King, L. S., "Of Autopsies," (Editorial). *J.A.M.A.*, 191: pp. 1078-1079, 1965.

cal science will advance, are actually pleading not for more autopsies but for persons who can profitably utilize the data of autopsies, persons who have imagination, originality, persistence, mental acuity, sound education and background, the indispensable prepared mind without which observations are quite sterile. It is a grave disservice to confuse the performance of autopsies with the spark of insight which the autopsy may trigger. We want the insight; and autopsies alone, no matter how numerous, are not the equivalent. We must not confuse the performance of postmortem dissection with the autoptic attitude. They may indeed coincide, but they need not.

From the religious viewpoint, however, even where an autopsy is sanctioned, different answers must be provided, particularly to the question of how an autopsy is to be done. In most religions, including Judaism, the physical remains of a deceased person must be treated with honor and respect. Judaism requires not only that the dead be treated with utmost dignity and honor but that no desecration of the dead be performed except where such an act may immediately save a life. Even in such a situation, all organs examined and/or removed must be returned to the body prior to burial. Burial must not be delayed. No benefit may be derived from the dead except where a life is at stake.

Autopsy and Jewish Law

This essay will discuss the Jewish attitude towards anatomical dissection and post mortem examinations as developed in the Biblical, Talmudic and Rabbinic literature. There is a desperate need for Orthodox Jewish physicians to obtain answers to the following perplexing questions: When, if ever, does Jewish law sanction or even demand an autopsy? When is it permissible for a Jewish physician to request permission for an autopsy from the next of kin, as required by American law? Does Jewish law require permission in the cases where autopsy is allowed? From whom must permission be sought—the bereaved family or the deceased prior to his demise? What if the deceased specifically asked that his body be dissected after his death?

What constitutes desecration of the dead? Can one not use cadaver organs for transplantation to live recipients who are desperately in need of a kidney, an eye or even a heart?[7a] How do autopsies affect the double commandment of burying the dead without delay?

The earliest leading responsum on autopsy is authored by 18th century Rabbi Ezekiel Landau.[8] It is this responsum upon which all subsequent inquiries and Rabbinic and legal decisions are based. Rabbi Landau was asked by the rabbinical authorities in London concerning a patient with a bladder calculus (probably urinary bladder, but possibly gallbladder) who had died following an unsuccessful operation for this condition. The question posed was whether it was permissible to make an incision into the body of the deceased at the site of the previous surgery, and to directly observe the root of the illness. The purpose was to learn what the proper therapy should be in future cases and to avoid unnecessary surgery. Rabbi Landau answered that autopsy constitutes a desecration of the dead, and is only permissible to save the life of another patient who is immediately at hand (*lefanenu*). In the case before him, however, the life of no specific living patient was under consideration, and the autopsy was solely to learn therefrom for a future patient with a similar affliction. This possibility was too remote to permit an autopsy. Furthermore, continues Rabbi Landau, "if we would be lenient in this matter, heaven forbid, they would dissect all dead people in order to learn the arrangement of the internal organs and their functions, so as to know what therapy to give to the living."

The only other 18th century Rabbinic responsum dealing with autopsy is that of Rabbi Yaakov Emden[9] who was asked by a medical student whether he could participate in the dissection of dogs on the Sabbath as a part of his anatomy training. Rabbi Emden replied that numerous prohibitions relating to the Sabbath are involved. Dissection

---

7a. See "Heart and Other Organ Transplantation and Jewish Law," *Jewish Life*, Vol. 37, pp. 28-51, Sept.-Oct., 1969 and the chapter on this subject in this book.

8. Landau, E., Responsa *Nodah Biyehudah. Mahadura Tanina. Yoreh De'ah*, No. 210. Paris, Lang Press, 1947.

9. Emden, Y., Responsa *She'elatz Yavetz*. Section 1, No. 41. Altona, 1739.

of human bodies, he continued, are prohibited because one is not permitted to derive any benefit from the deceased.

In the nineteenth century, there are five recorded Rabbinic Responsa dealing with autopsy by Rabbis Schreiber,[10] Ettlinger,[11] Schick,[12] Auerbach[13] and Bamberger.[14] All take an essentially negative view towards the performance of autopsy except if the lives of other existing (not future) patients might thereby be saved. Rabbi Ettlinger also allows autopsy if the deceased had willed his body for that purpose during his lifetime.

Twentieth century Responsa on permitting autopsies are numerous and, rather than present an exhaustive enumeration of them, it seems more appropriate to discuss the principles upon which is based the Jewish legal attitude toward autopsy. These are described in detail by Rabbi Yitzchak Arieli,[15] and others.[16] The questions discussed by Rabbi Arieli include whether autopsies are permitted for the following:

10. Shreiber, M., Responsa *Chatam Sofer. Yoreh De'ah*, No. 336. Grossman Press, New York, 1958.
11. Ettlinger, J., Responsa *Binyan Tzion*, No. 170-171, Altona, 1868.
12. Schick, M., Responsa *Maharam Schick. Yoreh De'ah*, No. 347, Muncacz, 1881.
13. Auerbach, B. Z., *Nachal Eshkol*, Part 2, No. 117 ff. 1868.
14. Bamberger, S., Responsa *Zekher Simchah*, No. 158.
15. Arieli, Y., "Bayath Nituchay Methim," *NOAM Jerusalem* 6: pp. 82-103, 1963. Arieli, Y., "Bayath Nituchay Methim," *Torah She Be'al Peh*, Jerusalem. Mossad Harav Kook, 1964, pp. 40-60.
16. Rubinstein, S. T., *"Lishe'elath Nituchay Methim Behalacha,"* *Torah She-Be'al Peh*, Jerusalem. Mossad Harav Kook, 1964, pp. 67-74. Silberstein, V., *"Nituach Methim Le'ohr Koroth Harefuah Vehitpathchutah,"* *Torah She-Be'al Peh*, Jerusalem. Mossad Harav Kook, 1964, pp. 82-86. Wilner, M. D., *"Nituach Methim Letzorchay Limud Veshimush Bechelkay Guphoth Methim Letzorchay Refuah,"* *Hatorah Vehamedinah*, Vol. 5-6, 1953-1954, pp. 202-212. Yisroeli, S., editor, *"Beshe'elat Nituach Hamethiim,"* *Hatorah Vehamedinah*, Vol. 5-6, 1953-1954, pp. 213-226. Hedaya, O., *"Nituach Methim Latzorchay Limud Urefuah,"* *Hatorah Vehamedinah*, Vol. 5-6, 1953-1954, pp. 191-201. Hirshenson, Ch., *"Nituach Hamethium,"* *Malki Bakodesh*, Part 3, pp. 6-9 and 137-152, 1923, Hoboken, New Jersey. Raphael Y., *"Leshe'elat Nituchay Methim Upitronah,"* *Or Hamizrach*, New York, Vol. 16, No. 1 (55), pp. 5-13, Nov. 1966. Schechter, N. S., *"Be'inyan Nituach Metim,"* *NOAM*, Vol. 5, pp. 165-181, 1962. Wachtfogel, Y. Y., *"Bedin Pinuy Hameth Meekivro Ubayath Nituchay Methim,"* *NOAM*, Vol. 5, pp. 159-164, 1962. Sharshafsky, S., *"Al Nituach Methim,"* *NOAM*, Vol. 7, pp. 387-392, 1964. Feinstein, M., *"Be'inyan Nituach*

1) the sake of studying anatomy; 2) as a general procedure to gain knowledge; 3) to determine the cause of death; 4) to save an existing seriously ill patient; 5) to save future patients who may present with a similar disease; 6) in the case of a common disease; 7) in the case of a rare disease; 8) in the case of a genetic disorder; 9) on a person who asked that this procedure be performed after his death; 10) transplantation of an organ from a dead person to a living individual; and 11) on a stillbirth.

The prohibition of desecrating or disgracing the dead is based upon the Biblical passage "And if a man has committed a sin worthy of death, and he be put to death, and thou hang him on a tree, his body shall not remain all night upon the tree but thou shalt surely bury him the same day . . ." (Deut. 21:22-23). The Talmud (*Sanhedrin* 47a) interprets this phrase to mean that just as hanging all night is a disgrace to the human body, so too any other action which constitutes a disgrace to the deceased is prohibited. If the Torah was concerned for the body of a convicted criminal, certainly, *a fortiori*, the body of a

Methim," *NOAM*, Vol. 8, pp. 9-16, 1965. Hedaya, O., "*Be'inyan 'Lo Talin' Be'meth*," *NOAM*, Vol. 8, pp. 68-74, 1965. Grossberg, H. Z., "*Nituach Hameth*," *NOAM*, Vol. 10, pp. 204-207, 1967. Levin, Y. H., "*Leshe'elat Nituach Methim*," *Hatorah Vehamedinah*, Vol. 7-8, pp. 222-227, 1955-57. Levine, S. Y., "*Nituach Methim*," *Hapardes* (Rabbinical Monthly Journal), Jubilee Book, New York, 1951, pp. 138-141. Greenwald, Y. Y., "*Kavod Hameth*," *Kol Bo Al Aveyluth*, New York, Vol. 1, pp. 33-63, 1947. Tooktzinski, Y. M., "*Nituach Ha Methim*," in *Gesher Hachayim*, 2nd edit., Jerusalem, Vol. 1, 1960, pp. 70-74. Margalit, D., "*Lebayat Netichat Goofat Niftarim*," *Korot* (Jerusalem), Vol. 4, No. 1-2, pp. 41-64, Dec. 1966. Globus, E. L., "*She'eloth Utshuvoth Al Chukay Nituchay Methim*," *Harefuah*, Jerusalem, Vol. 60, No. 6, pp. 196-200, March 15, 1961. Uziel, B. Z., *Responsa Mishpetay Uziel*, *Yoreh De'ah*, Part 1, No. 28-29 and Part 2, No. 110, Tel Aviv, 1935. See also A. D. Kook (*Da'ath Kohen*, No. 199), M. J. Zweig (*Responsa Ohel Mosheh*, Part 1, No. 4), Y. Zweig (*Responsa Parat Yosef*, No. 17), D. Hoffman (*Responsa Melamed Leho'il*, *Yoreh De'ah*, No. 109), M. T. Halevy (*Responsa Diveri Malkiel*, Part 2, No. 95), E. Y. Waldenberg (*Responsa Tzitz Eliezer*, Vol. 4, No. 14), Y. M. Shapira (*Responsa Ohr Hameir*, Part 1, No. 74), E. H. Shapira (*Responsa Minchat Elarzar*, Part 4, No. 25), D. M. Manesh (*Chawatzeleth Hasharon*, *Yoreh De'ah*, No. 95), A. Safer (*Responsa K'taw Sofer*, *Yoreh De'ah*, No. 174), and M. Winkler (*Responsa Levishei Mordechai*, *Orach Chayim*, Part 2, No. 29), among many others.

AUTOPSY

good citizen should be treated with the proper respect, and be properly interred without being subjected to shame or disgrace.

Two Talmudic passages dealing with autopsy should be mentioned, although neither deals directly with dissection of the dead for purely medical purposes. One case deals with criminal law, the other with civil law. The first case, described in *Chullin* 11b, deals with a murderer for whom the Divine Law prescribes death. The Talmud asks:

> Why do we not fear that the victim may have been afflicted with a fatal organic disease, for whose killing a person is not punishable as a murderer? Is it not because we follow the majority and most victims of murderers are not so afflicted? And should you say that we can examine the body—this is not allowed because it would thereby be mutilated. And should you say that since a man's life is at stake, we should mutilate the body, then one could answer that there is always the possibility that the murderer may have killed the victim by striking him in a place where he was suffering from a fatal wound, thus removing all traces of the wound. In such a case it is clear that no amount of postmortem examination would show that the victim was afflicted with a fatal illness.

Therefore it is proved, concludes the Talmud, that we follow the majority and do not perform an autopsy. In this case, the findings of an autopsy, even if it were permitted, would have been irrelevant to the conviction of the murderer, and insufficient to acquit him.

The second case is described in *Baba Batra* 154a where the story is told that in Bene-Berak a person once sold his fathers' estate and died. The members of the family, thereupon, protested that he was a minor at the time of his death and therefore not eligible to sell any of his father's estate. Hence, the property he sold should belong to the surviving members of the family. They came to Rabbi Akiba and asked whether the body might be exhumed and examined, so as to ascertain his age by performing a post mortem examination. Rabbi Akiba replied that one is not permitted to dishonor the dead; and furthermore, the signs of maturity usually undergo a change after death. Hence, the examination would not produce reliable evidence of his age. Neither Talmudic case deals with autopsy for medical purposes but both illustrate the objection to this procedure on the grounds that it would constitute a desecration of the dead, a Biblically prohibited act.

The next major objection in Jewish law against autopsy is the multi-faceted problem of burial of the dead. Firstly, the Biblical phrase, "Thou shalt surely bury him . . ." (Deut. 21:23), tells us that it is a positive commandment to bury the dead (*Sanhedrin* 46b). Secondly, whoever keeps his dead unburied overnight transgresses a negative commandment. This is deduced from the earlier part of the same Biblical phrase: "His body shall not remain all night . . ." Thirdly, the body must be interred whole, for if one leaves out even a small portion, it is as if no burial at all took place (Jersualem Talmud, Tractate *Nazir* 7:1). According to Maimonides (*Hilkhoth Sanhedrin* 15:8) the infinitive "Thou shalt surely bury him . . ." indicates that the command regarding burial concerns all dead, not only those executed by the Court. A fourth facet of the burial problem is the question as to whether burial, in addition to averting disgrace (by later putrefaction of the body), also represents atonement for the sins committed during life (*Sanhedrin* 46b). If one performs an autopsy, one is in fact transgressing the prohibition of delaying burial of the dead. If one fails to return all removed organs to the body for burial, one also prevents atonement since such a burial is incomplete.

Another serious objection to autopsy in Jewish law is the prohibition of deriving any benefit from the dead as deduced in the Talmud (*Avoda Zara* 29b and *Nedarim* 48a). The question of whether observation alone consitutes a benefit, or whether parts of the deceased must be used, such as for organ transplantation in order to be considered deriving benefit from the dead, is a legal technicality, as is the question of whether the prohibition is Biblical or Rabbinic in origin.

Other halakhic questions are also raised concerning autopsies. For example, can a priest ritually defile himself for the burial of a first degree relative if the deceased has had an autopsy, particularly if organs are removed? Or can mourning begin if burial is effected but parts of

AUTOPSY

the body have not been buried? Thirdly, do the prohibitions regarding autopsy apply to a stillbirth? Fourthly, according to the Jewish concept of the soul being bound to the body, does not the soul suffer pain and/or disgrace if the body is dissected? Is permission for autopsy required to avoid the problem of stealing, particularly in regard to organ transplants? Who may give such consent? The deceased in his lifetime? The family? Society?

Rabbi Arieli arrives at 14 conclusion:

1. A post mortem examination is a desecration and disgrace to the dead and Biblically forbidden.
2. There is suffering to the soul which is bound to the body when the latter is desecrated.
3. The body of a Jew is holy.
4. If one leaves unburied any part of the deceased, then one transgresses the positive commandment of burying the dead, and the negative commandments of delaying the burial and defiling the land. There is no rest to the deceased until his entire body returns to the earth.
5. If the relatives are able to effect burial of the entire body then the laws of *Aninut* (time prior to the onset of mourning) apply until they have done so.
6. If any part of the body is missing, then priestly relatives may not actually defile themselves for the deceased.
7. Autopsy on a stillbirth is prohibited.
8. In addition to the reasons mentioned above, dissection for medical studies is prohibited because one derives benefit from the dead, which some but not all Rabbis also state is not allowed.
9. Dissection of the dead to save another person's life is permitted, provided such a patient is available, and there is a reasonable prospect that the autopsy will directly save that life. But to save the life of a patient who may present at a future time, autopsy is prohibited.

10. Autopsy to establish the cause of death is adjucated like the case of a patient who may present in the future (i.e., prohibited).

11. Autopsies are permitted in cases of hereditary diseases, just as if a patient whose life could be directly saved is at hand.

12. If the deceased in his lifetime freely consented to an autopsy, then many authorities allow it, and it is permitted.

13. Corneal grafts[7a] from the dead to the living are permitted, but the transplantation of other organs requires further investigation.

14. The family, while not empowered to permit autopsies, may prevent them. In some cases, anyone can prevent an autopsy.

Rabbi Arieli, as well as most 20th century Rabbis base their decisions primarily on the classic responsum of Rabbi Ezekiel Landau who allows autopsies only if they would save the life of a patient immediately available (*Lefanenu*). Rabbi Jakobovits points out:[17]

> Rabbi Arieli is prepared to extend this principle even to patients who are not locally at hand, but who—through modern means of communication—may benefit from the findings of autopsies elsewhere, provided the ailment concerned is widespread enough to warrant the assumption that some other sufferer at the same time may be cured through these findings. But in fact, adds Rabbi Arieli, while the disease may be widespread, the likelihood of a cure being discovered as a result of any particular

---

17. Jakobovits, I., "Bayath Nituach Hametim Lehalacha Ullemasseh," in *Torah She-Be'al Peh*, Jerusalem, Mossad Harav Kook, 1964, pp. 61-66. See also the following by Rabbi Jakobovits: "The Religious Problem of Autopsies in New York Jewish Hospitals," *Harofe Haivri* 2: pp. 233-238, 1961; "The Dissection of the Dead in Jewish Law: A Comparative and Historical Study," *TRADITION*, 1: pp. 77-103, Fall, 1958; "The Dissection of the Dead in Jewish Law: An Historical Study," *Harofe Haivri*, 1: pp. 210-222, 1960 (Part 1) and 2: pp. 212-221, 1960 (Part 2); *Jewish Medical Ethics*, New York, Bloch Publishers, 1959, pp. 132-152; *Jewish Law Faces Modern Problems*, New York, Yeshiva University Press, 1965, pp. 81-87; *Journal of a Rabbi*, New York, Living Books, 1966, pp. 173-193.

autopsy is very remote indeed. In these circumstances, therefore, one would not be justified in setting aside the ban on disfiguring the dead for the (almost hypothetical) sake of saving life. . . . Equally restrictive is Rabbi Arieli's rejection of autopsies to establish the cause of death, since he regards the link between such operations and the saving of life once again too tenuous . . . he is inclined (however) to permit autopsies on bodies or persons who gave their consent in their lifetime . . .

The consensus of Rabbinic opinion today seems to permit autopsy only in the spirit of the famous responsum of the *Nodah Biyehudah,* Rabbi Ezekiel Landau, i.e., if it may directly contribute to the saving of a life of another patient at hand. In the case of hereditary diseases, the family or future offspring of the deceased are considered to represent patients at hand and thus autopsies are allowed. However, as pointed out by Rabbi Jakobovits,[17] in applying the 18th century ruling of the *Nodah Biyehudah,* one must take into account the following new circumstances:

1. With the speed of present-day communications, such patients are in fact at hand all over the world, and the findings of an autopsy in one place may aid a sufferer in another immediately.

2. Without autopsies, some of the worst scourges still afflicting mankind cannot be conquered. Indeed any autopsy nowadays, when medical science is so advanced, is more likely to help in the saving of life than the case permitted by the *Nodah bi-Yehudah* under the relatively primitive conditions of two centuries ago.

3. Autopsies now bear a relationship to the saving of life not only in the hope they hold out for finding new cures for obscure diseases, but also in testing the effects and safety of new medications, and in demonstrating errors of diagnosis and treatment.

4. On the other hand, the very frequency of autopsies increases the danger that they will become a sheer routine, without

any regard for their urgency, and without proper safeguards for the respect due to the dead.

5. With some patients in Israel refusing to be admitted to hospitals for fear of autopsies, the consideration of the saving of life now also operates in reverse.

The problem of autopsy today is not the same as that confronting the *Nodah Bi'yehudah* two centuries ago. Medicine has advanced since then, and the whole matter of post mortem examination requires a new look and a new appraisal by Jewish legal authorities. Rabbis must be made to understand the importance of autopsies and the benefits to be derived therefrom for mankind in the battle against disease. Physicians too must be made to appreciate the Jewish legal position on the matter. The human body is the creation of G-d in His image and cannot be treated with less than the utmost dignity and respect. Rabbis and physicians must sit at the same table to discuss their mutual problems and to arrive at a mutually satisfactory working relationship. Certain concrete proposals have already been made by Chief Rabbi Jakobovits who stated:

> While no general sanction can be given for the indiscriminate surrender of all bodies to post mortem examinations, the area of the sanction should be broadened to include tests on new drugs and cases of reasonable suspicion that the diagnosis was mistaken; for autopsies under such conditions, too, may directly result in the saving of life. . . .
>
> Any permission for an autopsy is to be given only on condition that operation is reduced to a minimum, carried out with the greatest dispatch, in the presence of a Rabbi or religious supervisor if requested by the family, and performed with the utmost reverence and with the assurance that all parts of the body are returned for burial.
>
> Just as it is the duty of Rabbis to urge relatives not to consent to an autopsy where the law does not justify it, they are religiously obliged to insure that permission is granted in cases where human lives may thereby be saved, in the same way as the violation of

the Sabbath laws in the face of danger to life is not merely optional but mandatory.

Another step forward is the pronouncement by Rabbi Moses Feinstein that post mortem needle biopsies of various organs are permitted by Jewish law, as long as the chest or abdomen are not opened. Such needle biopsies do not constitute a desecration of the dead, because such procedures are often performed on the living in order to ascertain the proper diagnosis of disease. Similarly, continues Rabbi Feinstein, to remove a sample of blood after death, through a needle puncture, for medical examination, is certainly permissible. Finally, post mortem peritoneoscopy, where the physician looks into a body cavity with an electric instrument, is also permitted, according to Rabbi Feinstein.[16]

THE ISRAELI AUTOPSY CONTROVERSY

Nowhere has the controversy over autopsies been more intense and bitter than in the State of Israel where we have often seen Jew pitted against Jew, Rabbi against physician and friend against friend. It was first raised prior to Israel's establishment in 1948 when the Hadassah Hospital in Jerusalem asked whether it was permitted to perform anatomical dissections for medical student teaching. The Chief Rabbinate, in answering the inquiry, stated that no objection exists for such anatomical dissections in cases where the deceased had freely willed his body for such purposes prior to his death. Chief Rabbi Herzog's Responsum on this subject was publicized in the Hebrew periodical *Kol Torah* (Vol. 1, 1947). Regarding autopsy or the dissection of bodies to discover pathologic anatomy, the agreement reached between Rabbis Herzog and Frank, and Dr. Yasky, the then director of the Hadassah Hospital, stated that the Chief Rabbinate would not oppose autopsy in the following situations:

a) if the autopsy is required by law;

b) if the cause of death cannot be established without an autopsy; and where three physicians attest to this fact;

c) to save a life, and

d) in cases of genetic or inherited disease where the family may be guided or counselled concerning future children . . .

The deceased must be buried in accordance with Jewish law and all organs removed for examination must be returned for burial.

THE ANATOMY AND PATHOLOGY LAW OF 1953

On August 26, 1953, the Israeli Parliament (*Knesset*) passed the present Anatomy and Pathology Law. One of the major provisions of this law (section 2) is that if a person agreed, in writing, that his body be used for science it is permitted to dissect that body for medical instruction and research. A second major provision of the law states that a physician may perform an autopsy to establish the cause of death, or in order to use one or more of the organs of the deceased for transplantation to a critically ill recipient (section 6). The Ministry of Health was empowered to make amendments and decrees to implement and interpet the law. The law was unclear as to who had the final word over whether an autopsy should be performed or not, the family of the deceased or the medical authorities. Some clarification emerged from the "Collected Amendments" (*Kovetz Hatakanoth*, 10 Shevat, 5714) in which section 2 of the Anatomy and Pathology Law is explained as follows.

If a person dies without leaving written consent for autopsy, his next of kin may request that the body not be disturbed, and no autopsy should then be performed. Next of kin is specifically defined. Furthermore, if the deceased had no family, the burial society (*Chevrah Kadishah*) may also object to autopsy, in which case it is not to be done. If the body is unclaimed, then the medical school can utilize the body for teaching and research purposes. However, a panel of three physicians was still empowered to order an autopsy if the cause of death could not be established without such a procedure.

Physicians were accused of taking advantage of this ambiguity in the law, overruling the wishes of families against performing autopsies in many instances. It was alleged that blank autopsy forms were signed by two physicians even prior to the death of the patient so that only one physician would need to sign the order for an autopsy once the patient died, a practice contrary to the spirit of the law, and against the wishes of the family. Physicians were accused of desecration of the dead, because they removed internal organs and filled the body cavities with rags.

When Yitzchak Raphael became Deputy Minister of Health late in 1961, the Israeli Parliament charged him with the formation of a committee to consider the law concerning autopsies, and to present its conclusions and recommendations to the government for action. The desires of the family of the deceased were to be considered in the committee's deliberations. In 1962 a committee was appointed by Dr. Raphael:

> to make a thorough study of the *de facto* and *de jure* situations, including all the relevant ordinances and operational directives and to present to the Ministry of Health conclusions to guide the Ministry's future actions in the matter. The committee is to take into consideration the needs of medical practice and research, the sensibilities of the public in the matter, the law of the land and Jewish legal (Halakhic) law.

The full committee met 17 times and its sub-committees held additional meetings. It took testimony from 14 experts. All the members of the committee made a sincere effort to work in a spirit of mutual understanding, despite the difference of opinion between some of them. They found a common language, and it transpired that for the needs of real life a solution could be found in Halakhic literature which provides for all contingencies. A detailed report was submitted by the committee which said in part:

> Having carefully weighed the data put before us, the testimony we have heard and the pamphlets and articles we have read, we have come to the conclusion that, despite the great gap that appears to exist between the two points of view expressed before

us, there is a way of satisfying at least part of the demands of both sides.

The following recommendations were accepted unanimously:

1) The 1953 law should be amended to include halakhic principles as follows:
   a. An autopsy should be performed only when, by thus establishing the exact cause of death, it will provide information which will make it possible to save lives, and
   b. in order to perform a transplant to treat a patient who has been specifically marked for this particular transplant.

2) An autopsy shall not be performed if the deceased had, in his lifetime, expressed opposition to it, or if, after his death, certain specified next of kin express opposition, except
   a. if there are grounds to suspect that not establishing the cause of death might constitute a danger to the public or to the family, or
   b. if there are grounds to suspect that death was caused by a medical error which, if not ascertained, might lead to deaths.

3) The next of kin shall be given enough time to express their opposition.

4) The section of the law concerning penalties (section 6) should be extended to apply also to false autopsy certificates.

5) A control committee should be set up consisting of a doctor, a Rabbi and a Christian clergyman.

These very restrictive amendments to the 1953 Anatomy and Pathology Act also required that in a case where physicians invoke item 2 above (danger to society or a medical error), the matter should come for adjudication before a Rabbi or Christian clergyman. An appeals board was also to be established by the Ministry of Health. Deputy Minister of Health Yitzchak Rafael, writing in the Hebrew periodical *Gevilin* (vol. 25), stated that he was certain that the

Knesset would not adopt such a restrictive law where the family has the final word. The rate of autopsy would drop to near zero, and the non-religious elements in the government would defeat any such proposal. After much deliberation and discussion with various members of the cabinet, Minister Rafael presented to the *Knesset* on December 25, 1964, the following compromise bill:

1) The concept of objection to autopsy by the burial society or a relative to the deceased is added to the 1953 law.

2) Autopsy is permitted to establish the cause of death if this will make possible the saving of lives.

3) An organ from a deceased may be used for transplant purposes for a patient who has been specifically designated for that transplant.

4) Autopsy will not be performed if the deceased had, in his lifetime, expressed opposition to autopsy after his death.

5) Autopsy will not be performed if there is opposition to autopsy from the person whose name appears in the hospital chart, and who is to be called in case of emergency, or from certain specified relatives, or a specified burial society.

6) Items 4 and 5 above are overruled if there are grounds to suspect that not establishing the cause of death might constitute a danger to the public, or to the family, or if there is a suspicion that death was caused by a medical error which, if not ascertained, might lead to further danger to life. Such a suspicion must be certified in writing by a panel of three physicians.

7) Autopsy is not to be performed until at least 5 hours have elapsed from the time of notification of death to the responsible family member or burial society as in item 5. Sabbaths and Jewish Holy Days are not included in the five hour waiting period.

8) The Minister of Health will appoint a control commission to supervise the implementation of the law. Among the

members of this commission should be a physician, Rabbi and Christian clergyman.

9) Penalties are to be imposed upon a physician who falsely certifies to the need for an autopsy, punishment to consist of three years imprisonment.

This new proposal was much more restrictive than the 1953 law but more moderate than the earlier proposal in that it did not require each case to be presented for Rabbinic judgment. In spite of strong objections from many sides, particularly the medical profession and the non-religious elements in the government, the proposal was presented to the Israeli Parliament as the "Anatomy and Pathology Law. Revised 1965." Renewed controversy among the various factions in the government brought the debate to fever pitch. Some demanded that the earlier version of the bill, as originally proposed by the Special Wahl Commission, be brought to the floor for a vote. Yet others had intermediate or compromise suggestions, but none were adopted because the parliamentary debate took place shortly before election time, and members of the *Knesset* felt that votes might be influenced by that consideration. The whole matter was referred back to the Special Commission and to a Committee made up of members of the Coalition Parties. As a result of these new deliberations, the following modification of the earlier proposal was made:

1) To delete the concept of the burial society objecting to an autopsy, except as it was defined in the 1953 law.

2) To allow autopsy in exceptional cases, even if this means overruling the expressed wishes of the deceased before his death or the objections of the next of kin.

The exceptional cases are where three physicians certify in writing that there exists the possibility that death was due to an unusual, unknown cause, or due to an accident, and without establishing the cause of death there may result damage to life; or where there is suspicion that a danger to society or to an individual exists which may be overcome by establishing the precise cause of death, or where a need exists to use an organ from the deceased for transplantation purposes. Corneas may be preserved in an eye bank.

3) To delete completely the paragraph dealing with a control commission to supervise implementation of the law.

4) To broaden the matter of transplantation.

This new "revision of the revision," which was now acceptable to the medical community but not to the religious elements in the Government, was presented to the fifth *Knesset* at the end of the session in 1965. In the haste of adjourning, the bill was referred back to a parliamentary committee. The sixth *Knesset* failed to act on the bill. In the meantime, autopsies continued to be performed in the major hospitals of Israel over the opposition of families of the deceased, burial societies and the Rabbinate. Polarization between the medical and religious communities reached a climax with an incident in the Kaplan Hospital in Petach Tikvah. An autopsy had been performed and the family of the deceased stormed the hospital, wreaked havoc causing extensive property damage, and physically assaulted members of the medical staff of the hospital. As a result of this incident, the Ministry of Health issued a circular to all hospitals in Israel directing that patients who stipulate that their bodies not be dissected if they die, should not be admitted to the hospital.

This directive outraged both the religious and non-religious public. Demonstrations were held in Israel and throughout the world demanding that indiscriminate autopsies cease at once. Many violent incidents ensued in the various confrontations. The Chief Rabbinate of Israel published a statement on October 15, 1966 which asserted that:

> In view of the great calamity in the matter of autopsy, we express our opinion that autopsy in any form whatsoever is prohibited by the law of the Torah. And there is no way to allow it except in a matter of immediate danger to life, and then only with the approval in each instance of a brilliant Rabbi who is authorized to do so.

The statement was signed by Chief Rabbis Isaac Yehuda Unterman and Yitzchak Nissim, Rabbi Yechezkel Abramsky and three hundred and fifty-six Rabbis from the entire State of Israel (56 from Jerusalem, 68 from Tel Aviv, 30 from Haifa, 10 from Petach Tikvah, 6 from Rechovot, five each from Ramat Gan, Cholon, Be'er Sheba, Bnei Brak, Tiberias and Bat Yam, 4 from Nathanya, etc.). The 14 pages of signatures end with the following pronouncement: "This judgment is a warning against the passage of any law which would negate it."

Needless to say, this extreme viewpoint of the Chief Rabbinate, generated more protest, more controversry, more violence. Accusations, counter-accusations and denials, flew between the Hadassah Medical Center in Jerusalem and *ad hoc* organizations such as the "Committee for Safeguarding Human Dignity." The Association of Orthodox Jewish Scientists, headquartered in New York, sent a letter to Prime Minister Levi Eshkol on May 5, 1967, part of which follows:

> We would like to emphasize that in spite of our appreciation of the contributions of post-mortem examination to modern medicine, we are firm in our conviction that the primary rights of disposition of the remains of a deceased individual—not merely the right to object to an autopsy—must be granted to the next of kin. This practice is almost universal in scientifically advanced countries. We are certain that non-coercive means can be found to assure adequate numbers of post-mortem examinations to preserve Israel's position in the medical world.
>
> We urge you to act immediately to achieve passage of legislation, vesting permission for autopsy in the hands of the family of the deceased. Until such legislation is passed, we urge you to prevail upon the medical community to declare a voluntary moratorium on autopsies, except when specific consent is obtained from the family of the deceased.
>
> With the prevailing climate of distrust and controversy, your personal intervention is urgently needed to terminate this destructive internecine war within the Jewish community. We urge you to act now.

The controversy did not abate, however. Stories were published in the Israel lay[18] and medical[19] presses as well as in American lay[20] and medical publications.[21] Acts of incitement and provocation, slanders, derogations, disturbances and personal threats and abuse against physicians continued. On the other hand, autopsies continued to be performed at major Israeli hospitals in spite of the objections of next of kin. People are now afraid to be admitted to an Israeli hospital for fear their body might be dissected if they should die.

The solution can only come about when tempers subside and rational thinking substitutes for emotional panic. When physicians and Rabbis will, face to face, discuss their mutual problems, then a major hurdle will have been surmounted. A new law concerning autopsy necessarily must take into account the religious and social sensitivities of the population, as well as the needs of the medical community in its dedication to provide the best possible medical care for the sick. In those circumstances where Jewish law does permit an autopsy, the procedure must be performed according to all halakhic principles including the return of all removed organs to the body for burial. Only in an atmosphere of mutual trust can the Rabbinate and medical profession arrive at a compromise solution which will satisfy the requirements of both.

18. Gillon, P., "Autopsies," *The Jerusalem Post*, Friday, March 24, 1967. Rosenthal, Y., "*Netichath Geviyoth Raq Behetar Rav*," *Haaretz*, December 4, 1966.

19. Resnekov, V., Editorial on Autopsies. *Quarterly Review of the Israel Medical Association*. (Tel Aviv). 23: No. 1, pp. 3-11, Jan.-April, 1967.

20. Greenberg, M. M., "The Autopsy Crisis in Israel," *The Jewish Observer*, September 1966, pp. 5-9, Chalef, M. N. and Goldberg, J., "Are Autopsies Really Prohibited?", *The Jewish Press*, Friday, Sept. 2, 1966, pp. 20-21 and Birnbaum, M., "Eye Witness to Autopsy Mill Tells of Experiences in Israel," *Ibid.*, Friday, Oct. 7, 1966. Robbins, P., "Unauthorized Autopsy on Israel Hero Performed," *The Guardian*, Vol. 3, No. 2, November, 1967, p. 1. Maeir, D. M., "An Examination of the Autopsy Problem," *Yeshiva University Alumni Review*, Vol. 7, No. 4, Summer, 1967, pp. 2 and 8.

21. Sohn, D., "Israeli Autopsy Debate," *New York State J. Med.*, 68: pp. 398-401, Feb. 1, 1968. "Autopsy Dispute Brings Israeli M.D.'s Under Fire," *Medical World News*, June 9, 1967, p. 45.

It is hoped that more Rabbis will speak out in the near future concerning the areas of disease (i.e., genetic and infectious diseases, experimental drug therapy and others) where autopsy may be permitted and how it should be conducted. Physicians, on their part, particularly pathologists, must make arrangements to perform autopsies without undue delay. They must return all organs to the body for burial, removing only minute pieces for microscopic examination. Photographs of the gross pathology can be taken for later use rather than saving whole organs, an act prohibited by Jewish law. Only with a recognition of the problems of medicine and Jewish law by both sides—that is physician and Rabbi—can progress be made towards a mutually acceptable solution. This is true not only in the United States, but also in Israel, because in the matter of autopsy, medicine and Judaism do, in fact, strive toward a common goal, the eradication of disease.

Chapter X

Heart and Other Organ Transplantation and Jewish Law

Introduction

Recent advances in medical knowledge and technology have made possible the transplantation of a human heart from a deceased person into another individual[1-2]* stricken with severe, advanced heart disease refractory to all other medical and surgical approaches. The life and health of the recipient may thereby be prolonged considerably. These operations have raised many moral, theological, legal, social and philosophical problems which seem to cry out for answers. The present paper is an attempt to present the Halachic (Jewish legal) aspects of heart and other organ transplantation procedures as derived from classical Biblical and Talmudic sources, as well as the more recent Rabbinic literature on the subject.

Theological, Moral, Ethical, Social, Legal and Philosophical Problems of Heart Transplantation

It would seem useful prior to embarking on the substance of this chapter to briefly outline some of the questions, other than those of Jewish law, revolving around cardiac transplantation in man. First,

---

* Titles of articles in Hebrew periodicals are given in English.

1. Barnard, C. N., "A Human Cardiac Transplant: An Interim Report of a Successful Operation Performed at Groote Schuur Hospital, Capetown," *S. Afr. Med. J.*, 41:1271-1274, (Dec. 30) 1967.

2. Cooley, D. A., Bloodwell, R. D., Hallman, G. L. and Nora, J. J., "Transplantation of the Human Heart. A Report of Four Cases," *J.A.M.A.*, 205(7):479-486, (Aug. 12) 1968.

theological questions arise. For example, is one interfering with G-d's will by "artificially" prolonging a person's life by providing him with a new heart when G-d may have ordained a shorter life span for this person? Is one interfering with the patient's right to die in dignity without extraordinary heroic efforts to extend the duration of his life?

Moral and ethical issues also stimulate our thinking. Is the publicity surrounding heart transplants in excess of that dictated by usual medical practice and ethics? Is cardiac transplantation premature? Is it still in the experimental stages or have we reached therapeutic application? What of the physical and emotional stresses on the family of the donor at the time of their bereavement? Some of these moral issues have been discussed by Tendler[3] and Schimmel[4] and others.[5–10]

Social problems regarding heart transplantation are also self evident. Who shall pay for the enormous expense of the procedure and the pre and post operative care? The patient? Society? Are only the rich entitled to benefit from this medical advance? Who should select the

3. Tendler, M. D., "Medical Ethics and Torah Morality, *Tradition*, 9(4):5-13, (Spring) 1968.
4. Schimmel, E. D., "Medical Ethics and Torah Morality. A Rejoinder," *Tradition*, 9(4):14-19, (Spring) 1968.
5. Hamburger, J. and Crosnier, J., *Moral and Ethical Problem in Transplantation. In Human Transplantation.* Edit. by F. T. Rapaport and J. Dausset, New York. Grune and Stratton, 1968, pp. 37-44.
6. Elkinton, J. R., "Moral Problems in the Use of Borrowed Organs, Artificial and Transplanted." Editorial. *Annals of Int. Med.*, 60(2):309-313, (Feb.) 1964 and 61(2):355, (Aug.) 1964.
7. Appel, J. A., "Ethical and Legal Questions Posed by Recent Advances in Medicine," *J.A.M.A.*, 205(7):513-516, (Aug. 12) 1968.
8. Reemtsma, K., *Ethical Problems with Artificial and Transplanted Organs: An Approach by Experimental Ethics. In Ethical Issues in Medicine. The Role of the Physician in Today's Society.* Edit. by E. F. Torrey, Boston, Little, Brown and Co., 1968, pp. 263-294.
9. Wolstenholme, G. E. W. and O'Connor, M., *Ethics in Medical Progress: With Special Reference to Transplantation.* Ciba Foundation Symposium. Boston, Little, Brown and Co., 1966, X and 257 pp.
10. Ladimer, I. and Newman, R. W. Editors: *Clinical Investigation in Medicine: Legal, Ethical and Moral Aspects, an Anthology and Bibliography.* Boston University Law-Medicine Research Institute. 1963, XXIII and 517 pp.

recipients? Since there are many more potential recipients than donors available, who should decide "who shall live and who shall die"? The physician? A group of physicians? Society? Should not society be investing billions of dollars in medical research to attempt to find the cure for heart disease and thus obviate the need for cardiac transplantation? These questions cry out for answers.

Philosophical questions also crop up. The heart is considered to be the seat of the soul. In removing the patient's diseased heart prior to implantation of a "new" heart, has one removed his soul? The famous expression of Descartes "I think. therefore, I am" would take on new meaning. Who am I?

Finally, legal problems[7,11] are of great concern to many people. The donor heart in one instance of cardiac transplantation performed in Texas was derived from a 36 year old sailor who had been fatally beaten. The County Medical Examiner feared for the possible legal problems involved in this homicide case, problems that might affect the prosecution and autopsy procedures. Further legal stumbling blocks include the fact that only 36 states currently have laws allowing the donation of an entire body and 5 additional states allow an individual to will his eyes. Donation of a heart specifically is not dealt with in the legal statutes of any state. A Uniform Anatomical Gift Act reforming the current legal structure relating to the donation and use of organs and tissues for transplantation and other medical purposes has been formulated[11a] and endorsed by the American Bar Association. In Italy, a new law governing kidney transplants was recently adopted.[11]

The answers to some of the above questions seem to be forthcoming. Medical and ethical guidelines for heart transplantation have been established by numerous hospitals, states, medical societies and also the prestigious American Medical Association[12] and National Academy of

11. "Organ Transplantation and Our Laws: A Warning and a Need," Medical News Section, *J.A.M.A.*, 203(2):31-32, 38, (Jan. 8) 1968.

11a. Sadler, A. M., Sadler, B. L. and Stason, E. B., "The Uniform Anatomical Gift Act. A Model for Reform," *J.A.M.A.*, 206(11):2501-2506, (Dec. 9) 1968.

12. Judicial Council, "Ethical Guidelines for Organ Transplantation," *J.A.M.A.*, 205(6):341-342, (Aug. 5) 1968.

Sciences.[13] Recommendations in these guidelines include the requirements that the surgical team shall have had extensive laboratory experience in cardiac transplantation, that death of the donor shall be certified by an independent team of physicians and that the information and knowledge gained should be rapidly disseminated to the medical world. All aspects of cardiac transplantation were considered at a meeting held on September 29 and 30, 1968 at Bethesda, Maryland under the sponsorship of the American College of Cardiology. Present at the meeting were surgeons, internists, biomedical scientists concerned with transplantation and immunology, government representatives, private philanthropists and lawyers concerned with cardiac and other organ transplantation. The proceedings of that conference have been published[13a] and cover the following subjects: scientific background of cardiac transplantation, clinical and experimental status of cardiac transplantation, procurement of organs and their storage, tissue matching, and the "nature of the regional and national effort required for realization of the full potential of this new approach to heart diease."[13a]

HALACHIC QUESTIONS IN HEART TRANSPLANTS

The problems in Halacha (Jewish Law) concerning transplantation of the human heart may be conveniently subdivided into those which pertain to the recipient, those that concern the donor and those which primarily affect the physician.

Recipient: Is the recipient allowed to subject himself to the danger of the operative procedure? We know that it is not proper for someone to wound himself.[14] Does this apply to the surgical cut of an operation

---

13. "Cardiac Transplantation in Man." Statement Prepared by the Board on Medicine of the National Academy of Sciences. *J.A.M.A.*, 204(9):805-806, (May 27) 1968 and editorial comment thereon in the same issue, pp. 820-821.

13a. Moore, F., Burch, G. E., Harken, D. E., Murray, J. E. and Lillihei, C. W., "Cardiac and Other Transplantation In the Setting of Transplant Science as a National Effort," *J.A.M.A.*, 206(11):2489-2500, (Dec. 9) 1968.

14. Babylonian Talmud *Baba Kamma* 91b; Maimonides' Mishneh Torah: *Hilchoth Shevuoth* 5:17 and *Hilchoth Chovel Umazik* 5:1.

in general, and of a heart trarnsplant operation in particular? Furthermore, does the recipient transgress the commandment of *Take heed to thyself and keep thy soul diligently* (Deut. 4:9) or *Take ye therefore good heed unto yourselves* (Deut. 4:15) which both the Talmud[15] and Maimonides[16] interpret to mean the removal of all danger to one's physical well being?

Another halachic problem concerning the recipient revolves around the need for burial of his "old" heart. This problem is not unique to heart transplants but applies to any organ removed from the body of a live human being. Thus, a gallbladder, stomach, lung or other diseased internal organ may require burial by Jewish law (there is some dispute on this point) and so might the excised "old" heart.

A third halachic question regarding the recipient is the status of his new heart after he dies. Does the new heart revert back to the original owner?

Another problem concerns the recipient who happens to be a priest (*Kohen*). Does the question of avoidance of ritual defilement[17] apply to the heart of the dead donor which is now to be implanted into a priest?

Finally, what halachic priorities are there in choosing a recipient? We know, for example, that a woman takes precedence over a man when both desperately need food[18] because it would be less dignified and more shameful for a woman to go begging than a man.[19] A woman is ransomed before a man if both are captives,[20] but a man takes precedence over a woman if both are drowning[21] because he is subject to more commandments.[22] Additional priorities are enumerated

---

15. Babylonian Talmud *Berachoth* 32b.
16. Mishneh Torah: *Hilchoth Rotzeach Ushemirath Hanefesh* 11:4.
17. Karo's *Shulchan Aruch*. Section *Yoreh Deah* 369:1 and 374:2.
18. *Ibid.* 251:8 and Mishnah *Horayoth* 3:7.
19. Commentary of Rabbi Shabbtai Hakohen known as *Sifsei Cohen (Shach)* on Karo 251:8.
20. Karo's *Shulchan Aruch* Section *Yoreh Deah* 252:8 and Mishnah *Horayoth* 3:7.
21. *Ibid.*
22. Commentary of Rabbi David Halevi known as *Turey Zahav (Taz)* on Karo 252:8.

in the Talmud[23] and mentioned by Rabinovitch.[24] Do any of these priorities apply to heart transplant recipients? Should medical criteria be used exclusively in the selection of recipients?

Physician: After the recipient's old heart has been removed and prior to the implantation of the new heart, the patient is without a heart. Is he considered halachically dead during this interim? If so, is the surgeon guilty of the Biblical prohibition of *Thou shalt not kill* (Exod. 20:13 and Deut. 5:17) as enunciated in the decalogue.

Does heart transplantation constitute human experimentation or is it a therapeutic procedure? The former would only be sanctioned under specific regulations and conditions,[25] whereas the latter would fall under the purview of the physician's permissibility to heal: *"And heal he shall heal"* (Exod. 21:19). From this verse we deduce the physician's license to practice medicine.[26]

Donor: The major considerations from the Jewish legal viewpoint in cardiac transplantation are the halachic questions that concern the donor. These are five in number. First, there is a prohibition of deriving any benefit whatsoever from the dead.[27] Second, there is a prohibition of desecrating or mutilating the dead body.[28] A third problem regarding the donor is the prohibition of delaying the burial of the dead[29] and the positive commandment of burying the dead.[30] Another halachic consideration is that of ritual defilement (*Tum'ah*) for priests in

23. Mishnah *Horayoth* 3:7 and 3:7 and the Talmud *Horayoth* 13a, 13b and 14a.
24. Rabinovitch, N. L., "What is the Halakhah for Organ Transplants?", *Tradition*, 9(4):20-27, (Spring) 1968.
25. Jakobovits, I., "Medical Experimentation on Humans in Jewish Law," *Proc. Ass'n. Orthodox Jewish Scientists*. New York, 1:1-7, 1966.
26. Babylonian Talmud *Baba Kamma* 85a; Karo's *Shulchan Aruch*, Section *Yoreh Deah* 336:1.
27. Babylonian Talmud *Avodah Zara* 29b; Karo's *Shulchan Aruch*, Section *Yoreh Deah* 349:1-2; Maimonides' Mishneh Torah, *Hilchoth Avel* 14:21.
28. Babylonian Talmud *Arachin* 7a; *Chullin* 11b; and *Baba Bathra* 154b.
29. Babylonian Talmud *Sanhedrin* 46b; Karo's *Shulchan Aruch*, Section *Yoreh Deah* 357:1; based on "His body shall not remain all night upon the tree" (Deut. 21:23).
30. Jerusalem Talmud *Nazir* 7:1; Babylonian Talmud *Sanhedrin* 46b; Maimonides' Mishneh Torah: *Hilchoth Avel* 12:1; based on "but thou shalt certainly bury him on that day" (Deut. 21:23).

the same room with either the donor or only with the donor's heart.[31] Does this heart transmit ritual defilement? The final and perhaps most crucial question concerns the establishment of the death of the donor. Since the chances of successfully resuscitating a transplanted heart diminish with time following death of the donor, it is imperative to define the criteria for death in order for physicians not to be accused of "heart snatching" from donors prior to their demise. This would constitute an act of murder on the part of the physician who is bound to prolong life but not to prolong the act of dying.[32] The halachic definition of death has recently been reviewed.[33] This classic definition of death in the Talmud[34] and Codes[35] would be set aside if prospects for resuscitation of the patient, even remote, are deemed feasible.[36]

The Halachah in Eye Transplants

Most of the Rabbinic Responsa literature concerning organ transplantation deals with eye (cornea) transplants. The basic halachic principles governing eye transplants, however, are applicable to nearly all other organ transplants and will thus be considered here. Kidney and heart transplants involve several additional unique questions and these will be discussed separately below.

The classic responsum on eye transplants is that of the present Chief Rabbi of Israel, Isaac Yehuda Unterman.[37] Rabbi Unterman states that the prohibitions of deriving benefit from the dead, desecrating the dead and delaying the burial of the dead are all set aside

---

31. Maimonides' Mishneh Torah: *Hilchoth Tum'ath Meth* 3:1; Karo's *Shulchan Aruch*, Section *Yoreh Deah* 369:1.
32. Rosner, F., "Jewish Attitude Toward Euthanasia," *New York State J. Med.*, 67(18):2499-2506, (Sept. 15)1967.
33. Rosner, F., "The Definition of Death in Jewish Law," *Tradition*, 10(4):33-39, (Fall) 1969.
34. Mishnah *Yoma* 8:6-7; Babylonian Talmud *Yoma* 85a; Jerusalem Talmud *Yoma* 8:5.
35. Mishneh Torah: *Hilchoth Shabbath* 2:19; Karo's *Shulchan Aruch*, Section *Orach Chayim* 329:4.
36. Jakobovits, I., Personal Communication. Aug. 1, 1968.
37. Unterman, I. Y., *Shevet Miyehudah*. 1955, Jerusalem, pp. 313-322.

because of the consideration of saving a life (*Pikuach Nefesh*). These prohibitions would remain if there is no threat to life involved for which the transplant is being done. For example, there is no *Pikuach Nefesh* involved in a bone or nose transplant. The question then arises: is an eye transplant in the category of *Pikuach Nefesh*? Attempting to answer this question, Rabbi Unterman cites the Talmud (*Avodah Zara* 28b) where it states: "if one's eye gets out of order, it is permissible to paint it on the Sabbath because the eyesight is connected with the perception of the heart." Thus, eye damage does seem to constitute *Pikuach Nefesh* since one may desecrate the Sabbath to save an eye. Rabbi Unterman argues, however, that this case deals with preventing blindness whereas in eye transplantation one attempts to restore vision, a totally different matter.

On the other hand, Rabbi Unterman does agree that blindness is considered a life-threatening situation since the person so afflicted may fall down a flight of stairs or into a ditch and be killed. Thus, since blindness constitutes a true *Pikuach Nefesh,* the problems of desecrating and benefiting from and delaying the burial of the dead are put aside.

What of a person blind in one eye? The concept of *Pikuach Nefesh* does not apply and thus on what grounds would corneal transplants be permitted? To answer this question, Rabbi Unterman provides us with an enlightening and original pronouncement. Once the eye is implanted into the recipient, it is not considered dead but a living organ. Thus, the prohibitions of deriving benefit from the dead and delaying the burial of the dead are not applicable since no dead organ is involved. Furthermore, the problem of ritual defilement (*Tum'ah*) is non-existent since *Tum'ah* relates only to a dead organ or a dead body. Confirmation of this last point can be found in the Talmud (Tractate *Niddah* 70b) where it states "The men of Alexandria asked R. Yehoshua . . . was the (dead) son of the Shunammite woman (revived by Elijah the Prophet) unclean? He replied: "A corpse is unclean, but a living person is not." Thus, when the boy came back to life, the problem of *Tum'ah* was eliminated.

One problem remains, however, in Rabbi Unterman's dissertation and that is the prohibition of desecrating the dead to obtain an eye for a person with unilateral blindness. One still has to make an incision into the donor and one doesn't have the concept of *Pikuach Nefesh* to set the question of desecration aside. A brilliant answer is offered by Rabbi Unterman who states that since the eyes of a deceased person are always closed, removing one or both would not constitute a desecration. Only a visible incision into the body or the removal of externally visible or internal organs represents a true desecration and this would be permitted for a real *Pikuach Nefesh* such as blindness in both eyes or advanced renal disease requiring a kidney transplant. An exhaustive review of the Rabbinic literature on eye transplants is beyond the scope of this book and does not seem to be desirable or necessary since it would probably add little if anything to the halachic principles enunciated in Rabbi Unterman's book.[37] However, the following additional Rabbinic Responsa dealing primarily with eye transplants have been selected because each makes a new point.

Rabbi Yekusiel Yehuda Greenwald[38] states that the prohibition of deriving benefit from the dead applies only to flesh (*Bassar*) or organs but not to skin (*Orr*). The cornea of the eye, according to Rabbi Greenwald, is considered as skin and not as flesh. This is based on a passage in the Talmud (*Niddah* 55a) and the Commentary of *Tosefoth* (*S.V. Sheme Yaaseh shetichin*) thereon. Rabbi Unterman and many others, however, reject this differernce between skin and flesh.

Another point brought out by Rabbi Greenwald is that the engrafted or transplanted cornea becomes nullified on the recipient. An analogous situation is described in the Talmud (*Sotah* 43b) where it states: "If he grafted a young shoot on an old stem, the young shoot is annulled by the old stem and the law of *Orlah*[39] does not apply to it." Similarly, when a cornea is transplanted, it does not retain its original status but becomes annulled on the recipient.

The conclusion to be drawn from Rabbi Greenwald's arguments is that one cannot remove the whole eye from a deceased donor for transplantation; only the cornea may be used since a whole eye repre-

38. Greenwald, Y. Y., *Kol Bo al Aveluth*. Vol. 1, New York, 1947, pp. 45-48.
39. Prohibition of using fruit during the first three years after planting a tree (Levit. 19:23).

sents flesh whereas the cornea alone is considered skin. Furthermore, one cannot overcome the problems of desecrating and delaying the burial of the dead without invoking the concept of *Pikuach Nefesh*. Thus, Rabbi Greenwald, as most authorities, would only permit eye grafts for a person blind in both eyes.

Rabbi Itzchak Glickman[40] reiterates and agrees with all of Rabbi Unterman's theses described above. Rabbi Glickman adds, however, that one may only perform a transplant if the donor gave permission prior to his death. Otherwise the donor is hindered from achieving atonement (*Kaparah*) for his sins through his death since one of his organs remains alive. If he gave permission, then he has voiced his acquiescence to delaying his atonement until his organ is later buried following the eventual death of the recipient. In the meantime, he has performed a charitable act (*Gemilas Chesed*). Most other Rabbinic Responsa agree with the need for permission from the donor or his family. There is one dissenting viewpoint.[41]

Rabbi Meyer Steinberg[42] raises the problem of eye banks. Is the permissibility for corneal transplantation only applicable to an immediate transfer of the cornea from donor to recipient or may one place an eye in an eye bank for later use? Since the permissibility of organ transplantation rests primarily on the overriding consideration of *Pikuach Nefesh*, it would seem that the recipient would have to be at hand (*Lefoneinu*. literally: before us). Rabbi Steinberg answers that since the number of blind people is so large, it is as if there is always a recipient at hand. The Chief Rabbi of the British Commonwealth, Dr. Immanuel Jakobovits, also permits[43] "organs or blood to be donated for deposit in banks provided there is a reasonable certainty that they will be eventually used in life-saving operations (including

---

40. Glickman, I., "Regarding the Law of Grafting Organs from the Dead onto the Sick," *Noam*, Vol. 4, pp. 206-217, Jerusalem 5721 (1961).

41. Pirer, B. Z., "In the Matter of Grafting an Organ from the Dead to a Living Person," *Noam*, Vol. 4, pp. 200-205, Jerusalem 5721 (1961).

42. Steinberg, M., "In the Matter of Grafting an Eye from the Dead to a Blind Person," *Noam*, Vol. 3, pp. 87-96, Jerusalem 5720 (1960).

43. Jakobovits, I., Personal Communication. Jan. 8, 1968.

the restoration or preservation of eye-sight)." Even Rabbi Unterman had already stated at the end of his remarks on eye transplants[37] that blood donations to blood banks are permissible for the same aforementioned reason.

Rabbi Moshe Feinstein, in a lengthy responsum[44] devoted exclusively to the prohibition of deriving benefit from the dead, raises the problem of a Gentile donor for an eye transplant. Rabbi Feinstein's conclusion is that it is permissible.

Rabbi Jacob Weinberg[45] takes exception to nearly all of Rabbi Unterman's arguments[37] but concludes that since Rabbinic authorities that preceded him permitted eye transplants, he would also be in accord with this ruling, providing, however, that the recipient is blind in both eyes.

Most other Rabbinic Responsa on our subject agree with Rabbi Unterman's ruling.[37] One outstanding exception is Rabbi Shmuel Huebner[46] who admits that most Rabbis permit eye transplants but he himself does not consider a blind or deaf person to be in the category of a dangerously ill person (*Choleh Sheyesh Bo Sakana*). Therefore, the concept of *Pikuach Nefesh* cannot be invoked and thus, states Rabbi Huebner, the prohibitions of desecrating, deriving benefit from, and delaying the burial of the dead cannot be set aside.

THE HALACHAH IN KIDNEY TRANSPLANTS

All the halachic principles discussed above relating to eye transplants are equally applicable to kidney transplants. In fact, many of the

---

44. Feinstein, M., In the Matter of Attaching an Organ or Flesh or Bone from a Dead to a Live Person, Whether This is Prohibited Because of the Law Prohibiting the Derival of Benefit from the Dead, if the Dead Person is a Jew or if He is a Gentile. *Responsa Iggroth Moshe*. Section *Yoreh Deah*. No. 229, New York, 1959, pp. 459-469.
45. Weinberg, J., *Responsa Sereedai Aish*. Section *Yoreh Deah*. No. 120, Vol. 2, Jerusalem, 1962, pp. 276-277.
46. Heubner, S., "The Utilization of Eyes from a Dead Person to Restore the Vision of the Blind," *Hadarom (Kovetz Torani)* of the Rabbinical Council of America). Vol. 13, New York, Nissan 5721 (1961), pp. 54-64.

Responsa deal with both eye and kidney transplants. A kidney transplant is only undertaken when both kidneys of the recipient are so diseased that life cannot continue without the removal of the body's waste products that accumulate in the blood. Elimination of such wastes can be accomplished by the intermittent use of an artificial kidney or its equivalent, or by the definitive implantation of a healthy human kidney to replace the non-functioning patient's own kidneys. All Rabbinic authorities would agree that such a case constitutes *Pikuach Nefesh* and, therefore, the prohibitions revolving around the dead donor would all be set aside for this overriding consideration of saving a life.

In addition to cadaver kidneys, physicians also employ kidneys from live donors for transplantation. Here, new halachic questions arise. Is the donor allowed to subject himself to the danger, however small, of the operative procedure to remove one of his kidneys in order to save the life of another? Does the donor transgress the commandment of *Take heed to thyself and keep thy soul diligently* (Deut. 4:9) or *Take ye therefore good heed unto yourselves* (Deut. 4:15)? We have already mentioned that the Talmud[15] and Maimonides[16] interpret these verses to refer to the removal of all danger to one's physical well being. We have also already stated that it is not permitted to intentionally wound oneself.[14] We also know that one may not set aside one person's life for that of another.[47] The question then remains: can one endanger one's own life by donating a kidney in order to save another's life?

The answer is found in commentaries on Maimonides[48] and on Karo[49] and later Codes[50] in nearly identical language:

---

47. Mishnah *Oholoth* 7:6; Maimonides' Mishneh Torah: *Hilchoth Rotzeach Ushemirath Hanefesh* 1:9; Karo's *Shulchan Aruch,* Section *Yoreh Deah* 425:2.

48. Commentary of *Keseph Mishnah* (Rabbi Joseph Karo) on Maimonides' Mishneh Torah: *Hilchoth Rotzeach Ushemirath Hanefesh* 1:14.

49. Commentary of *Me'eerath Ainyim* (Rabbi Joshua Valk Cohen) on Karo's *Shulchan Aruch.* Section *Chosen Mishpat* 426:1.

50. *Aruch Hashulchan* by Rabbi Yechiel Michael ben Aharon Halevi Epstein. Section *Chosen Mishpat* 426:4.

"the Jerusalem Talmud concludes that one is obligated to place oneself even into a possibly dangerous situation (to save another's life). It seems logical that the reason is that the one's (death without intervention i.e. the kidney recipient) is a certainty whereas his (the donor's) is only a possibility."

Some authorities claim that since many of the Codes including Maimonides, *Alfasi* (Rabbi Isaac Alfasi), *Tur* (Rabbi Jacob ben Asher), and *Asheri* (Rabbi Asher ben Yechiel) omit this passage from the Jerusalem Talmud, the final ruling is not in accord therewith. However, based upon this passage, Rabbi Immanuel Jakobovits[43] has stated that a donor may endanger his own life or health to supply a "spare" organ to a recipient whose life would thereby be saved only if the probability of saving the recipient's life is substantially greater than the risk to the donor's life or health. This principle is applicable to all organ transplantation where live donors are used as a source of the organ in question.

Rabbi Eliezer Yehuda Waldenberg[51] discusses at length the question of whether a healthy person must or may donate one of his organs for transplantation into a desperately ill individual in order to save the latter from certain death. Rabbi Waldenberg concludes that kidney transplants from a live donor are only permissible if a group of trustworthy physicians testify that there is no danger to life to the donor and if the donor is not coerced into consenting to the procedure. If one were to understand Rabbi Waldenberg literally, then it would be impossible ever to use a live donor as a source for an organ, for there is always a very small risk involved. Fortunately, anesthetic and surgical deaths in this type of operation are exceedingly rare, but they do occur. Perhaps Rabbi Waldenberg means that one is not obligated to endanger one's life to save another, but one may do so on a voluntary basis.

51. Waldenberg, E. Y., Whether there is an Obligation or any sort of Commandment for a Healthy Person to Donate one of his Organs for Transplantation into the Body of a Dangerously Ill Person and to thereby Save the Latter from Death. *Responsa Tzitz Eliezer.* Vol. 9, No. 45, Jerusalem, 1967, pp. 179-185.

The majority viewpoint[43,48,50] seems to be that a small risk may be undertaken by the donor if the chances for success in the recipient are substantial.

The Halachah in Heart Transplants

In the case of transplantation of a human heart from a dead donor, the prohibitions dealing with desecrating the dead, delaying the burial of the dead and ritual defilement are all set aside by the overriding consideration of *Pikuach Nefesh*, saving a life. The major halachic problem remaining is the establishment of the death of the donor. Prior to death, the donor is in the category of a *Gossess* (hopelessly ill patient) and one is prohibited from touching him or moving him or doing anything that might hasten his death.[52]

There are many types of death: intellectual death when a person's intellect ceases to function; social death when a person can no longer function in society; spiritual death when the soul leaves the body; and physiological or medical death. We are concerned with the halachic definition of death. The Jewish legal definition of death based upon Talmudic and Rabbinic sources has recently been reviewed[33] and summarized earlier in this paper. Cessation of respiration and absence of a heartbeat for a given time period represents the classical halachic interpretation of death. Today, an additional halachic criteria is the impossibility of resuscitation.[36]

On the assumption that the donor is absolutely and positively dead, many Rabbinic authorities permit heart transplants. Rabbi Immanuel Jakobovits states[43]:

> "An organ may never be removed for transplantation from a donor until death has been definitely established. The prohibition of *nivul hameth* (desecration of the dead) would then be suspended by the overriding consideration of *pikuach nefesh*. Hence,

---

52. Mishnah *Semachoth* 1:2; Babylonian Talmud *Shabbath* 151b; Maimonides' Mishneh Torah: *Hilchoth Avel* 4:5; Karo's *Shulchan Aruch*, Section *Yoreh Deah* 339.

in principle, I can see no objection in Jewish law to the heart operations recently carried out, provided the donors were definitely deceased at the time the organ was removed from them."

Rabbi Yitzchak Arieli is also quoted[53] as having said that heart transplants are permissible if the donor is definitely dead, but only with the family's consent. A similar pronouncement was made by Rabbi David Lifshutz[54] of the Rabbi Isaac Elchanan Theological Seminary of Yeshiva University.

A published responsum dealing specifically with heart transplants is that of the Chief Rabbi of Israel, Rabbi Isaac Yehuda Unterman[55] and represents remarks made in an address to the Eleventh Congress on Jewish Law in Jerusalem late in August, 1968. Rabbi Unterman begins by stating that consent from the family of the donor must be obtained. Otherwise, the doctors and the recipient would transgress the prohibition of *Thou shalt not steal* (Exod. 20:13 and Deut. 5:17). The Chief Rabbi then reviews the halachic definition of death. He states that under ordinary circumstances, death occurs when respiration ceases. However, sudden unexplained death in young otherwise healthy individuals should be followed by resuscitative measures. A *gossess* (hopelessly ill dying person with less than 3 days of life left) need not be resuscitated when respiration ceases. Rabbi Unterman then briefly mentions the problem of organ banks by stating that freezing organs for later use is allowed provided there is a good chance they will be used to save a life. Then, the situation would be comparable to having the recipient at hand (*Lefaneinu*).

A novel pronouncement by the Chief Rabbi[55] is that heart transplants may not be halachically sanctioned until such time that the chances for survival from the surgery are greater than those for failure.

---

53. Arieli, Y.: Cited by Abraham Ben Melech in *Panim el Panim*. Jerusalem, No. 458, March 1, 1968, p. 16.

54. Lifshutz, D., Personal Communication. Feb. 16, 1968.

55. Unterman, I. Y., Points of Halacha in the Question of Heart Transplantation (From an address to the Congress of Oral Law), Jerusalem, Elul, 5728 (August, 1968). Reprint.

That is, we invoke the requirement that the probability of success of the surgery shall be greater than the risk to the recipient. This ruling seems to be contrary to the pronouncements of earlier Rabbis[56] who allow a sick person to submit to very dangerous surgery or a very dangerous medication if there is a small chance for cure even if the risk of the operation or the treatment is much greater than the chance for cure.

Rabbi Unterman explains that the recipient of a new heart is in a different situation from all other desperately ill (but not necessarily dying) people. After his diseased heart is removed and before the new heart is implanted, the recipient has lost his *Chezkath Chayim* (hold on life, or preseumption of still being alive). Once he loses his *Chezkath Chayim,* the heart transplant recipient is no longer permitted to risk his life if the chances for success are not greater than the chances of failure. A person dying of cancer, on the other hand, never loses his *Chezkath Chayim* and, therefore, may subject himself to any risk, however great, if there is a small chance for cure.

The definition of *Chezkath Chayim* is exemplified in the Talmud (*Gittin* 28a) where it states that if a messenger brings a divorce from a distant place and the husband was an old man or sick at the time the messenger left, he should still deliver it to the wife on the presumption that the husband is still alive. Thus, unless we have positive information to the contrary, a person retains his *Chezkath Chayim* until he is pronounced dead. There are numerous other examples of *Chezkath Chayim* in the Talmud.[55]

That the heart is the seat of life and that its removal causes one to lose one's *Chezkath Chayim* is exemplified by the well known case of a chicken that was slaughtered in accordance with Jewish law and was found to have no heart. Two Sages gave diametrically opposing rulings regarding this chicken. Rabbi Zvi ben Yakov Ashkenazi, known as the *Chacham Zvi,* decreed that the chicken is kosher because without a heart, there is no life and, since the chicken walked and ate in a normal

---

56. Rabbi Jacob Reischer, (*Responsa Shevuth Yaakov*), Part 3, No. 75 and Rabbi Chayim Ozer Grodzinski, (*Responsa Achiezer*), Section *Yoreh Deah,* Chapter 16.

manner, the heart must have been present. After the chicken was opened, a cat must have snatched the heart away and eaten it. The *Chacham Zvi* also cites the *Zohar* in which it is written that without a heart, life cannot exist for even a moment. Furthermore, says the *Chacham Zvi*, Rabbi Joseph Karo, author of the *Shulchan Aruch* (under the pen name of *Keseph Mishnah*), in his Commentary on Maimonides' *Mishneh Torah,* points out that Maimonides omits absence of the heart from his list of animals with defects which cannot be slaughtered for food (*Terefoth*) because such an animal would not be viable. Finally, says the *Chacham Zvi,* even if witnesses were to come and say that they saw the chicken at all times and nothing was removed from it, they are not believed since that is impossible and against nature. The opposing viewpoint is that of Rabbi Jonathan Eyebeschutz, author of *Keresi Upelesi.* This Rabbi ruled that the chicken is not kosher and the witnesses are believed. He also claims that physicians in Prague assured him that another piece of flesh that did not look like a heart might in fact have functioned as a heart. Thus, without a normal heart, the chicken is a *Terefah* (non-kosher).

In either event, we see from both Sages involved in this case that the heart is essential to life, and life is impossible without it. Therefore, concludes Rabbi Unterman,[55] in the case of a human heart transplant recipient, removing the patient's old heart removes from him his *Chezkath Chayim,* and thus the removal of the recipient's heart can be sanctioned only if the risk of death resulting from the surgery is estimated to be smaller than the prospect of lasting success. On the other hand, one must desecrate the Sabbath to rescue someone from under a collapsed building[57] even if the person may be already dead because he retains his *Chezkath Chayim* (presumption of being alive) until proven otherwise. Similarly, a patient dying of an incurable illness may subject himself to a potentially lethal medication or operation[56] on the small chance that cure might be achieved, because this patient never lost his *Chezkath Chayim.*

57. Mishnah *Yoma* 8:6-7; Babylonian Talmud *Yoma* 85a; Maimonides' Mishneh Torah: *Hilchoth Shabbath* 2:19; Karo's *Shulchan Aruch,* Section *Orach Chayim* 329:4.

This original concept of Rabbi Unterman regarding the loss of the *Chezkath Chayim* by the heart transplant recipient after his diseased heart is removed raises numerous questions. What is the status of this "lifeless" patient until the new heart is implanted? Is he legally dead? Is his wife considered a widow? Can she remarry? Are his children considered orphans and how do the inheritance laws apply here, if at all? After he receives his new heart, he is certainly alive again. Does he have to remarry his wife? All these questions have already been answered negatively by Rabbi Azriel Rosenfeld.[58] Rabbi Rosenfeld discusses the case of a person who has just died of an incurable disease and whose body is stored at a very low temperature for eventual thawing out and revival when the cure for the disease will be found. If the answer to all the above questions is NO as Rabbi Rosenfeld proves for a refrigerated person who "is certainly dead—by any ordinary definition—once he has been frozen,"[58] then certainly a heart transplant patient who has only lost his *Chezkath Chayim* temporarily should be considered not to have lost his status as husband and father. He might be considered lifeless during this interim period between heart exchanges but certainly not legally dead.

Dissenting from Rabbi Unterman's permissiveness towards heart transplants under the conditions described above is Rabbi Yitzchak Yakov Weiss of Manchester, England. Rabbi Weiss, answering an extensive inquiry from the Chief Rabbi of the British Commonwealth, Dr. Immanuel Jakobovits, strongly condemns cardiac transplants.[59] Rabbi Jakobovits wrote to Rabbi Weiss that a transplant operation may require artificial extension of the donor's life by the use of a respirator until the recipient can be prepared to receive the new heart. As a result, the following halachic question arises. Is it lawful to

---

58. Rosenfeld, A., "Refrigeration, Resuscitation and the Resurrection," *Tradition*, Vol. 9, No. 3, pp. 82-94, (Fall) 1967.

59. Weiss, Y. Y., "Whether It is Permissible to Transplant the Heart of a Sick Person about to Die into Another Ill Person as Therapy," *Hamoar*, Rabbinical Monthly Journal. Brooklyn, New York. 20th year, Part 5, No. 178, Elul, 5728 (Aug.-Sept.) 1968, pp. 3-9.

artificially prolong the life of the donor solely to preserve his heart long enough to effect the transplant and, having done so, is it lawful to then shut off the respirator thus, in effect, manipulating the life and death of the donor at will? This question, which Rabbi Jakobovits believes is highly relevant to the whole problem,[60] was answered negatively by Rabbi Weiss, while Rabbi Auerbach of the Kol Torah Yeshiva in Jerusalem offered an affirmative reply.[60]

Another responsum dealing with heart transplantation is that of Rabbi Chaim Dov Gulewski of Brooklyn, New York.[61] Rabbi Gulewski discusses the question of whether a person can renounce his desire to live in order to give his heart to another and, if this is permissible, whether the potential recipient is allowed to accept this heart and whether the surgeon is guilty of murder if he performs the transplantation. Rabbi Gulewski further offers legal definitions for a person who is considered a *Terefah* (suffering from a serious organic disease and who cannot live more than twelve months) and a dying individual (Hebrew: *Gossess*). The law differs whether this person is dying by Divine decree (*Gossess Biyeday Shamayim*) such as from incurable cancer or old age, or by human intervention (*Gossess Biyeday Adam*) such as a car accident or homicide victim. At the end of his article, Rabbi Gulewski offers a rebuttal to Rabbi Unterman's responsum.[55]

Another unpublished responsum on heart transplants is that of Rabbi Aryeh Leib Grosnas of the London *Beth Din* (Court of the Chief Rabbi). Rabbi Grosnas writes[62] that a person is still alive by Jewish law if his breathing is maintained either spontaneously or artificially even if all cerebral function has ceased. Such an individual is classified as a *Terefah* upon whom one may not operate save to heal

---

60. Jakobovits, I., Personal Communication. December 18, 1968.

61. Gulewski, C. D., "Regarding the Law of the Pursuer Who Commits No Act, The Problems of Heart Tarnsplantation and the Laws of a *Gossess* and a *Terefah*," *Hamoar*, Rabbinical Monthly Journal. Brooklyn, New York. 21st year, Part 1, No. 179, Tishri-Cheshvan, 5729 (Oct.-Nov.) 1968, pp. 3-16.

62. Grosnas, A. L., Personal Communication to Rabbi C. D. Gulewski dated 2nd day of Chanukah 5729 (Dec. 17, 1968).

him but not to use his heart even with his permission to save another. Once a person reaches the status of a *Nevelah* as defined in the Talmud (*Chullin* 21a), then one may remove his heart and transplant it into another. Rabbi Grosnas also discusses the status of the recipient after his diseased heart was removed and before his "new heart" is implanted. Although legally dead, if the operation is successful, then the matter becomes clear that the patient was never really dead at all. A long discussion follows in Rabbi Grosnas' responsum dealing with the question as to whether one is required or allowed to donate an organ such as a kidney to save another if there is a risk involved to the donor.

The Dean of the Yeshiva Tifereth Jerusalem in New York, Rabbi Moses Feinstein, has added his voice[63] to those condemning heart transplantation. Rabbi Feinstein, considered by many to be the leading Rabbinic scholar in the United States today, as England's Rabbi Weiss, considers this procedure to involve a double murder. However, a personal interview with Rabbi Feinstein by this writer as well as careful reading of Rabbi Feinstein's lengthy unpublished responsum on this subject discloses the following clarification of his position. If the donor is absolutely and positively dead by all medical and Jewish legal criteria, then no murder of the donor would be involved and the removal of his heart or other organ to save another human life would be permitted.

Concerning the recipient, when medical science will have progressed to the point where cardiac transplantation becomes an accepted therapeutic procedure with reasonably good chances for success, then murder of the recipient would no longer be a consideration. Additional animal experimentation, continues Rabbi Feinstein, is essential to overcome major obstacles such as organ rejection, tissue compatibility typing and immuno-suppressive therapy before heart transplantation in man can be condoned. In the present state of medical knowledge,

---

63. Feinstein, M., "Final Legal Judgement in the Matter of Heart Transplantation," *Hapardes,* Monthly Rabbinical Journal (New York). 43(6):4, March-April, 1969.

however, where chances for success are minuscule and the recipient's life is probably shortened rather than lengthened by this procedure, heart transplantation must still be considered murder of the recipient.

Another recent responsum on cardiac transplantation is by Rabbi Yehuda Gershuni of Yeshiva University.[64]

The major concern of most, if not all, the Rabbis attempting to give legal rulings in heart transplant cases is the establishment of the death of the donor. This is the identical problem that the medical and legal professions are now wrestling with. The majority of Rabbinic opinion expressed to date[43,53,54,55,61,62] in regard to heart transplants is of a permissive nature *provided* the donor was definitely deceased at the time his heart was removed. Even Rabbis Feinstein and Weiss who voice the most stringent opposition might also agree under these conditions.

Final Note

On December 3, 1967, Dr. Christian Barnard performed the world's first cardiac transplant at Groote Schuur Hospital in Capetown, South Africa. Exactly one year and two days lalter, on December 5, 1968, Professor Morris Levi at the Belinson Hospital in Petach Tikva performed Israel's first heart transplant and the world's one hundredth. Because the donor's name was not revealed, a furor of speculation and religious dispute emerged with reverberations throughout the world press.[65] The major concern seemed to have been the possible lack of permission from the donor's family to use his heart for transplantation thus raising the issue of "organ stealing." The operation itself was sanctioned by Chief Rabbi Unterman under the conditions described in his responsum.[55] Sephardic Chief Rabbi Yitzchak Nissim said that transplants are acceptable "in the case of danger to life and as long as clinical death is insured."

64. Gershuni, Y., "Heart Transplantation in the Light of Jewish Law," *Or Hamizrach* (Religious Zionists of America, New York). 18(3):133-137, April, 1969.
65. "Heart Transplant Spurs Dispute in Religious Circles in Israel." *The New York Times,* December 9, 1968.

Heart transplantation is probably here to stay. As of the date of the writing of this paper, over 100 such operations have been performed in South Africa, the United States, Canada, France, England, Chile, Argentina, Brazil, Venezuela, Czechoslovakia, Japan, India, Spain and the Soviet Union. Many medical problems such as availability of donors, tissue typing, rejection control remain to be solved. However, just as answers to the legal, moral and religious issues seem to be forthcoming, so too, it is hoped, strict medical evaluation and careful consideration of the prerequisites before a transplantation is performed, will improve the likelihood of successes.

As a motto to our survey of Jewish legal attitudes toward heart and other organ transplantation, we might cite the prophecy of Ezekiel as promised by Almighty G-d: *And a new heart will I give you and a new spirit will I put within you, and I will take away the stone heart out of your flesh and I will give you a heart of flesh* (Ezekiel 11:19 and 36:26). Although this Scriptural reference is obviously meant in a purely figurative and spiritual sense, it seems to vividly depict the present epoch of cardiac transplantation.

ADDENDUM TO CHAPTER X

Since the original publication of this essay in 1969, several additional papers on heart transplantation have appeared (66-69) by leading Rabbinic authorities in Israel, including the country's Chief Rabbi (67) and the armed forces Chief Rabbi (69). Finally, an exposition on brain transplants and the Jewish legal questions involved has also been published (70).

66. Levi, J., "In the Matter of Transplanting Organs from the Dead," *Noam*, Vol. 12, pp. 289-313, Jerusalem, 5729 (1969).
67. Unterman, I. Y., "The Problem of Heart Transplantation from the Viewpoint of Halachah," *Noam*, Vol. 13, pp. 1-9, Jerusalem, 5730 (1970).
68. Kasher, M. M., "The Problem of Heart Transplantation," *Noam*, Vol. 13, pp. 10-20, Jerusalem, 5730 (1970).
69. Goren, S., "Heart Transplantation in the Light of Halachah," *Machanayim*, No. 122, pp. 7-15, Marcheshvan, 5730 (1970). Published by the Israeli armed forces.
70. Rosenfeld, A., "The Heart, the Head and the Halakhah," *New York State Journal of Medicine*, Vol. 70:2615-2619, (Oct. 15) 1970.

Chapter XI

Suicide in Biblical, Talmudic and Rabbinic Writings

INTRODUCTION

Every day in the United States, about sixty people kill themselves by poisoning, hanging, drowning, shooting, stabbing, jumping from high places or other means. Although nearly 25,000 deaths from suicide are recorded annually in the United States,[1] the actual figure according to the National Institute of Mental Health is probably closer to 50,000 yearly.[2]

Worldwide, more than 500,000 suicides are registered yearly, according to the World Health Organization[3] and there are approximately eight times as many suicide attempts. The problem of suicide has reached such proportions that the United States Public Health Service created the National Center for Studies of Suicide Prevention in October 1966, headed by Dr. Edwin S. Schneidman. Presently there are 90 regional suicide prevention centers in 26 states in this country whereas in 1965 there were only 15 such centers.

The medical, psychological, psychiatric, legal and social literatures are replete with articles, monographs, symposia and other publications on suicide. Factors such as age, sex, marital status, day of week, month

---

1. Solomon, P., "The Burden of Responsibility in Suicide and Homicide," *J.A.M.A.,* 199:321-324, 1967.
2. Nelson, B., "Suicide Prevention: NIMH Wants More Attention for 'Taboo' Subject," *Science,* 161:776-777, 1968.
3. "Campaign Against Suicide," *Medical World News,* 10:7, (Jan. 3) 1969.

of year, method, religion, race, motivation, living conditions, repetitive attempts, medical and psychiatric histories of patients attempting and committing suicide are amply covered in these writings as well as the many books published on this subject.[4] A periodical devoted exclusively to suicide is the Bulletin of Suicidology published by the United States Public Health Service since 1967.

Several salient features of the problem deserve mention. Suicides are three times as frequent in men than in women although there are more attempts by women than men. Twice as many White Americans commit suicide than do Negro Americans and twice as many single people kill themselves than do married individuals. College students have a suicide rate 50 percent higher than non-college students of comparable age, sex and race. In industrialized countries, physicians, dentists and lawyers have a higher rate of suicide than other professionals. Although the suicide rate has remained relatively constant in the United States over the past decade or so, poisoning by drugs,

---

4. See Shneidman, E. S. and Farberow, N. L., editors, *Clues to Suicide* (New York: McGraw Hill, 1957), pp. XII and 227; Morielli, E. A., *Suicide: An Essay on Comparative Moral Statistics* (New York: D. Appleton & Co., 1903), pp. XI and 388; Bohannan, P., editor, *African Homicide and Suicide* (Princeton: Princeton Univ. Press, 1960), pp. XIX and 270 and appendix; Douglas, J. D., *The Social Meanings of Suicide* (Princeton: Princeton Univ. Press, 1967), pp. XIV and 398; Yochelson, L., editor, *Symposium on Suicide* (Washington, D.C.: George Washington Univ., 1967), pp. 150; Yap, P. M., *Suicide in Hong Kong with Special Reference to Attempted Suicide* (Hong Kong Univ. Press, 1958), pp. X and 101; Stengel, E. and Cook, N. G., *Attempted Suicide: Its Social Significance and Effects* (London: Chapman and Hall, 1958), pp. 136; Sainsbury, P., *Suicide in London: An Ecological Study* (London: Chapman and Hall, 1955), pp. 116; Hendin, H., *Suicide and Scandinavia: A Psychoanalytic Study of Culture and Character* (New York: Grune & Stratton, 1964), pp. XII and 153; Leonard, C. U., *Understanding and Preventing Suicide* (Illinois: Charles C. Thomas, 1967), pp. XII and 351; Durkheim, E., *Suicide: A Study in Sociology* (Glencoe Free Press, 1951), pp. 405; Farberow, N. L. and Shneidman, E. S., *The Cry for Help* (New York: McGraw Hill, 1961), pp. XVI and 398; Murphy, G. E. and Robins, E., "Social Factors in Suicide," *J.A.M.A.*, 199:303-308, 1967; "The Burden of Responsibility," *J.A.M.A.*, 199:334, 1967; "Changing Concepts of Suicide," *J.A.M.A.*, 199:752, 1967; "Suicide and Suicidal Attempts in Children and Adolescents," *Lancet*, 2:847-848, 1964; "Of Suicide and Folly," *Canad. Med. Ass. J.*, 96:1167-1168, 1967.

especially barbiturates, has become much more popular as a method of choice.[5]

The age group with the highest suicide rate is that above 65 years. Suicide ranks third as a cause of death among teenagers.[6] It has also been estimated that the ratio of suicide attempts to actual successes in adolescents is 100 to 1.

One phase of suicide hardly discussed at all is the religious aspect. This chapter attempts to organize and present in a systematic fashion the subject of suicide as found in Jewish sources. The closely related topic of martyrdom will be discussed briefly at the end.

Suicide in the Bible

During the period of the Judges in approximately the 11th or 12th century B.C.E., lived Samson of the tribe of Dan whose story is known to all. Samson's final effort in bringing down the Philistine temple upon himself as well as his enemies is vividly described in the Book of Judges (16:23-31):

> And Samson said: "Let me die with the Philistines." And he bent with all his might; and the house fell upon the lords, and upon all the people that were therein. So the dead that he slew at his death were more than they that he slew in his life.

At the end of the First Book of Samuel (31:1-7), we read of King Saul's final battle against the Philistines on Mount Gilboa in the 11th century B.C.E. Here, Saul saw his three sons Jonathan, Abinadab and Malchishua and most of his army slain. Not wishing to flee nor to be taken prisoner and exposed to the scorn of the Philistines, King Saul entreated his armor bearer to kill him. The latter refused and so

---

5. Berger, F. M., "Drugs and Suicide in the United States," *Clin. Pharmac. & Therap.*, 8:219-223, 1967.
6. Bakwin, H., "Suicide in Children and Adolescents," *J. Pediatr.*, 50:749-769, 1957; Faigel, H. C., "Suicide Among Young Persons. A Review of Its Incidence and Causes, and Methods for Its Prevention," *Clin. Pediatr.*, 5:187-190, 1966; Jacobziner, H., "Attempted Suicides in Adolescence," *J.A.M.A.*, 191:7-11, 1965.

the king fell upon his own sword. The Biblical passage concludes (I Samuel 31:5):

> And when his armor bearer saw that Saul was dead, he likewise fell upon his sword and died with him.

From these events it would appear as if Saul committed suicide. However, later on when David is informed of Saul's death, we read as follows (2 Samuel 1:5-10):

> And David said unto the young man that told him: "How knowest thou that Saul and Jonathan his son are dead?" And the young man that told him said: "As I happened by chance upon Mount Gilboa, behold, Saul leaned upon his spear; and lo, the chariots and the horsemen pressed hard upon him. And when he looked behind him, he saw me, and called upon men. And I answered: Here am I. And he said unto me: Stand, I pray thee, beside me, and slay me, for the agony hath taken hold of me because my life is just yet in me. So I stood beside him and slew him, because I was sure that he could not live after that he was fallen..."

Biblical commentators differ in their interpretation of this passage. R. David Kimchi explains that Saul did not die immediately when he fell on his sword but was mortally wounded. In his death throes, Saul asked the Amalekite to render the final blow of mercy to hasten his death. *Rashi, Ralbag* and *Metzudat David* agree with Kimchi and consider the death of King Saul as a case of euthanasia. Others view the story of the Amalekite as a complete fabrication.

In any event, Saul did attempt suicide. Only the question of his success is debated. As to Saul's armor bearer, no one disputes that he committed suicide.

King David's faithless counsellor, Ahitophel, committed suicide by hanging himself in his native town of Gilo. One of several reasons probably prompted suicide. First, he knew that Absalom's attempt to overthrow David was doomed and that he would die a traitor's death. Second, and less likely, is the disgust of Ahitophel at Absalom's conduct in setting aside his counsel, thus wounding Ahitophel's pride and disappointing his ambition.[7] Finally, David's curse (*Makkot* 11a) may have prompted Ahitophel to hang himself.

> And when Ahitophel saw that his counsel was not followed, he saddled his ass and arose, and got himself home unto his city, and set his house in order, and strangled himself; and he died and was buried in the sepulchre of his father.[8]

King Baasha of Israel reigned from 911 to 888 B.C.E. and was succeeded by his son Elah. The latter was addicted to idleness and drunkenness and passed the days drinking in his palace while his warriors were battling the Philistines at Gibbethon.[9] Zimri, a high ranking officer, took advantage of the situation, assassinated Elah and mounted the throne. His reign, however, lasted only seven days. As soon as the news of King Elah's murder reached the army on the battlefield General Omri was elected king and laid siege to the palace. When Zimri saw that he was unable to hold out against the siege, he set fire to the palace and perished in the flames. It is written in I Kings 16:18:

> And it came to pass, when Zimri saw that the city was taken that he went unto the castle of the king's house, and he burnt the king's house over him with fire, and he died.

Some Biblical commentators, notably *Radak* and *Metzudat David*, to whom the thought of suicide was abhorrent, interpret that Omri burned the house over Zimri. Most commentators, however, interpret the Biblical passage literally.

SUICIDE IN THE APOCRYPHA

In the Second Book of Maccabees two acts of suicide are recorded. The first occurred when King Demetrius I of Syria (162 to 150

---

7. Graetz, H., *History of the Jews,* [six volumes] (Philadelphia: Jewish Publication Society), p. 143.
8. 2 Samuel 17:23.
9. Graetz, H., *History of the Jews,* p. 192.

B.C.E.) escaped from his imprisonment in Rome and returned home as an invader.[10] Attempting to put down a rebellion of his Judean subjects, King Demetrius sent Nicanor, one of the warriors who escaped with him from Rome, to Judea, to treat the insurgents with the utmost harshness. Nicanor, in order to induce surrender from the Judeans, ordered that the most respected man in Jerusalem, Ragesh (or Razis) be seized. When the arresting soldiers were forcing open the courtyard door to Ragesh's house ". . . he fell upon his sword preferring to die nobly rather than to fall into the wretches' hands..." (2 Book of Maccabees 14:41-42). The ghastly tale of his lack of success in the first suicide attempt, his subsequent attempt by throwing himself down from a wall and his final success by self-disembowelment is vividly described (*ibid.* 14:43-46).

The second act of suicide is that of Ptolemy, an advocate of the Judeans at the Syrian Court, who was called a traitor before King Antiochus Eupator. Unable to maintain the dignity of his office, Ptolemy poisoned himself (2 Book of Maccabees 10:12).

Other Suicides and Near Suicides in Ancient Jewish Writings

All the suicides mentioned in the Bible and Apocrypha are psychologically understandable. Each knew what lay ahead if he remained alive, namely a prolonged, torturous martyrdom and/or disgrace to the G-d of Israel. All were prominent people. Except, perhaps, for King Saul, none could be accused of having experienced temporary insanity to excuse his act of self-destruction. Perhaps Ragesh and Ptolemy were influenced by the Greek philosophy of their times in which suicide was highly acceptable.

There are several individuals mentioned in the Bible, Apocrypha and other ancient Jewish writings who considered suicide and perhaps wished to attempt it, but did not.

---

10. *Ibid.*, pp. 482-485.

Job, during his quest for an explanation of his wretchedness, speaks of suicide (Job 7:15):

> And my soul chooseth strangling, and death rather than these my bones.

He did not attempt suicide perhaps out of either love or fear of G-d as he himself states (Job 13:15):

> Though He slay me, yet will I trust in Him.

Possibly Job did not mean to even consider suicide but was remarking that he would prefer death to life. This question remains unresolved.

One of the most famous "near suicides" is Flavius Josephus who failed to commit suicide at Jotapata in the year 69 C.E. when all other zealots there did so in a mass suicide pact. Flavius Vespasian, successor to Nero as Emperor of Rome, had come to conquer Judea. Strong resistance was offered at the fortress of Jotapata. After a 40 day siege, the fortress fell. Many chose suicide by flinging themselves over the walls or falling on their weapons. Josephus, however, sought concealment in a huge cistern in which he found 40 of his own soldiers. They all swore to die by their own hand in a mass suicide pact. When his turn came Josephus reneged and surrendered to the Romans.[11] In Josephus' *Antiquities of the Jews,* there are numerous examples of suicide cited, including the mass suicide at Masada.

SUICIDE IN THE TALMUD

The Talmud is replete with stories concerning suicide and martyrdom as well as discussions relating to the laws of burial and mourning for the deceased.[12]

---

11. *Ibid.,* pp. 276-290.
12. See also *Avodah Zarah* 17b; *Taanit* 18b; *Taanit* 29a; *Berakhot* 61b; *Pesachim* 50a; *Baba Batra* 10b; *Sanhedrin* 11a; 14a; 74a, b; 110b; and Unterman, I. Y., *Shevet Miyehudah* (Jerusalem, 1955), pp. 38ff; and Jakobovits, I., *Jewish Medical Ethics* (Block, New York, 1959), pp. 52-54.

Avodah Zarah 18a describes Rabbi Hanina ben Teradion's death by burning at the hands of the Romans. He was wrapped in the Scroll of the Law, bundles of branches were placed around him and these were set ablaze. The Romans also brought tufts of wool which they had soaked in water, placing them over his heart to prevent a quick death. When his disciples pleaded with him to open his mouth so that the fire consume him more quickly, he replied that one is not to accelerate one's own death. The executioner asked him: "Rabbi, if I raise the flame and remove the tufts of wet wool from your heart, will I enter the life to come?" Yes was the reply. The executioner did as he proposed and the Rabbi died speedily. The executioner then jumped into the fire and was burned to death. A voice from heaven exclaimed that Rabbi Hanina ben Teradion and his executioner had been assigned to the world to come.

Another case of suicide is related in *Baba Batra* 3b. Herod was the slave of the Hasmonean house of the Maccabees and had set his eyes on a certain maiden of that house. One day he heard a voice from heaven saying that every slave that rebels now will succeed. So he killed the entire household but spared the maiden. When she saw that he wanted to marry her, she ran up to the roof and cried out: "whoever comes and says that he is from the Hasmonean house is a slave since I alone am left of it and I am throwing myself down from this roof." Herod loved her so that he preserved her body in honey for seven years.

The suicide of a Roman officer who saved the life of Rabbi Gamliel is portrayed in Tractate *Taanit* (fol. 29a). When Turnus Rufus the wicked destroyed the Jewish Temple, Rabbi Gamliel was condemned to death. A high officer came to the house of study to search for him but Rabbi Gamliel hid. The officer found him and asked him secretly: "If I save you, will you bring me into the world to come?" The answer was affirmative. The officer made Rabbi Gamliel swear to it and then he (the officer) mounted the roof and threw himself down and died. The Romans annulled the decree against Rabbi Gamliel according to their tradition that the death of one of their leaders (i.e. the officer's suicide) is a punishment for an evil decree. Thereupon a voice from

SUICIDE

heaven was heard saying that this high officer was destined to enter the world to come.

Two nearly identical stories are told in Tractates *Chullin* (fol. 94a) and *Derech Eretz Rabbah* (Chapter 9, fol. 57b). Because of an incident that once occurred, it was decreed that guests may not give any of the food that is set before them to the host's son or to his servant or deputy unless they have received the host's permission to do so. The incident was that in a time of scarcity a man invited three guests to his house and only had 3 eggs which he set before them. When the host's (hungry) child entered and stood before them, one of the guests took his portion and gave it to him; the second guest did the same and so did the third. When the father came in and saw his son with one egg in his mouth and holding two in his hands he picked him up to his full height and flung him to the ground so that he died. When the mother saw her child dead, she went up to the roof, threw herself down and died. On seeing this, the father also went up to the roof, threw himself down and died. Rabbi Eliazar ben Jacob said: "Because of this, 3 souls perished."

A related incident that terminated in suicide is told in Tractate *Chullin* (fol. 94a). A man had sent his friend a barrel of wine and there was oil floating at the mouth of the barrel leading the recipient to believe that the whole barrel contained oil. He invited some guests to partake of it. When he came and found that it was only wine, he went and hanged himself out of shame because he had nothing else prepared to set before his guests. As a result, it was decreed that a man should not send to his neighbor a barrel of wine with oil floating on top of it.

Another Talmudic episode of suicide is found in the commentary of Rashi on *Avodah Zarah* 18b. Rabbi Meir is said to have fled to Babylon. One of the reasons given is "because of the incident of (his wife) Beruria." The incident concerns the fact that Rabbi Meir's wife once taunted him regarding the Rabbinic adage that women are temperamentally light headed. He replied that one day she would testify to its truth. Subsequently she was enticed by one of her husband's disciples proving she was too weak to resist. She then committed suicide by strangulation.

A mass suicide is described in Tractate *Gittin* (fol. 57b) where 400 boys and girls are said to have been carried off for immoral purposes. They guessed what they were wanted for and said to themselves that if we drown in the sea we shall attain the life in the future world as portrayed in Psalms 68:23. The girls leaped into the sea first and the boys followed.

In *Gittin* 57b is related the story from the Second Book of Maccabees of the woman and her seven martyred sons. The sons were killed one by one by Emperor Antiochus Epiphanes for refusing to serve an idol. As the last son was being led away to be killed, his mother said to him: "My son, go and say to your father Abraham: Thou didst bind one (son to the altar, i.e. Isaac), but I have bound seven altars." Then she went up on a roof and threw herself down and was killed. A voice thereupon came forth from heaven saying, *"A joyful mother of children"* (Psalms 113:9).

Another incident is related in Tractate *Berakhot* (fol. 23a). A certain student once left his phylacteries on the side of the road in a hole before entering a privy. A harlot passed by and took them. She came to the house of learning and said: "See what so and so gave me for hire." When the student heard this, he went to the top of a roof and threw himself down and killed himself.

The rules and regulations governing suicide are discussed in at least two Tractates of the Talmud. In *Baba Kamma* 61a is found the following: "No Halakhah may be quoted in the name of one who surrenders himself to meet death for the words of the Torah." Further in the same Tractate (91b) we find: ". . . who is the *Tana* that maintains that a man may not injure himself? It could hardly be said that he was the *Tana* of the teaching: *'And surely your own blood of your souls will I require'* (Genesis 9:5) which Rabbi Eleazer interpreted to mean that I will require your blood if shed by the hands of yourselves (i.e. suicide), for murder is perhaps different . . ." Rashi interprets this Scriptural verse to mean that even though one strangles oneself so that no blood flows, still I will require it.

The major Talmudic discussion of rules governing suicide is found in Chapter 2 of Tractate *Semakhot*. Here we are told that we do not occupy ourselves at all with the funeral rites of someone who committed suicide willfully. Rabbi Ishmael said: we exclaim over him "Alas for a lost (life). Alas for a lost (life)." Rabbi Akiba said to him: "Leave him unmourned; speak neither well nor ill of him." Further "we do not rend garments for him, nor bare the shoulder (as signs of mourning), or deliver a memorial address over him. We do, however, stand in a row for him (at the cemetery after the funeral to offer condolences) and recite the mourner's benediction for him because this is respectful for the living (relatives). The general rule is that we occupy ourselves with anything that is intended as a matter of honor for the living . . ."

The Talmud (*Semachot*, Chapter 2, Rule 2) defines an intentional suicide. It is not he who climbed to the top of a tree and fell down and died, nor he who ascended to the top of a roof and fell down and died as these may have been accidents. Rather, a willful suicide is one who calls out: "Look, I am going to the top of the roof or to the top of the tree, and I will throw myself down that I may die." When people see him go up to the top of the tree or roof and fall down and die, then he is considered to have committed suicide willfully. A person found strangled or hanging from a tree or lying dead on a sword is presumed not to have committed suicide intentionally and none of the funeral rites are withheld from him.

The Talmud (*ibid.*, Rules 4 and 5) next relates two childhood suicides and considers neither an intentional suicide. One case concerns the son of Gornos of Lydda who ran away from school, and the other case is that of a child in Bnei B'rak who broke a bottle on the Sabbath. In each case, the father threatened to punish the child and out of fear each child destroyed himself in a pit. Rabbi Tarfon in the former case, and Rabbi Akiba in the latter case ruled that these are not willful suicides and therefore none of the funeral rites should be withheld.

Suicide in the Midrash

In the Midrash Rabbah, Ecclesiastes (Chapter 10, 7; fol. 26b) the story is told of Rabbi Akiba walking (barefoot) to Rome when met by a eunuch officer of the Emperor riding on a horse. The officer asked him whether he was the famous Rabbi of the Jews and he answered yes. In order to embarrass Rabbi Akiba, the eunuch said three things: "he who rides on a horse is a king, he who rides on a donkey is a free man and he whose feet have shoes on is a human being; he who has none of these is worse than a dead person." Rabbi Akiba replied saying three things: "one's beard is one's majestic countenance, happiness of heart is one's wife and the inheritance of G-d is to have children; woe is the man who is lacking all three. Not only that but Scriptures states, *"I have seen servants upon horses and princes walking as servants upon the earth"* (Eccles. 10:7). When the eunuch officer heard these words, he knocked his head against a wall until he died.

Another case of intentional suicide is related in Midrash Rabbah on Genesis (65:22; fol. 130b). The case is that of Jakum of Tzeroroth, nephew of Rabbi Jose ben Jo'ezer of Tzeredah. Jakum taunted Rabbi Joseph Meshitha and, as self punishment, subjected himself to the four modes of execution inflicted by the courts: stoning, burning, decapitation and strangulation. He took a post, planted it into the earth, raised a wall of stones around it and tied a cord to it. He made a fire in front of it and fixed a sword in the middle of the post. He hanged himself on the post, the cord was burned through and he was strangled. The sword caught him while the wall of stones fell upon him and he was burned.

Suicide in the Codes of Jewish Law

In his *Mishneh Torah* (Laws of Mourning, Chapter 1, Section 11), Maimonides states:

> For one who has committed suicide intentionally we do not occupy ourselves at all (with the funeral rites), and we do not mourn for him nor eulogize him. However, we do stand in a row

for him and we recite the mourner's benediction and we do all that is intended as a matter of honor for the living.

Maimonides then defines an intentional suicide exactly as defined in Tractate *Semakhot*.

The commentators on Maimonides' code, Rabbi David ben Zimra (*Radvaz* 1479 to 1598), Rabbi Joseph Karo (*Keseph Mishneh* 1488 to 1575) and Rabbi Abraham di Boton (*Lechem Mishneh* 1560 to 1609) all point out that Maimonides considers mourning an honor for the dead and therefore prohibited.

Code of Jacob ben Asher (Tur):

Rabbi Jacob ben Asher (Section *Yoreh Deah* No. 345) codifies the section of the Talmud from Tractate *Semakhot* (vide surpra) nearly verbatim. He states that we do not rend garments, bare the shoulder or eulogize the willful suicide victim. However, we do stand in a row to offer condolences to the family at the cemetery and we utter the mourner's benediction for these are intended as a matter of honor for the living relatives. Rabbi Jacob ben Asher then continues by saying that the prohibition of rending the garments refers only to distant relatives but the immediate relatives who have to mourn the deceased should rend their garments as a sign of mourning. This is diametrically opposed to Maimonides. The *Shulkhan Arukh* follows Maimonides.

Rabbi Jacob ben Asher (*Tur*) defines a willful suicide as it had been defined in Tractate *Semakhot*. However, a child who committed suicide even willfully is not considered to have attained his full measure of intelligence. Similarly, he continues, anyone who commits suicide in unusual circumstances such as King Saul is not considered a willful suicide and he is entitled to all funeral rites. According to Rabbi Joseph Karo (*Bet Josef*) and Rabbi Joel Sirkash (*Bet Chadash*) in their commentaries on Jacob ben Asher, the latter statement in the *Tur* is based upon Rabbi Moses ben Nachman's (*Nachmanides* 1092 to 1167) work entitled *Sefer Ha'adam*.

Code of Joseph Karo (Shulkhan Arukh):

Karo's Code is based primarily upon the earlier Codes of Isaac Alfasi, Maimonides and Asher ben Yechiel (father of Jacob ben Asher). Karo seems to combine the Talmudic (Tractate *Semakhot* vide supra) and Maimonidean regulations regarding suicide. He states (Section *Yoreh Deah* No. 345) that we do not occupy ourselves at all for anyone who has committed suicide willfully. We do not mourn for him (contrary to Jacob ben Asher but in agreement with Maimonides) nor eulogize him nor rend garments for him nor bare the shoulder. However, all that is in honor of the living, such as standing in a row to offer condolences to the relatives of the deceased, is performed.

Several commentators on Karo including Rabbi Shabbetai Hakohen (*Sifsei Kohen* 1621 to 1662), Rabbi Zechariah Mendel of Cracow (*Be'er Hetev,* 17th century) and Rabbi Abraham Zvi Eisenstadt (*Pitchei Teshuva* 1813 to 1868) point out that Jacob ben Asher's Code differs from Karo in that the former does require garment rending and mourning of close relatives of the deceased. Rabbi Shabbetai Hakohen also quotes Rabbi Solomon ben Abraham Adret (*Rashba* 1215 to 1310) who in one of his several thousand Responsa (No. 763) explains that "we do not occupy ourselves at all" as cited from the Talmud and Maimonides does not refer to the burial itself. Rather, only the rites surrounding the funeral are withheld but the deceased must be buried.

Suicide in Recent Rabbinic Writings

Responsa literature on suicide is rather sparse. Rabbi Moses Schreiber (*Responsa Chatam Sofer—Yoreh Deah* No. 326) was asked concerning a person found drowned in a river. Rabbi Schreiber defines in great legal detail what a willful suicide is in Jewish law. He seeks legal technicalities such as fear, anger, emotional instability on the part of the victim which, if present, would remove the deceased from being considered an intentional suicide. He thus justifies the actions of Saul and Ahitophel. Rabbi Schreiber concludes that laws of mourning, including the recitation of the Kaddish prayer, are observed even for an intentional suicide victim.

Rabbi Yechiel Michel Toktzinski, in his two volume work entitled *Gesher Hachayim* (Jerusalem 1960) devotes an entire chapter (no. 25) to a discussion of suicide. The person who commits willful suicide is considered a murderer. It matters not whether he kills someone else or himself since his own soul is not his, just as someone else's soul is not his. Would we be able to bring this man to justice in this world, he would be adjucated as any murderer. In fact, he may be so judged in Heaven above.

The thirteenth century *Sefer Chasidim* written by Rabbi Judah the Pious One states (No. 675) that even one who neglects the preservation of his health is guilty of partially murdering himself. Rabbi Toktzinski states that it may even be a graver sin to commit suicide than to murder someone else for several reasons. Firstly, by killing himself, a person removes all possibility of repentance. Secondly, death in most circumstances is the greatest atonement for one's sins (Tractate *Yoma* 86); however, in a suicide's death there has been committed a cardinal transgression rather than expiation. A third reason why Judaism abhors suicide is that the person who takes his own life asserts by this act that he denies the Divine mastery and ownership of his life, his body and his soul. The willful suicide further denies his Divine creation. Our Sages compare the departure of a soul from a human body to a Torah Scroll which has been consumed by fire. Thus, a person who commits suicide can be likened to one who burns a Sefer Torah.

He who takes his own life is also one who denies in the Judaic teaching of the immortality of the soul and in the eternal existence of Almighty G-d. Such a person will have to answer to Heavenly judgment in the world to come as our Rabbis of Blessed memory stated "He who willfully destroys himself has no share in the world to come."

Martyrdom in Judaism

The subject of suicide is intertwined with the topic of martyrdom since many suicides are committed as an act of martyrdom. The Jewish attitude toward martyrdom is based upon the following passage in Leviticus (18:5): *Ye shall therefore keep my ordinances and my judgments which, if a man do, he shall live in them: I am the Eternal.* The Rabbis deduce from the words "he shall live" that martyrdom is prohibited save for idolatry, adultery and murder (*Sanhedrin* 74a). All other commandments may be transgressed if life is in danger in order that "he shall live." Martyrdom includes both the ending of one's own life for the sanctification of the Name of G-d (Levit. 22:32) or allowing oneself to be killed in times of religious persecution rather than transgress Biblical commandments. Perhaps the best known example of martyrdom in Jewish life are the ten famous scholars executed or martyred by the Roman state at different times for their insistence on teaching the Torah. The martyrdom of Hananiah, Mishael and Azariah, friends of Daniel, is portrayed in the Book of Daniel and in Genesis *Rabbah* (Chapter 34, 13 fol. 72). The martyrdoms of Rabbi Hanina ben Teradion and his wife are depicted in Tractate *Avodah Zara* (fol. 17b). In Tractate *Taanith* (fol. 18b) is related the story of Shemaiah and his brother Achiyah (identified as Julianus and Pappus), the martyrs of Lydda, who took upon themselves the guilt for the death of the Emperor's daughter in order to save the people as a whole. In the same Tractate (fol. 29a) is the legend which declares that when the First Temple was destroyed by fire, many priests leaped into the flames. Numerous other incidents of martydom are related in the Talmud (Tractates *Berachoth* fol. 61b, *Pesachim* fol. 50a, *Baba Bathra* fol. 10b, *Sanhedrin* fols. 11a, 14a, 74a, 110b).

In addition the Codes of Jewish Law including Maimonides (*Yesode Hatorah,* Chapter 5) and Karo (*Yoreh Deah,* Chapter 157) deal with the subject of martyrdom in detail.

Summary and Conclusions

Judaism regards suicide as a criminal act and strictly forbidden by Jewish law. The cases of suicide in the Bible as well as from the Apocrypha, Talmud and Midrash took place under unusual and extenuating conditions.

In general a suicide is not accorded full burial honors. The Talmud and Codes of Jewish Law decree that rending one's garments, delivering memorial addresses and other rites of mourning which are an honor for the dead are not to be performed for a suicide victim. The strict definition of a suicide for which these laws apply is one who had previously announced his intentions and then killed himself immediately thereafter by the method he announced. Children are never regarded as deliberate suicides and are afforded all burial rites. Similarly, those who commit suicide under extreme physical or mental strain, or while not in full possession of their faculties, or in order to atone for past sins are not considered as willful suicides and none of the burial and mourning rites are withheld.

These considerations may condone the numerous acts of suicide and martyrdom committed by Jews throughout the centuries, from the priests who leaped into the flames of the burning Temple to the martyred Jews in the time of the Crusades, from the Jewish suicides during the medieval persecutions to the martyred Jews in recent pogroms. Only for the sanctification of the Name of the Lord would a Jew intentionally take his own life or allow it to be taken as a symbol of his extreme faith in G-d. Otherwise intentional suicide would be strictly forbidden because it constitutes a denial of the Divine creation of man, of the immortality of the soul and of the atonement of death.

Chapter XII

Creation Versus Evolution

INTRODUCTION

Few books have created such a lasting storm of controversy as did Charles Darwin's *The Origin of Species,* published on November 24, 1859. Darwin's theory of evolution stirred up popular debate to fever pitch. Today, in almost every country throughout the world, the theory of evolution is accepted and taught. No textbook on biology, at high school, college or graduate school level is devoid of Darwinism. Even some children's books contain instruction in evolutionary theory.

This seemingly total acceptance of the theory of evolution is not confined to schoolbooks. Whenever the subject of the origin of life or the origin of man is discussed in newspapers, on the radio or on television, the opening comments usually begin with a phrase such as "millions of years ago . . .". If evolution is a fact, then what the Bible says about G-d must be wrong.

The other extreme is to totally deny the validity of the theory of evolution and to look solely at the Biblical account of creation and the origin of man. Must a religious person, Jew or non-Jew, necessarily adopt the latter viewpoint? Must the scientist, of necessity, subscribe to the former opinion? Cannot a scientist also be religious and, conversely, cannot a religious person also be a scientist?

The argument of creation versus evolution is only a small part of the larger question of religion versus science. Here too one might ask: Is religion right and science wrong? Or is science right and religion wrong? I would like to subscribe to the third possibility, namely that both science and religion can coexist and that both creation and evolution may be right. Such an approach should not be construed by the reader as "straddling the fence" or "buttering one's bread on both sides" or "having one's cake and eating it too." Rather it is an attempt to rationalize the two seemingly opposing viewpoints as seen through the eyes of a deeply religious Jewish physician.

Parenthetically one might mention the fourth alternative, namely that both science and religion are wrong and that both evolution and creation are wrong. Very few, if any people at all, subscribe to this viewpoint by offering another explanation for the existence of man and the world.

Science and Religion

Before discussing evolution and creation, a brief mention of the science and religion debate seems in order. One can approach the problem from several viewpoints. It would be very easy to say that science and religion deal with totally different aspects of the same subject and therefore, cannot conflict. For example, if one analyzed New York City from social, political, economic and other viewpoints, one would arrive at three different analyses of the same subject but from totally different, not necessarily contradictory, but perhaps interrelated aspects. Similarly religion and science may look at the same subject but on separate levels, not necessarily contradictory.

Such an approach is depicted by Spero[1] who quotes Rabbi Abba Hillel Silver who said: "The conflict between religion and science is more apparent than real. There is no fundamental issue between them. . . . As soon as religion and science discover their legitimate sphere, the conflict ceases. . . . Science investigates, religion interprets. One seeks causes, the other ends. . . ."

In a similar vein, Spero quotes a famous scientist who said: "Science . . . seeks the answer to the question, HOW does the natural world function? The supernatural world is the sphere of religion. The question which religion seeks to answer is WHY does the universe

---

1. Spero, S., "Does the Science-Religion Conflict Rest on a Mistake?", *Tradition*, 9(4):119-130, (Spring) 1968.

work as it does." Here again we see the "distinct spheres" approach to science and religion. Sol Roth, whose work[2] is analyzed in depth by Spero, also challenges the fundamental assumptions on which the conflict between science and religion is based. He shows that science and religion "belong to different universes of discourse precluding the possibility of contradiction." He further charges that the centuries old conflict between religion and science is fictitious and is based on misunderstanding.

A more erudite enunciation of this point of view is that of Kasher who states[3]: "The whole problem of conflicts between religion and science is a pseudo-problem. The various disciplines, through their differing methodologies, construct systems of acceptable established propositions and theories. There can be no contradiction between the affirmation of a particular proposition within the context of one discipline and the negation of the same proposition within the context of another discipline since what we are really confronted with here are two totally different concepts of truth — the one defined by the methodology of the other . . ." Kasher examines the fundamental assumptions for all discussions of religion and science. Among these are assumptions that participants in such discussions share a common language, in a uniform manner, directly intelligible to all, and that various different disciplines which are defined each by its use of its own methodology, are autonomous and self contained, from the point of view of content. Thus Kasher describes not the CONTENT of discussions about science and religion but the METHODOLOGY of the discussions.

Another similar but not identical approach is to look at science and religion as converging on a common goal from two opposite directions. A religious person conforms to the ancient Israelite pronouncement "let us obey first and then we will listen." That is, explanations for the

2. Roth, S., *Science and Religion*. Studies in Torah Judaism, New York. Yeshiva University Press, 1966.
3. Kasher, A., "Fundamental Assumptions for Discussion on Religion and Science," *Tradition*, 10(1):87-99, (Summer) 1968.

things we do and the rituals we perform are sought after first complying with the commandments by accepting them on blind faith. For some Biblical precepts (*Chukim*), no logical explanations will ever be found. For others (*Mishpatim*), continuing education and learning and study of Torah will provide insights into the why and wherefores of those precepts. In either the case of *Chukim* or *Mishpatim* we accept and perform on blind faith and this is, in essence, the definition of Judaism.

On the other hand, a scientist seeks explanations in advance before he believes in the scientific truths he discovers. Thus, if he cannot smell, touch, feel, see or hear something, it does not exist. This oversimplified contrast between the scientist and the religious person is perhaps fallacious in that both are really based on unprovable axioms or assumptions. The religionist believes in faith although he cannot prove it. The scientist begins with unprovable axioms such as "matter cannot be destroyed or created."

Berkovits[4] expresses the aforementioned thought more vividly when he says: "A scientific world view is not science, but the *leap of faith* undertaken by the scientist who ventures to interpret the whole of reality on the basis of the exact knowledge gained from the scientific investigation of a relatively small segment of the whole. Neither is a religious world-view religion. It too, is a *leap of faith,* which attempts to grasp the essential nature of the whole in the light of a necessarily limited experience and a specific insight." Berkovits thus indicates that both science and religion are based on unprovable axioms and assumptions i.e., faith. Therefore, it is not at all unreasonable to espouse the thought that since the basic assumptions of both religion and science are not within the realm of provability, they may both be compatible and need not be contradictory.

One definition of a scientific theory[5] is that it is a "body of logically

---

4. Berkovits, E., "The Scientific and the Religious World View," *Intercom* (Association of Orthodox Jewish Scientists), 6(2):6-12, (January) 1965.

5. Klahr, C. N., "Science versus Scientism," *Intercom,* 6(2):13-16, (January) 1965.

related hypotheses i.e., guesses, based on an incomplete collection of facts and concerned with things still unmeasured. But the things discussed must be susceptible to measurement . . . otherwise it is not a scientific theory. . . ." Such a declaration affirms that certain measurable things are subject to scientific proof but science remains, in general, only part fact and part theory.

The entire discussion so far concerning the possible conflict of religion and science emphasizes that these two areas of learning actually blend with each other and perhaps harmonize mankind's quest for both moral exactitude and scientific precision. Many of today's deeply religious Jewish scientists espouse this viewpoint. Psychologist Boris Levinson states[6] that "the domains of science and religion are in no way antagonistic to each other even though the individual functions are entirely different. The purpose of science is to learn facts and data . . . the purpose of religion is to develop the ideals, the consciences and aspirations of mankind. . . . Far from being antagonistic, science and religion can be mutually supplementary . . . it was not a rare occurrence that good teachers of Judaism were at the same time well at home in the sciences of their age . . .". We need mention only a few, such as Maimonides and Nachmanides in the middle ages, and Samuel, Rabbi Chiya, Rabbi Ishmael and Mar Bar Rav Ashi in Talmudic times. All were simultaneously physicians and great Talmudic scholars.

Radiologist Melvin Zelefsky[7] asserts that "faith does not falter before the scientific advance. Scientific information transforms faith into a more deep and profound religious experience. Science expands religion, it does not contain it."

In all fairness, it must be said that not all Orthodox Jewish scientists subscribe to the blending and harmony of science and religion. Some still propound the thesis that science and religion conflict. For example, physicist Alvin Radkowsky[8] states that "it is acknowledged today by

---

6. Levitan, T., "The Scientist and Religion," *The Synagogue Light,* 35(5):5-7, (February) 1969.

7. *Ibid.,* 36(5):5-6, (January) 1970.

8. *Ibid.,* 35(8):5-6, (May) 1969.

philosophers of both science and religion that the controversy arising out of conflict between these two types of knowledge . . . is not a thing of the past. . . . The claims of secularism which challenge the intellectual integrity of the Jewish faith . . . are fallacious." Mathematician Lewis Berenson[9] asserts that all science is based on theory and subjectivity and that new facts disprove old theories.

Before proceeding to the discussion of evolution and creation, I would like to illustrate, using three examples, the synthesis of religion and science and the lack of contradiction and antagonism in spite of much controversy.

The first example is the exodus from Egypt. The truly orthodox Jew believes in the many miracles wrought by G-d for the Israelites during their exodus from Egypt several thousand years ago. Professor Immanuel Velikowsky, in a book entitled *Worlds in Collision,* attempts to explain every miracle of the exodus from Egypt by natural means. Even the splitting of the Red Sea is described by Velikowsky as having transpired due to a unique occurrence of a complex constellation of astronomical events. Certainly, no religious Jew could accept such an interpretation as the sole explanation of the historical events described in the Book of Exodus. It is conceivable, however, although not provable, that G-d wrought all the miracles of that era through natural means.

A second example is the story of prophet Elisha and the Shunammite woman's son who died of sunstroke. The child's revival by Elisha is described (II Kings 4:34-35) as follows: "And he went up and lay upon the child, and put his mouth upon his mouth, and his eyes upon his eyes, and his hands upon his hands; and he crouched over him; and the child sneezed seven times and the child opened his eyes." Some consider this incident to have been nothing less than a miracle. Rabbi David Kimchi (*Radak*), however, states that Elisha attempted to breathe on the child to provide warmth from his natural body heat that emanated from his mouth and eyes. *Radak* further asserts that most miracles are performed with direction and guidance from natural

9. *Ibid.,* 35(9):5-6, (June-July) 1969.

or worldly actions. Rabbi David Altschul (*Metzudath David*) states that Elisha tried to pour some of the life of his own body into the limbs of the child. Rabbi Levi ben Gershon (*Ralbag*) gives an identical interpretation but adds ". . . he (Elisha) did this after he prayed." These commentators thus seem to consider a combination of natural and miraculous events as having contributed to the child's revival. Once again it is conceivable and even plausible that G-d wrought the miracle of restoring the child's life through natural means i.e., artificial respiration applied by Elisha.

The third example is the Six-Day War of 1967 between Israel and her Arab adversaries. The two sides of the picture are depicted by parasitologist Morris Goldman[10]: "For millions of Jews, myself included, the sequence and confluence of events in May and June of last year (1967) which led finally to the recovery of Old Jerusalem, were so improbable and had such apocalyptic overtones, that they could only be viewed as the clearest demonstration of Divine intervention that we could expect to see in our lifetimes. And yet all took place between men of flesh and blood wielding tangible fire and steel, all is describable at a secularist level, and all is no doubt so entombed in State Department memoranda." I would only add that once again it seems conceivable and even plausible that Divine intervention in this war was effected by natural means i.e., the tools of war and the spirit of the Israeli soldiers.

CREATION AND/OR EVOLUTION

We cannot ignore the theory of evolution, because of its wide acceptance throughout the world, and must therefore make attempts to cope with it. The authoritative *Encyclopedia Britannica* asserts: "We are not in the least doubt as to the fact of evolution. . . . The evidence by now is overwhelming." The standard biology text called *Biology for Today,* used in New York schools, states: "Living things

---

10. Goldman, M., "Man's Place in Nature," *Tradition,* 10(1):101, (Summer) 1968.

probably originated as single-celled organisms. These developed into more complex organisms. Effects of mutations accumulated, species changed and varied until thousands of different types of organisms existed." Even the famous children's book *The Giant Golden Book of Biology* says: "About 400 million years ago, plants and a few animals emerged onto the land . . . some of them began to be human, and about 50,000 years ago one such creature came to be our kind of man . . .". Other books proclaim apes to be our distant cousins, and that both man and the living apes descended from some ancient common ancestor.

Do the above and other "authoritative" sources make evolution an established fact? The evidence in support of evolution is not overwhelming and evolution is not an established fact. Evolution was, and still is, called the theory of evolution because it began as a theory, not as a fact. There are many gaps and failures in the theory of evolution. The hypothesis was formulated and facts were sought to support or reject it. Some facts have emerged to support evolution (e.g. mutations do occur) but even these facts are open to varying interpretations. The theory of evolution is a satisfying explanation of *some* of the evidence. All living forms, however, cannot be explained by evolution.

A recent writer[11] states that one should not become encased in scientific dogmatism but from time to time one must stop to think things out for oneself. Moses Maimonides, eight centuries ago, in both his philosophical and medical writings, attempts to eradicate preconceived notions and dictated dogmas. He encourages people to observe and experiment for themselves and to develop an attitude of keen criticism and skepticism toward accepted traditions and teachings even if these originate from as renowned a scholar or authority as Galen. Using this Maimonidean approach we can view the conflict, or lack thereof, between evolution and creation in four different ways: either

11. Kerkut, G. A., *Implications of Evolution*. Pergamon Press, New York, 1960. Chap. 2, pp. 6-17.

evolution is right and creation is wrong; or creation is right and evolution is wrong; or creation and evolution are both right and do not conflict or contradict each other; or creation and evolution are both wrong and some other explanation must be offered to explain the existence of the world.

I would like to reject outright the last of these possibilities since I know of no one, even the most outspoken atheist, who espouses the suggestion that both evolution and creation are wrong. Many scientists accept evolution as fact whereas most religious Jews would reject evolution entirely believing solely in creation as described in the Bible to explain life, man and the universe. As an Orthodox Jew, I would like to agree with the late Chief Rabbi of the British Commonwealth, J.H. Hertz, in support of the other alternative, namely that both creation and evolution are correct. Hertz asserts[12] that even if one accepts the fundamental dogma of Judaism that the "world was called into existence at the will of the One, Almighty and All-good G-d, . . . there is nothing inherently un-Jewish in the evolutionary concept of the origin and growth of forms of existence from the simple to the complex, and from the lowest to the highest . . .". Before expounding further on this theme, I would like to briefly define the theory of evolution and to discuss the two perhaps most complex questions in the evolution versus creation controversy, namely the age of the world and the origin of man.

What is the Theory of Evolution?

So many books have been written since Darwin's *The Origin of Species* that it would be superfluous to give a detailed account of the theory of evolution. The interested reader is referred to a massive three volume work entitled *Evolution After Darwin* (Edit. S. Tax, Chicago Univ. Press, 1960) which was published in honor of the centennial of the appearance of Darwin's *magnum opus*. One of many

12. Hertz, J. H., Additional Notes to Genesis, in his *The Pentateuch and Haftorahs*. London, Soncino Press, 1960, 2nd edition, pp. 193-202.

ways to summarize the theory of evolution is that of Kerkut[11] who lists seven basic assumptions which collectively form the basic theory of evolution:

1. Non-living things gave rise to living things i.e. spontaneous generation.
2. Spontaneous generation occurred only once.
3. Viruses, bacteria, plants and animals are all interrelated.
4. One-celled animals gave rise an many-celled animals.
5. Various invertebrates are interrelated.
6. Invertebrates gave rise to vertebrates.
7. Within vertebrates, fish gave rise to amphibia, amphibia to reptiles and reptiles to birds and mammals.

These seven assumptions are not capable of experimental verification. They assume that a certain series of events has occurred in the past. Even if one could today change a reptile into a mammal, it would not prove that this is the way it happened in the past. The scientist accepts upon faith that biogenesis occurred, that is life began somehow. But how? Some invoke the "primeval-atom theory" which says that a burst of radioactivity which began life occurred ten billion years ago. After the burst, natural laws took over. Others subscribe to the "steady state hypothesis" which says that there never was a creation. The Jewish view is enunciated by Maimonides in his 13 principles of faith — "I firmly believe that the Creator, blessed be His name, is both Creator and Guide of all created beings and that He alone has made, does make and will make all things." This belief, of course, is based on the first chapter in Genesis. None of these three points of view is provable, and thus the evolutionist stands on no firmer ground than the religionist in regard to the origin of life.

The second assumption in the theory of evolution holds that life was formed (or created) only once. If living material had developed on several occasions, one would expect a large number of distinct unrelated groups of animals. Yet, assumptions three through seven say that all living things are related in that the "higher forms evolved from the lower forms." Once again we theorize in an area that is not subject to scientific experimental verification.

The major evidence for evolution is that obtained from paleontology (study of fossils) and to a lesser degree from zoology, comparative anatomy and embryology. Thus, for example, the earliest rocks from the Cambrian era have no vertebrate fossils, rocks from the Devonian era contain fish fossils, rocks from the Carboniferous era have amphibia fossils, rocks from the Cretaceous, Jurassic and Triassic eras contain reptile fossils and rocks from the more recent Coenozoic era contain mammal fossils. It is beyond the scope of this paper and the competence of this writer to critically review all the evidence propounded in favor of the theory of evolution. Suffice it to say that there are many gaps and failures and the little evidence available is fragmentary. Darwin himself, in his *The Origin of Species*, stressed the imperfections in the geological and fossil evidence for evolution. We have to conclude that[13] "past events which can never be subjected to direct observation have to be inferred from the data provided by the material which is presently existing . . .".

How Old Is The World?

Is the world as we know it 5732 years old or is it ten billion years old? How can one tell? Is one to accept the Jewish calendar which uses the lower number? Or should one adhere to the higher number propounded by many natural scientists? Is 5732 reconcilable with ten billion? Are these two necessarily contradictory? I say no.

Let us briefly examine the ten billion figure. There are two major scientific approaches to dating the age of the world, the radioactive decay method and the stratigraphical method. In the radioactive decay approach, one measures the amount of radiation of certain isotopes such as carbon, potassium, uranium and others in rocks and plants. From this measured amount of radioactivity one can "back-

---

13. Le Cros Clark, W. E., "The Crucial Evidence for Human Evolution," *Proc. Amer. Philos. Soc.*, 103(2):159-172, 1959.

calculate" the duration of time the element must have been present, using the concept of half-time decay, that is the duration of time it takes for the radioactivity to halve. The major fallacy in this method is that it is based on the assumption that the rate of radioactive decay has remained constant over many centuries and eons. This may or may not be true. There are conflicting reports even in the scientific literature concerning deviations in radioactive decay rates, particularly of carbon 14. Furthermore, using different radioactive isotopes, one obtains results for the age of the world that differ widely. Finally, when samples of the same rock were given to several laboratories for carbon dating, differences of many thousands of years were reported by the individual laboratories.

The stratigraphical or geological method of estimating the age of the world measures the thickness of each layer of stratum of rock and earth. From the known rate of deposition and erosion of layers, one calculates the age of the earth. This method is also crude, no more than an estimate, and also assumes that no sudden changes occurred. The few centuries where man has been observing nature form too brief an interval by which to measure geological action in all past time. Rabbi Dr. Elie Munk (*Das Licht Der Ewigkeit*, 1935, p. 115) specifically asserts that changes in natural phenomena did in fact take place. He states that when man left paradise, he succumbed to the forces of nature with a progressive decline in physical strength. Nature too progressively weakened. Evidence cited by Rabbi Munk are the dinosaur skeletons which he interprets as extinct supercreatures, perhaps the giants or *Bnei Anakim* of the Pentateuch. Therefore, concludes Rabbi Munk, since nature changed, one cannot calculate the age of the world from natural phenomena.

Although the major scientific methods of estimating the age of the world can be strongly criticized, is it still not possible that the 5732 and the 10 billion figures are both correct? One explanation is that each of the seven days of creation as described in the first chapter of Genesis represented a thousand or a million years. Such an opinion is enunciated by Rabbi Menachem Kasher (*Encyclopedia of Biblical Interpretation*. Genesis Vol. 1, 1953) who explains the phrase *and there was evening and there was morning, the sixth day* to mean that our system of time reckoning begins after the creation of heaven, earth and planets was finished; that is on the seventh day. The system of time measurement for the six days of creation was comprised of a separate and relative time for each day.

Another possible way of reconciling the 5732 and the 10 billion figures for the age of the world is the Midrash in Genesis which says that the Holy One blessed be He used to create worlds and destroy them again. That is, prior to the existence of the present universe which is presumably 5732 years old, certain "formless worlds issued... and then vanished, like sparks which fly from a red hot iron beaten by a hammer, that are extinguished as they separate themselevs from the burning mass . . . ours is the best of all possible worlds."[12] Thus the total duration of the "Fountain of Existence" including all the previous worlds which G-d created and destroyed, may perhaps be several billion years.

Maimonides denies the concept of earlier worlds being formed and annihilated. He asserts that time itself is one of the things created by Almighty G-d. Maimonides' own words speak eloquently for themselves[14]:

> "Now the world has not been created in a temporal beginning . . . because time belongs to the created things. . . . On the other hand, the statement which you find formulated by some of the Sages that affirms that time existed before the creation of the world, is very difficult to comprehend. For that is the opinion of Aristotle, which I have explained to you: he holds that time cannot be conceived to have a beginning; that is incongruous. Those who made this statement were conducted to it by their finding in Scripture the terms: *one day* (Genesis 1:5), a *second day* (Genesis 1:8). He who made this statement understood these terms according to their external sense and as follows: Inasmuch as a rotating sphere and a sun did not yet exist, whereby

---

14. Maimonides, M., *Guide of the Perplexed*. Part 2, Chapter 30 (translation of Shlomo Pines: Chicago Univ. Press, 1963, p. 349).

was *the first day* measured? They express their opinion in the following text (Midrash Genesis Rabbah, III): *The first day—Rabbi Judah, son of Rabbi Simon, said: Hence (we learn) that there existed before that an order of time. Rabbi Abuha said: Hence (we learn) that the Holy One may His name be blessed, used to create worlds and to destroy them (again).* This second opinion is even more incongruous than the first. Consider what was the difficulty for these two (Sages). It was the notion that time existed prior to the existence of this sun. . . . To sum up, you should not, in considering these points, take into account the statements made by this or that one. I have already made it known to you that the foundation of the whole law is the view that G-d had brought the world into being out of nothing without there having been a temporal beginning. For time was created, being consequent upon the motion of the sphere (i.e. the sun) which was created."

The Origin of Man

One cannot intelligently discuss the origin of man without commenting on the more general question of how did life originate. We have already mentioned that for evolutionists, a major and seemingly insurmountable hurdle to overcome is the problem of what started life or how did life begin. The concept of creation implies *"yesh may-ayin"* or creating something from nothing. No acceptable alternative has yet been offered by evolutionists although the primeval-atom theory and the steady state hypothesis briefly mentioned earlier in this paper are attempts to account for the origin of life. Nor can spontaneous generation be proved. Even Darwin himself, in his *Origin of Species* seems to believe in a Creator when he says that "there is grandeur in this view of life, with its several powers, having been originally breathed by the Creator into a few forms or into one."

The Biblical account of the origin of life, although not subject to scientific verification, is certainly reasonable and in harmony with the facts as we know them today. How logical and orderly the process of creation revealed in Genesis! First heaven and earth (*domem*), then plant life (*tzomeach*), then creatures of the sea and sky and then land animals (*chai*) and finally man (*medaber*). Evolution cannot explain the creation of the world, nor does the belief in the Creator of the world negate the possibility that evolution exists and occurs. Each created species is endowed with the ability to produce only its kind and no other kind. A dog cannot produce a kitten nor can an apple seed produce an orange tree. Within each species, however, evolution may or may not take place. Thus, the few scientifically proved facts concerning evolution can be readily explained and need not be refuted as untrue.

Turning to the origin of man, the same question arises as with the origin of the world. Evolutionists assert that humans have lived here on earth for hundreds of thousands of years but history offers no support for such a theory. The earliest records we have of human history i.e., civilization in Mesopotamia, go back only about 5000 years. The early stages of man's evolutionary progress remain a total mystery. It is perfectly reasonable to consider the creation of Adam and Eve by G-d to have been followed by "evolution" of man in the form we know him today. Perhaps Adam was a Neanderthal man. What is unacceptable to myself and other religionists is that man may have evolved from monkeys. No fossils have yet been found to liken man to apes.

With the creation of man, and perhaps his evolution from early man to modern man, begins a new non-biological evolution, the evolution of culture and ethics and morality. This process represents daily life of man practiced by the observant Jew according to the Torah, and possible by virtue of man's endowment with a feature non-existent in all lower forms of beings. I refer to the power of reasoning or intelligence, the power to select right from wrong. Such endowment, we believe, is a G-d given attribute of man that distinguishes him from animals. This concept is spoken of by evolutionists as cultural adaptation, which is an erudite expression that explains nothing however.

Jewish Views of Creation and Evolution

There is no doubt that every religious Jew believes that G-d created the world, including man. This creation of something from nothing is a feat that cannot be duplicated by any science or discipline. Many Rabbis and observant Jewish scientists espouse the view that evolution is totally and completely untrue and that creation alone explains everything we find in the world today. As already stated before, I disagree with this one-sided approach, and consider the few facts that evolutionists have in their support to be valid, but only in the overall context of the belief in creation. This thought is perhaps depicted by mathematician Berenson[9] who asserts that "an evolutionary process makes sense only if we also assume the existence of a higher force which guides this process toward its desired ends . . .".

The *Lubavitscher Rebbe,* Menachem M. Schneerson, in a public letter dated 18 Teveth 5722, states that "science formulates and deals with theories and hypotheses, while the Torah deals with absolute truths. These are two different disciplines where reconciliation is entirely out of place." This perspective seems somewhat distorted. Science not only formulates theories and hypotheses but attempts and often succeeds in proving them. The absolute truths of Torah, on the other hand, are absolute truths because we believe them to be so, not because we can scientifically prove them. The *Rebbe* seems to contradict himself when he distinguishes between "empirical and experimental science dealing with, and confined to describing and classifying observable phenomena, and speculative science, dealing with unknown phenomena, sometimes phenomena that cannot be duplicated in the laboratory." He thus admits that science not only deals with theories and hypotheses, as he enunciated earlier in his letter, but experiments and accumulates data and information.

I would not dissent from the *Rebbe*'s statement that observable data concerning the universe are only available for a short period of time, and thus to extrapolate to billions of years is incorrect. However, I would object to the *Rebbe*'s dogmatic statements such as "all scientists universally admit that atmospheric pressure, radioactivity and other cataclystic factors are different today than many years ago"; some scientists do and some don't. Nor could I agree with the dogmatic assertion that "evolution has not a shred of evidence to support it. . . . The theory of evolution has no bearing on the Torah account of Creation. For even if the theory of evolution of species were proven in laboratory tests, this would still not contradict the possibility of the world having been created as stated in the Torah, rather than through the evolutionary process. . . ." Mutations have in fact been observed in the laboratory and thus the *Lubavitscher Rebbe* seems to be saying exactly what I've been proposing throughout this essay, namely Creation by G-d occurred as in the Torah, but certain things can evolve within their own species.

Another modern Talmudic scholar, Rabbi Avigedor Miller,[15] espouses the sentiment that creation is completely correct and evolution is all wrong. He also begins with a dogmatic assertion, unacceptable to me, that "we need not refute evolutionists, for they have not produced a single proof." He continues by stating that:

> "The mathematical improbability of accidental evolution is staggering. E.g. take 10 cards numbered 1 to 10 and shuffle them. The chances that they will fall in numerical order are one in a billion. If there were 100 cards the chance would be 1 in many zillion. The improbability that a single cell should by chance develop into an ant is of astronomical proportions. The accidental develpment of 1 cell into an ant's leg requires hundreds of various sized and various shaped cells of various materials, all precision made and all precisely proportioned and all united by structure and by nerve and muscle connection to function as a unit. The improbability of such an accidental arrangement defies mathematical calculation. But even this is nothing compared to the human eye (lid, ducts, fluids, lens, retina, nine layers of rods and cones and nerves, etc.). It seems childish to believe that a single cell had the infinite foresight, and the enormous technical

15. Miller, A., *Rejoice O Youth.* New York, 1962. Published by the author, pp. 10 to 30.

knowledge of chemistry, physics, engineering and logistics, far beyond the combined knowledge of all mankind, to develop even part of the eye."

All these arguments bespeak against accidental development, thus requiring belief in a Creator with wisdom and purpose in His creations. True, but evolution as a process after creation is not ruled out by Rabbi Miller's line of reasoning.

Whereas the *Lubavitscher Rebbe* dismissed the fossil evidence for evolution by stating that conditions of fossilization in prehistoric times are unknown, or that perhaps G-d created ready fossils, Rabbi Miller goes further by showing that many fossils are actually fakes. He ridicules the thought that living beings acquired new forms by virtue of changing environment as follows:

> "When fish found themselves in shallow bottoms where their fins were useless, they spent the next million years developing their fins into feet for crawling when the need for food and self-protection necessitated the ability to fly . . . the fish flippers and the reptile scales spent the ensuing million years developing into wings and feathers . . ."

He also ridicules the theory of sudden mutation to explain change. "Where are men with tails and horns . . . or 3 breasted women? Such a chain of accidents is nothing less than the wildest of fantasies!"

What Rabbi Miller fails to acknowledge is that mutations are an observable scientific fact, and can be induced in the laboratory by radiation, viruses and certain chemicals. In his unique style of refutation of the theory of evolution, Rabbi Miller continues:

> "The ear has whorls and hollows to collect sound waves and channel them to the eardrum. This membrane, 1/10 of a mm. in thickness, has three layers . . . the malleus, the incus and the stapes are each cunningly and efficiently shaped for their varied functions. They transmit the sound impulses to the lymph in the internal ear, which then arouses nerve impulses in the 20 to 30,000 hair cells of the hearing nerve. To maintain equal air pressure on both sides of the eardrum, the inner ear is connected

by the Eustachian tube or the pharynx to admit air. . . . Considering that the components of the ear number in the tens of thousands and all must be coordinated by a master-plan, only a *lunatic* can claim this to be the result of a number of accidents."

Rabbi Miller's use of such strong language is perhaps an exaggeration. He seems to be admiring the marvels of nature. Fine! G-d created nature and now it runs by itself with the Creator overseeing it. Why could G-d not have created the evolutionary process as part of nature. Its existence is not at all disproved by Rabbi Miller's eloquent rhetoric. He concludes by saying that "evolution is a religion and its adherents defend it at all costs. It is a religion which requires the most stubborn faith . . . they refuse to admit creation by a Creator . . ." But what about the observant Jews who believe in both creation and evolution? What religion do they belong to, according to Rabbi Miller; the religion of evolution or the religion of creation? I say they belong to the religion of Judaism which affirms creation but does not necessarily negate evolution.

I have presented in some detail the pronouncements in evolution by two prominent Rabbis to provide the reader with the most prevalent Rabbinic view toward evolution. Let us now examine briefly how some Orthodox Jewish scientists approach evolution and creation.

Biologist Morris Goldman, in an article entitled *The Doctrine of Evolution by Natural Selection: A Critical Review*, concludes that "the thesis of Darwinian evolution is not a scientifically self-sufficient hypothesis, as is so often assumed. Instead, it is a doctrine resting on faith that satisfies the secularist yearnings of our age. As such, it can be rejected by the religious Jew . . ." But Divine creation can also not be proved and belief therein rests on faith. Why must the religious Jew necessarily reject evolution as incompatible with creation?

Physicist Alvin Radkowsky attempts to show[16] that the doctrine of evolution ultimately leads to a logical inconsistency which throws into

---

16. Radkowsky, A., "Judaism and the Technological Dilemma," *Proc. Ass'n. Orthodox Jewish Scientists*, Vol. 1, pp. 68-78, New York, 1961.

question the validity of all science. Biologist Edward Simon[17] shows that the evolutionary process of random mutation for gene function leads to an absurdity in respect to the inordinate amount of time required. Physicist Lee Spetner[18] criticizes both the "fact" and the "theory" of evolution pointing out fossil record gaps and inconsistencies. Biologist S. B. Ullman[19] states that the strength of the doctrine of evolution lies in that it denies the existence of a Creator of heaven and earth and the act of creation.

All the above Orthodox Jewish scientists seem to say: Creation: yes; evolution: no! None accept the possibility of both creation and evolution being correct. Spetner goes even further when he asserts[20] that "the theory of evolution is retained not because it is adequate to explain the facts, since it is not. It is retained because there is no theory to replace it." This seems to be an unwarranted conclusion. Spetner's thesis ends with the following declaration:

> "It would therefore be foolish for one to mold his philosophy, morals and ethics on the assumption that man is a mere chance descendant of a sub-microscopic molecule that happened to form in the primordial ocean some three billion years ago. Faith of some kind is necessary in order to establish for oneself any ethical and moral code. One is free, of course, to choose his faith. Some would start by believing that the scientific theories in current vogue represent absolute truth. Others would accept a way of life derived from a revelation witnessed by more than a million people whose testimony has been handed down, withstanding the test of time for a hundred generations. I prefer the latter."

I ask again: why totally reject even the few facts concerning evolution? Why cannot the observant Jew who believes in Divine

---

17. Simon, E. H., "On Gene Creation," *Ibid.*, pp. 87-91.
18. Spetner, L. M., "A New Look at the Theory of Evolution," *Ibid.*, pp. 79-86.
19. Ullman, S. B., *Chinuch Umada Le'or Hayahaduth* (Education and Science in the Light of Judaism). Jerusalem, Newman Publishers, 1963, 291 pp.
20. Spetner, L. M., "Evolution — Fact or Theory," *The Jewish Observer*, January, 1966, pp. 16-19.

creation of the world and of man also accept the doctrine of evolution on a limited basis. Obviously the believing Jew cannot accept all that is propounded by strict evolutionists, but the concept of evolution with some factual support does not negate belief in the Creator.

I fully realize that the approach to evolution and creation that I have adopted is not accepted by the majority of Rabbinic or Orthodox Jewish scientific opinion which totally rejects evolution. However, the minority view should be heard and is most eloquently and forcefully enunciated by the late Chief Rabbi of the British Commonwealth, J. H. Hertz[12]:

> "Now, while the fact of creation has to this day remained the first of the articles of the Jewish Creed, there is no uniform and binding belief as to the manner of creation, i.e. as to the process whereby the universe came into existence. The manner of the Divine creative activity is presented in varying forms and under differing metaphors by Prophet, Psalmist and Sage; by the Rabbis in Talmudic times, as well as by our medieval Jewish thinkers.
>
> In face of this great diversity of views as to the manner of creation, there is, therefore, nothing inherently un-Jewish in the evolutionary conception of the origin and growth of forms of existence from the simple to the complex, and from the lowest to the highest. The Biblical account itself gives expression to the same general truth of gradual ascent from amorphous chaos to order, from inorganic to organic, from lifeless matter to vegetable, animal and man; *insisting, however, that each stage is no product of chance, but is an act of Divine will*, realizing the Divine purpose, and receiving the seal of the Divine approval. Such, likewise, is in effect the evolutionary position. Behind the orderly development of the universe there must be a Cause, at once controlling and permeating the process. Allowing for all the evidence in favour of interpreting existence in terms of the evolutionary doctrine, there still remain facts—tremendous facts —to be explained; viz. the origin of life, mind, conscience, human personality. For each of these, we must look back to the Creative Omnipotence of the Eternal Spirit.

MAN IS THE GOAL AND CROWN OF CREATION—he is fundamentally distinguished from the lower creation, and is akin to the Divine. Man, modern scientists declare, is cousin to the anthropoid ape. But it is not so much the descent, as the *ascent* of man, which is decisive. Furthermore, it is not the resemblance, but the *differences* between man and the ape, that are of infinite importance.

Nor is the Biblical account of the creation of man irreconcilable with the view that certain forms of organized being have been endowed with the capacity of developing, in G-d's good time and under the action of suitable environment, the attributes distinctive of man. 'G-d formed man of the dust of the ground' (Gen. II, 7). Whence that dust was taken is not, and cannot be, of fundamental importance. Science holds that man was formed from the lower animals; are they not too 'dust of the ground'? 'And G-d said, *"Let the earth bring forth the living creature"* '— this command, says the Midrash, includes Adam as well. The thing that eternally matters is the breath of Divine and everlasting life that He breathed into the being coming from the dust. By virtue of the Divine impact, a new and distinctive creature made its appearance—man, dowered with an immortal soul.

G-d the Creator and Lord of the Universe, which is the work of His goodness and wisdom; and Man, made in His image, who is to hallow his week-day labours by the blessedness of Sabbath-rest—such are the teachings of the Creation chapter. Its purpose is to reveal these teachings to the children of men—and not to serve as a textbook of astronomy, geology or anthropology. Its object is not to teach scientific facts; but to proclaim highest religious truths respecting G-d, Man and the Universe. The 'conflict' between the fundamental realities of Religion and the established facts of Science is seen to be unreal as soon as Religion and Science each recognizes the true borders of its dominion."

Epilogue

If one takes the trouble to read Darwin's *The Origin of Species,* one finds a very enlightening insight into Darwin's view of the world. It appears that Darwin himself believed in G-d the Creator as he himself states in the last paragraph of his book:

> "It is interesting to contemplate a tangled bank, clothed with many plants of many kinds, with birds singing on the bushes, with various insects flitting about, and with worms crawling through the damp earth, and to reflect that these elaborately constructed forms, so different from each other, and dependent upon each other in so complex a manner, have all been produced by laws acting around us. These laws, taken in the largest sense, being Growth and Reproduction; Inheritance which is almost implied by reproduction; Variability from the indirect and direct action of the conditions of life, and from use and disuse, a ratio of increase so high as to lead to a Struggle for Life, and as a consequence to Natural Selection, entailing Divergence of Character and the Extinction of less improved forms. Thus, from the war of nature, from famine and death, the most exalted object which we are capable of conceiving, namely, the production of the higher animals, directly follows. There is grandeur in this view of life, with its several powers, having been originally breathed by the Creator into a few forms or into one; and that, whilst this planet has gone cycling on according to the fixed laws of gravity, from so simple a beginning endless forms most beautiful and most wonderful have been and are being evolved."

The phrase . . . "life with its several powers having been originally breathed by the Creator into a few forms . . ." lends credence to the thought that perhaps Darwin himself believed in both creation and evolution. This synthesis of the two doctrines and attempted resolution of possible conflict between them has been the purpose of this essay.

STUDIES IN TORAH JUDAISM

* 1. (a) "The Philosophy of Purpose"
     by Dr. Samuel Belkin
     (b) "The Philosophy of Purpose" (in Yiddish)
     by Dr. Samuel Belkin

* 2. "Sabbaths and Festivals in the Modern Age"
     by Dr. Emanuel Rackman

* 3. "A Jewish Critique of the Philosophy of Martin Buber"
     by Dr. Eliezer Berkovits

  4. "The Kaddish — Man's Reply to the Problems of Evil"
     Rabbi Marvin Luban

* 5. "Prayer"
     by Dr. Eliezer Berkovits

  6. "Knowledge and Love in Rabbinic Lore"
     by Dr. Leo Jung

  7. "Luzzatto's Ethico-Psychological Interpretation of Judaism"
     by Dr. Noah H. Rosenbloom

* 8. "Jewish Law Faces Modern Problems"
     by Dr. Immanuel Jakobovits

  9. "The Nature and History of Jewish Law"
     by Rabbi Mendell Lewittes

  10. "Science and Religion"
      by Dr. Sol Roth

  11. "Rabbi Kook's Philosophy of Repentance"
      A Translation of "Orot Ha-Teshuvah"
      by Dr. Alter B. Z. Metzger

  12. "The Musar Movement"
      A Quest for Excellence in Character Education
      by Dr. Zalman F. Ury

  13. "Modern Medicine and Jewish Law"
      by Dr. Fred Rosner, M.D.

STUDIES IN JUDAICA

1. "Scholarship on Philo and Josephus" (1937-1962)
   by Dr. Louis H. Feldman
2. "Rabbinics and Research:
   The Scholarship of Dr. Bernard Revel"
   by Dr. Sidney B. Hoenig
3. "The Medical Aphorisms of Moses Maimonides"   Volume I
   Translated and Edited by Fred Rosner, M.D.,
   and Suessman Muntner, M.D.
4. "The Medical Aphorisms of Moses Maimonides"   Volume II
   Translated and Edited by Fred Rosner, MD.,
   and Suessman Muntner, M.D.

BOOKS

1. "In His Image"
   by Dr. Samuel Belkin
2. "Essays in Traditional Jewish Thought"
   by Dr. Samuel Belkin
3. "Judaism As A Philosophy"
   by Dr. Leon D. Stitskin
4. "The Great Sanhedrin"
   by Dr. Sidney B. Hoenig
* 5. "Currents in Modern Philosophy"
   by Dr. Gershon Churgin
6. "Urban Civilization in Pre-Crusade Europe" (second printing)
   by Dr. Irving A. Agus
7. "Horizons of Thought: Studies in Jewish
   and General Philosophy"
   by Dr. Gershon Churgin
8. "Isaac Halevy" (1847-1914)
   Spokesman and Historian of Jewish Tradition
   by Rabbi O. Asher Reichel
9. "Harmony and Discord"
   An Analysis of the Decline of Jewish Self-Government
   in 15th Century Central Europe
   by Dr. Eric Zimmer
10. "Jubilee Volume for Dr. Joshua Finkel"

---

*   No longer available